STEALTH
WARPLANES

STEALTH
WARPLANES

Doug Richardson

MBI Publishing Company

A SALAMANDER BOOK

This edition first published in 2001
by MBI Publishing Company,
729 Prospect Avenue, PO Box 1,
Osceola, WI 54020-0001 USA

© Salamander Books Ltd., 2001

A member of the Chrysalis Group plc

MBI Publishing Company books are also
available at discounts in bulk quantity for
industrial or sales-promotional use. For
details write to Special Sales Manager at
Motorbooks International Wholesalers &
Distributors, 729 Prospect Avenue, PO Box
1, Osceola, WI 54020-0001 USA.

Library of Congress Cataloging-in-
Publication Data Available

ISBN 0-7603-1051-3.

CREDITS

Project Manager: Ray Bonds
Designers: Interprep Ltd
Artworks: Stephen Seymour, Terry Hadler
and the Maltings Partnership
(© Salamander Books Ltd.) Profiles © Pilot
Press
Reproduction: Canale
Printed and bound in Italy

THE AUTHOR

Doug Richardson trained as an
electronics engineer in the
aerospace industry. He has been
Defence Editor of the aviation
journal *Flight International*, Editor
of the German journal *Military
Technology*, Editor of *Defence
Materiel*, and Technical Editor of
the Swiss defence magazine
Armada International. He is
currently the Editor of *Jane's
Missiles & Rockets*.

Published work has appeared
in many international magazines,
and covers areas such as avionics,
communications, computer
hardware and software, navigation
systems, satellite communications,
and satellite navigation systems,
plus a wide range of military
technologies ranging from small
arms and ammunition to military
aircraft, guided missiles, radar,
electronic warfare, information
warfare, stealth technology,
tanks, artillery, warships,
submarines, and even space
warfare and intelligence
gathering. He has also written
more than 20 books on
aerospace and defence topics.

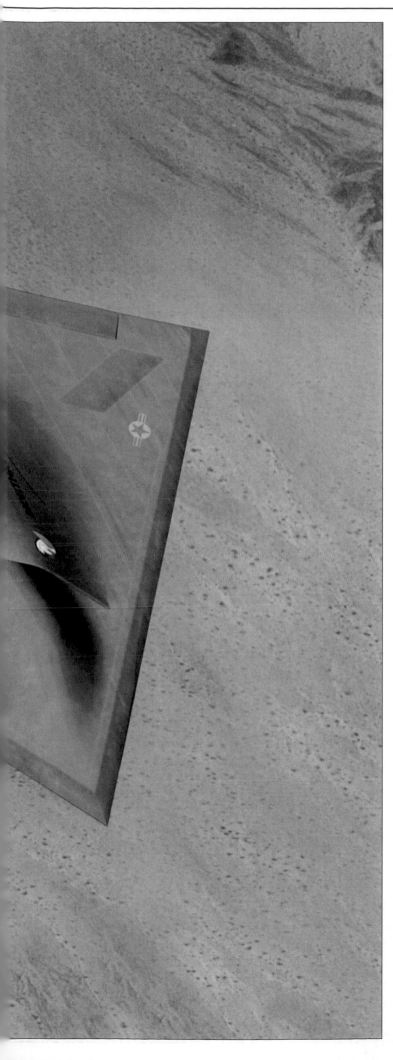

CONTENTS

Introduction	10
Deceiving the Eye	14
Radar and Radar Cross-Section	24
Designing a Stealth Aircraft	34
Early Stealth Aircraft	58
The World of Black Programmes	68
Stealth Aircraft	
Lockheed U-2S	106
Lockheed SR-71 Blackbird	108
Rockwell International B-1B	110
Eurofighter Typhoon	112
Dassault-Breguet Rafale C & M	114
Lockheed F-117A Nighthawk	116
Northrop B-2 Spirit	118
Lockheed Martin F-22A Raptor	120
Boeing and Lockheed Martin	
Joint Strike Fighter (JSF)	122
Mikoyan 1.42 and 1.44	124
Sukhoi S-37 Berkut (Golden Eagle)	126
Boeing Sikorsky RAH-66 Comanche	128
Aids to Stealth	130
Stealth in Action	146
Counters to Stealth	168
Index	186

INTRODUCTION

From the earliest times when men could recount the past, the tales which the poets sang included those telling of heroes and mighty warriors. The stories reflected a simple world in which enemies were overthrown by the manly virtues of strength, courage and force of arms. The poets were less kind to those who sought to achieve their end by trickery or stealth; Homer's "wily Odysseus" is less favourably depicted than valiant warriors such as Hector and Achilles.

In all these stories, deception and stealth are seen as evil or ill-intentioned, an opinion widely held in many societies. Throughout history, armies have not hesitated to execute enemies found guilty of wearing false colours, while in mediaeval Japan the black-robed ninja was much feared.

With the arrival in the 1930s and early 1940s of the cinema swashbuckling heroes, deception suddenly became innocent sub-plot, as Errol Flynn's Robin Hood and his Merry Men dressed as simple peasants in order to sneak into Nottingham. Such innocence was not to last. Wartime commandos, saboteurs, special forces and fifth columnists soon restored deception to its traditional rôle. In Tolkien's saga of elves and hobbits, the power of invisibility is given not by Gandalf's benevolent magic but by an evil ring of power. In the "Star Trek" TV series, it's the Klingons who equip their space vessels with invisibility-shrouding "cloaking devices". Such trickery is beneath the honour of the steely-jawed crew of the Starship Enterprise. Concealment by shape-changing reached its dramatic but gory cinematic climax in John Carpenter's 1982 movie "The Thing", a remake of the earlier black-and-white classic directed by Howard Hawks.

Yet in the late 1970s, the concept of stealth and deception suddenly became respectable. Within the aviation community, rumours began to circulate of a new and highly-secret technology which would make aircraft

Above: **President Carter inspects a SAC B-52. In 1977 he decided to re-equip these old bombers with air-launched cruise missiles.**

and missiles near-invisible to radar systems.

The Washington-based magazine *Aviation Week and Space Technology* was once described by an ex-astronaut as being "... to airplane and space people what *Rolling Stone* is to rock musicians". Around the aerospace industry, it is sometimes known as "Aviation Leak" because of its long record of being first into print with sensitive items of aviation news. (In 1947 it published the first news of Chuck Yeager's then-classified pioneering supersonic flight.)

LEAKS

For aerospace professionals, *Aviation Week* is essential reading. For anyone attempting to tell the story of stealth technology, it is an essential source. Its name will appear again and again throughout this book.

In the struggle for opinion and support among the key members of the defence community, aerospace industry executives, Pentagon "top brass", US politicians and the inevitable consultants and analysts, the US military often turn to the magazine as an ideal vehicle for judiciously-timed leaks. In 1980 just such an operation seemed to be under way, as stories of stealth appeared in its pages and in several US newspapers, lifting the veil on the new technology. Following a series

of stealth-technology stories in *Aviation Week*, President Carter and US Defense Secretary Harold Brown finally confirmed that radar-invisible stealth aircraft had been test flown but ordered a security clampdown on the entire topic.

It is simple to declare a brand-new technology secret but when the secret consists largely of a blend of existing technologies it is more difficult. Such is the case with stealth. For three years following these early revelations, very little useful information on stealth was published. Behind the scenes however, the new technology was creeping out of the closet.

Like so many "modern" ideas, stealth technology first appeared in the world of nature. The simplest stealth technique is that of camouflage. Any child will be able to list examples from the animal world such as the polar bear's white fur, the stick insect's ability to mimic a twig and the colour-changing capabilities of the chameleon.

Other examples of "low observable technology" can be found in nature. Many large marine predators such as killer whales, sperm whales, dolphins and

Below: Until the unveiling of the F-117A late in 1988, most analysts predicted that the aircraft would rely on rounding, wing/body blending and extensive use of RAM. Thanks to tight security, the concept of using faceting as a means of RCS reduction remained secret.

Above: When first released, this Testor/Italeri kit of the "F-19" was seen by some observers as a potential breach of security.

porpoises, search for their prey by means of a form of sonar. They emit beams of sound waves and measure how long the echo takes to return from "targets". To cope with this threat, some fish and cephalopods, such as squid and octopuses, have evolved "stealth" defences. The bodies of some fish and squid are poor reflectors of the whale's sonar waves, the result of their not having an air-filled swim bladder (a good sonar target) for depth control. One scientist has even speculated that the mucus on their skin may be a sound absorber, a natural prototype for the radar-absorbing materials (RAMs) carried by stealth aircraft.

CLASSIFICATION

Much the same concepts lay behind the new and secret stealth technology – avoid radar-reflective structural features and absorb the incoming energy – but they were shrouded in secrecy. Since the mid-1970s, all new work on scattering, shaping and RAMs had been highly classified (some observers would argue excessively so).

Despite this, a substantial amount of information remained in the public domain. Engineers and scientists working in the field could hardly be expected to surrender their files and personal libraries for security vetting, or to de-programme their brains.

Given the amount of information in the public domain, it was inevitable that stealth would begin to creep out of the closet. In 1982,

Right: Inward canted tail fins, plus "venetian blind" exhausts were seen as likely "F-19" features. In practice, the F-117A tail surfaces were tilted outwards (an equally effective low-RCS shape), but these engine exhausts are not too unlike those actually used by Lockheed.

Above: Taken by a ground-based photographer, this unauthorised picture of the F-117A revealed the true leading edge angle of the aircraft's highly-swept wing.

Professor Allen E. Fuhs of the US Naval Postgraduate School began to lecture on the subject of radar cross-section (RCS) while on a sabbatical to NASA's Ames Research Center. A short course on the subject was introduced at Georgia Tech in January of the following year.

STEALTH MODELS

In a special electronics supplement published in September 1984 by the journal *International Defense Review* my former *Flight* colleague Bill Sweetman pushed back the bounds of what was in the public domain in a six-page article simply entitled "Stealth". He returned to the subject again in 1985 with a three-page article, "The Vanishing Air Force", in the August issue of *International Defense Review* and again on "Stealth" in the pages of the November edition of *Interavia*.

By this point, Bill was rapidly becoming a one-man stealth industry whose detective work was not always appreciated by those

fighter. "Attention all foreign spies", announced the 26 July edition of *The Washington Post*, "if you want to know what the Air Force's supersecret stealth fighter jet looks like, try your local toy store". The $9.95 model was a product of the Testor Corporation of Rockford, Illinois. Within a few weeks it had registered orders of around 100,000.

Following the release of the Testor model, a Pentagon official told Congress that it was inaccurate and that any aircraft built to that shape would crash. Model designer John Andrews retaliated by claiming that the model was "80 per cent accurate" and that more than 100 copies had been sold by a model shop close to the Lockheed plant where the real aircraft was being built.

Right: The B-2 was assembled at Palmdale, so could not be kept under wraps indefinitely. Even so, guests at the rollout were allowed only a frontal view.

attempting to keep stealth technology under wraps. Behind the scenes, however, he was preparing the manuscript of an entire book on the subject.

Before it saw print, two textbooks on the subject appeared. Professor Fuhs's RCS lectures were printed in 1985 by the American Institute of Aeronautics and Astronautics in a volume soon dubbed "The No-See-Um Book", while the Georgia Tech course resulted in Eugene F. Knott, John F. Shaeffer and Michael T. Tuley publishing their massive textbook *Radar Cross Section: its prediction, measurement and reduction*.

These were both highly theoretical treatments of the subject, but 1986 saw the appearance of a popular account in the form of Bill Sweetman's *Stealth Aircraft – secrets of future airpower*. Stealth technology had "come in from the cold".

In July 1986 toy stores around the USA began to sell a plastic construction kit which claimed to depict the Lockheed "F-19" stealth

FIRST LOOK

Testor national field sales manager, Steve Kass, denied that classified information had been used to design the model. "Everything we got, you can get out of any library", he explained to a *Washington Post* reporter. The model revealed no information which haven't already been published in trade journals, he claimed. In practice, the model's rounded shape bore little resemblance to that of the still-classified F-117A. Indeed there has been speculation that its configuration, and the similarly rounded shapes shown in other unofficial artist's impressions of the US stealth fighter were the result of a successful US "disinformation" campaign.

By late 1988, the veil of secrecy had to be relaxed. As the

first edition of this book was being written, the US Department of Defense finally released the first photograph of the F-117A stealth fighter, while the roll-out of the first Northrop B-2 revealed the shape of the USAF's second stealthy combat aircraft. Here were the first aircraft designed specifically to operate in the radar equivalent of Tolkien's "land of darkness, where the shadows lie".

In the years that followed, two other US stealth aircraft were to be unveiled – the Lockheed Have Blue technology demonstrator which had preceded the F-117A, and the Northrop Tacit Blue technology demonstrator for a proposed stealthy radar-surveillance aircraft. The F-117A was to make its operational debut over Panama in 1989, and was to go to war in the skies of Iraq in 1991. In the previous year, Lockheed and

Northrop had rolled out their respective Advanced Technology Fighter (ATF) technology demonstrators for a combat aircraft which would combine the manoeuvrability of the F-15 with the stealth of the F-117A.

Stealth had now come out from under its cloak of secrecy. As the number of books on the subject increased, aerospace companies began to talk about the subject, and at the 1991 Paris Air Show, Lockheed even held a press conference to publicise the F-117A.

In the 1920s and 1930s, the nations of Western Europe were apprehensive about the threat posed by the primitive but near-unstoppable piston-engined bombers of the day. Within a few years, radar was to give the fighter an ascendancy over the medium-and high-altitude bomber.

At first sight it might seem that stealth technology has simply restored the *status quo* but, in practice, the situation is more complex. Applied to bombers, fighters and even missiles, stealth is completely rewriting the book of air combat operations and tactics.

In Bram Stoker's gothic classic *Dracula*, vampire hunter Professor Van Helsing describes the difficulties which his party will experience in their attempts to locate and destroy the evil Count. "He can, within limitations, appear at will, where and when, and in any of the forms which are to him ... he can grow and become small; and at times he can vanish and come unknown. How then are we to begin our strife to destroy him?" It is a good description of the problems faced by would-be vampire hunters but is almost

equally applicable to the problems faced by future air defences which must cope with a range of stealthy attackers.

Yet the task is not an impossible one. The sight of Yugoslavian civilians dancing triumphantly on the wreckage of an F-117A in late March 1999 showed that stealth aircraft are not invulnerable, although the exact circumstances under which the aircraft was shot down remain classified. This book will describe the underlying principles of stealth technology, give the history of the programmes which have used it, and look towards the future to report on the next generation of stealthy aircraft. It will also examine the technologies which help the stealth aircraft fulfil its mission, and those needed in order to detect and track them.

DECEIVING THE EYE

When the first military aircraft were fielded, little thought was given to colour schemes which might help reduce detection. The fact that they flew at all seemed more than adequate. Like their civil counterparts, military aircraft had no paint finish to speak of but were a pale yellow, the result of applying fabric-tautening dope and protective varnish to the linen or cotton covering.

Some work on reducing visibility had been done prior to the war. This had not been done by the application of deceptive colouring but rather by the even more obvious approach of trying to make the aircraft near-invisible by covering its wooden framework not with doped fabric but with a transparent skin. It may surprise those working with today's highly-classified stealth aircraft to learn that the first attempts to build aircraft of this type date back to the era of their great-grandparents.

In 1913 the United States War Department carried out experiments intended to assess the feasibility of building an aircraft which would be invisible to the naked eye when flying at an altitude of 1,000ft (300m). In an attempt to meet what by any standards must be seen as an impossible target, the

Below: **US First World War air ace Eddie Rickenbacker poses alongside his French-built Spad fighter. Although more complex than the contemporary British camouflage scheme shown above, the colour finish on the aircraft was probably no more effective as an antidetection measure.**

wings of an aircraft were manufactured with what a contemporary newspaper account described as "a material of a semi-transparent nature, composed partly of celluloid". Other trials involved the use of the same material in the "understructure" of airships. A secondary goal of the work

was to give aircrew a better view of the ground.

In 1914 the magazine *Flight* reported similar experiments. "Only the framework is dimly visible, and this and the outline of the motor and the pilot and passengers present so small an area for rifle or gun fire, that at the rate of speed at which aeroplanes are flown today, accurate aiming at such surfaces becomes nearly impossible."

CAMOUFLAGE

British troops had adopted khaki uniforms as a result of casualties to long-range rifle fire in the South African wars, so this colour was the logical choice for an aircraft finish. When the state-owned Royal Aircraft Factory (forerunner of the Royal Aerospace Establishment) developed a pigmented compound intended to protect the fabric covering of aircraft from the adverse effects of strong sunlight, the colour chosen for the resulting Protective Covering (PC) No. 10 was of the khaki type. The exact shade used is a matter of some debate, involving fading

Right: RAF Handley Page Hampden in typical early WWII bomber camouflage. The white ring is omitted from the wing roundels.

Below: This replica of the late WWI Sopwith Snipe has only nominal camouflage, heavily compromised by roundels and white lettering.

Below: The winning side can ignore camouflage rules. The bold insignia on this Bf 109E spoil the effect of the splinter green finish.

Bottom: For a brief period prior to the United States' entry into WWII, traditional tail stripes were retained despite the new olive drab.

memories and faded paint samples, and seems to have ranged from a greenish khaki to what can best be described as chocolate brown.

French aircraft started the First World War without camouflage. Early Nieuport fighters carried the company's standard silver-grey finish, for example. A nominally "standard" French camouflage scheme was later adopted, a distinctive finish made up of green and two or even three shades of brown. This was often retained by French built aircraft taken into Royal Flying Corps or US Army service. Describing the Spad XIII C.1 in a 1960s monograph, C.F. Andrews summed up the French attitude to camouflage: "The variations of French camouflage patterns during 1917 and 1918 have been somewhat obscure".

The Germans took a different approach. Initial experiments involved applying two or three shades of colour to the aircraft by means of paints or distempers but this was soon superseded by a scheme in which camouflage colouring was printed on the fabric used to cover the aircraft. This approach allowed the use of camouflage patterns too complex to be cost-effectively applied by hand. The pattern chosen was a complicated one, a dense network of hexagons in four or five colours, and there is no evidence that this "lozenge fabric" was any more effective than the RFC's single-colour PC No. 10.

NIGHT COLOURS

Bomber units operating by night adopted specialised colour schemes. Black seemed the obvious choice for an aircraft intended to operate under the concealment of darkness, but nobody seems to have realised that to be effective such a finish must be matt so that reflections from searchlight beams be minimised. So disappointing

were the results of tests on black aircraft that few service machines were painted in this manner. The huge Handley Page 0/400 – a twin-engined biplane of 100ft (30.5m) wingspan developed to meet Commodore Murray Sueter's requirement for a "bloody paralyzer of an aeroplane" – was finished overall in PC No. 10 compound.

A better paint finish for night operations emerged in early 1918. Developed by the Experimental Station at Orford Ness, Suffolk, the grey-green varnish known as "Nivo" was optimised for use on moonlit nights and had a surface sheen intended to match that of open water. It was too late for large scale wartime use.

With the arrival of peace, camouflage was soon abandoned by most squadrons in favour of brighter colours. The inter-war years were to prove the zenith in the art of aircraft decoration and nowhere was this more true than in Britain's Royal Air Force (RAF), successor to the Royal Flying Corps. A generation of pilots serving in what they sometimes termed "the best flying club in the world" flew silver-doped biplanes adorned with highly-conspicuous squadron markings. In the United States, the Army Air Corps preferred to leave aircraft in their natural finish but added brightly-coloured tail stripes and squadron insignia.

TONING DOWN

By the mid 1930s, Britain faced the growing air strength of a reborn German *Luftwaffe* which would soon re-equip with modern monoplane fighters and bombers. As the likelihood of war increased, bright colours gave way to drab low-visibility schemes.

Early WWII German Colours

1930s American Bomber Scheme

Reconnaissance Spitfires

black area was extended initially over the entire lower half of the aircraft then to all but the upper surfaces in 1941. From 1943 onwards, Coastal Command aircraft were finished in white, except for the upper surfaces which were dark slate grey/extra dark sea grey.

NEW COLOURS

The most novel colours were those applied to high-altitude photo-reconnaissance aircraft. These were finished in a single colour overall, varying from several shades of blue to pink. Night fighters of the RAF and USAAF were also painted black overall.

The US Army Air Force entered the war using its olive

Top: As WWII progressed, the Royal Air Force developed special low-visibility schemes. This recce Spitfire sports a blue finish.

Above: A pink colour was also found to be effective at high altitude, helping to match the aircraft with the sky background.

Camouflage was re-introduced. The basic RAF scheme involved upper surfaces painted in two colours – dark green and dark earth, applied in large areas with curving outlines.

At the same time, the RAF's night bomber units bade farewell to "Nivo". Tests had shown that the varnish's surface sheen reflected too much light if the aircraft were illuminated by a searchlight. Upper surfaces were finished in dark green and dark earth, while the undersides received a matt black known as RDM2. The low-visibility roundel was retained, however, and also applied to the wings of camouflaged aircraft which operated mainly by day.

Other nations similarly toned down their aircraft. The United States opted for olive drab upper surfaces and sides and grey or azure undersides. The US Navy's pale grey or even bare metal gave way to finishes based on blue or grey. A typical scheme had upper surfaces in non-specular blue/grey and under surfaces in non-specular light grey.

For much of the war, the *Luftwaffe* used a distinctive two-tone "splinter" colour scheme for the upper surfaces of its aircraft. This used two shades of green – dark green *(dunkelgrün)* and a very dark green *(schwarzgrün)* applied in large patches with angular outlines. Undersides were painted in light blue *(hellblau)*.

As the war progressed, camouflage finishes on both sides were improved and new schemes devised to suit

various specialised rôles or geographical regions. In the UK, the basic "Temperate Land" dark green/dark earth finish was altered in 1941 with sea grey replacing dark earth. This basic finish was supplemented by a combination of dark slate grey and extra dark sea grey ("Temperate Sea") better suited to the over water rôle, while aircraft assigned to the North African campaign and the Middle East were finished in a combination of dark earth and middle stone ("Middle East"). Undersurfaces were finished in grey or blue, depending on the geographical area in which the aircraft was operating.

RAF night bombers retained their dark green/dark earth upper surfaces but the matt

Above: Red outer wings and large red stars make nonsense of the white winter camouflage applied to these Soviet MiG-3 fighters.

Right: This 1918 photo of the Royal Navy battleship *Revenge* shows the disruptive "dazzle" camouflage scheme.

drab paint scheme, albeit without the brightly-coloured unit insignia and tail marking of the pre-war era. Tail stripes had been deleted from camouflaged aircraft in 1940. It was to retain this scheme until 1944.

The bright colours applied to some areas of *Luftwaffe* aircraft slowly disappeared and new paint schemes attempted to reduce the visibility of aircraft. For day operations the *hellblau* undersides were frequently retained but often merged gradually into the green upper surfaces.

Bombers assigned to the night-time *blitz* against the UK often carried hastily improvised camouflage. On the undersides, black replaced

German Nightfighter Colours

Above: Painstaking research resulted in the bizarre mottled blue/grey paint scheme used on WWII *Luftwaffe* night fighters.

Below: As USAAF strength rose and that of the *Luftwaffe* faded, US fighters and bombers flew combat missions in metal finish.

the traditional *hellblau* and was often carried up over the fuselage sides. In some cases, the fuselage crosses were toned down or even painted out completely.

New camouflage colours were devised to match the aircraft to their theatre of operation. For the North African campaign, a sand brown colour with a distinctly pinkish cast was used on upper surfaces. This worked well over the desert but, on aircraft operating in areas where scrub was common, this basic colour was often overlaid with areas of dark green. These varied in size from large sections of the aircraft down to small patches. Given the right circumstances, the effect of the latter was to make the aircraft near-invisible when seen from above.

WINTER COATS

Winter operations on the Russian front again demanded a custom paint job – in this case all-white upper surfaces intended to reduce visibility over a snow-covered landscape. As the spring saw areas of green breaking through the snow and ice, it is hardly surprising that many white-finished aircraft sported green patches. A non-drying glyptal paint was developed to aid the application and

removal of such temporary colour finishes.

For early night fighter operations, the *Luftwaffe* adopted an all-black finish similar to that used on Allied night fighters. So obvious did the virtues of black colouring seem that throughout the war the RAF and US Army Air Force never fielded a successor. Given the growing magnitude of the RAF's night bomber campaign against German cities, the *Luftwaffe* could not be so complacent and had to launch a research programme to test low-visibility paint schemes for night use.

One suspects that much to their surprise, they found that the ideal finish was very far from the traditional black. Tests showed that the night sky over Western Europe still contained sufficient light to silhouette a black-painted bomber when seen from the side or below. As the tests proceeded, lighter shades replaced black until aircraft were flying in an odd-looking scheme or overall pale blue with mottled grey. This was soon widely applied to nocturnal hunters such as the Ju 88 and He 219.

DAZZLE SCHEMES

At best, these traditional camouflage schemes could only delay visual detection. A more subtle approach involves applying markings intended to deceive the eye into wrongly identifying what it is seeing. The first military application of the concept had been during the First World War when Royal Navy warships sported what became known as "dazzle" camouflage. This took the form of large jagged panels of bold colouring and was intended to break up the vessel's visual outline. It could also help create a false perspective. Painted-on bow waves could complete the illusion, seen though a submarine periscope, giving the attacking U-boat a false idea of the warship's true course and speed. The idea was taken to its extreme in the Second World War when

the Japanese aircraft carrier *Zuiho* had its flight deck painted to represent a light cruiser.

With the end of the Second World War, camouflage was once more abandoned, with most air forces flying in natural metal finish. Navies stayed with camouflage for their carrier-based aircraft. Britain's Fleet Air Arm settled for medium blue upper surfaces, while the USN adopted light greys.

POST WAR

In 1955 the USN threw caution to the wind, adopting upper surfaces of non-specular light gull grey and lower surfaces finished in glossy insignia white which formed the background for brightly-coloured unit markings reminiscent of the 1920s and 1930s.

With the escalating Cold War, the UK re-adopted camouflage in 1947. Fighters once more sported grey and green upper surfaces. The new Canberra light bombers started life in 1951 with grey upper surfaces and black under sides. Soviet aircraft operating in North Korea followed suit, the result of Allied air superiority.

For the main part, the USA and Soviet Union stayed with natural metal for both fighters and bombers. This was a particularly good choice for supersonic aircraft since it reduced drag and posed no abrasion problems. In the late 1950s, the RAF fielded the Lightning in natural metal but the long-range V-bombers carried an all-white anti-flash finish designed to minimise

Above: **For almost a decade, USN F-14 Tomcats relied on a basic grey and white finish, and carried brightly-coloured unit insignia.**

Below: **Like Britain and the Soviet Union, France operated its first-generation Mach 2 warplanes in natural metal finish.**

the thermal effects of nuclear explosions. With the US Navy operating aircraft from its carriers in bright paint schemes reminiscent of the inter-war years, the concept of camouflage seemed to be nearly forgotten.

Two factors restored the need for visual stealth in the 1970s. One was the downing of Gary Powers's Lockheed U-2 spyplane over Soviet territory on 1 April 1960 and the other was the outbreak of the Vietnam War.

Early Vietnam War operations were flown by

Above: The Vietnam War saw US re-adopt camouflage, but the schemes used were little improved over those of two decades earlier.

uncamouflaged aircraft, but the growing threat posed by the North Vietnamese fighter force resulted in the re-introduction of camouflage. Upper surfaces of USAF fighters and fighter-bombers were given a three-tone treatment of Forest Green, Medium Green and Tan Brown, while the undersides were finished in the much lighter Very Pale Grey.

During the war, the USAF gradually reduced the size of the national insignia applied to its aircraft, the final version being only 15in (38cm) high.

Left: As these RAF Harrier GR3s show, the art of applying temporary winter camouflage schemes is still very much alive.

Another change applied to some aircraft later in the war, intended to reduce the demarcation between the insignia and the camouflage scheme, was the deletion of the blue outline from the "wings" of the insignia.

Other nations followed the US lead in readopting camouflage. Several broad patterns emerged, setting the style for many of today's colour schemes.

GREY AND GREEN

Camouflage finishes were not always the result of careful research or study. When the Indian Air Force hastily camouflaged its fighter force during the December 1981 war with Pakistan, considerable "artist's licence" seems to have been granted to those who wielded the paint brushes. Great variations in

Above: The "air superiority blue" finish used on prototype and early-production F-15 Eagles proved unsuccessful.

interpreting the new standard finish were displayed by the men who worked on individual aircraft, or even on different parts of the same aircraft. Some aircraft sported two-tone dark green and grey/green for example, while others displayed a finish reminiscent of the 1940s *Luftwaffe* "mirror" camouflage.

When the F-15 Eagle first entered service in the mid-1970s, it was finished all over in air-superiority blue. National insignia were small in size and had no border. It was short lived. The skies may be blue over Texas but grey is closer to the normal in Western Europe. Pale blue gave way to the grey-based "Compass Ghost" finish. This uses two different tones of grey in an arrangement known as "counter-shading" in which the lighter tone is applied to the parts of the aircraft likely to be in shadow.

The year 1983 saw the introduction of low-visibility markings for the USN. Overall grey replaced the long-established gull grey and insignia white, while national and unit insignia shrank in size and were applied in a medium grey only.

In 1979 the RAF tested an alternative to its then-current dark green and grey with light grey undersides. This took the form of an all-grey scheme retaining standard-sized national and squadron markings. Radomes remained black. This period also saw the introduction of the pale brown "hemp" finish on larger aircraft such as the Nimrod, Victor and C-130 Hercules. The latest RAF scheme sees tactical fighters given an all-green finish. This was first seen on the Harrier GR5 (British version of the AV-8B) and BAe's second Hawk 200 prototype single-seater.

Research into multicoloured camouflage continued. During the JAWS (Joint Attack Weapon System) trials of the A-10 in 1977, the Second World War *Luftwaffe* concept of temporary finishes was taken to its logical extreme. Aircraft were regularly repainted to match the

Right: **This mottled camouflage was just one of those tested on the A-10 during the 1977 Joint Attack Weapon Systems trials.**

current terrain and weather conditions.

In the early 1980s, the USAF recognised that its Vietnam-era scheme was not ideal for NATO low-level operations. As an interim measure, the pale grey of the undersides was replaced by the three colours used on the upper surfaces instead, creating a completely "wrap-around" finish.

Eventually the USAF settled on what it termed "European One" – a "wrap-around" scheme using medium green,

Below: **Dark tones on well-lit areas, plus lighter tones elsewhere are a feature of the USAF's current "Compass Ghost" finish.**

dark green and dark grey. This entered service in 1983, gradually replacing the older colours as paint stocks for the latter were used up. At the same time, Phantoms assigned to air defence were painted in the pale blue and grey finish used for other interceptors.

Experience showed that the USAF fighters spent more time at altitude than at low level. Since the green and grey scheme had been designed for low-level use, it was thus far from the optimum. Two permutations suitable for medium-altitude use were tested in the mid-1980s. "Hill Gray I" combined medium grey and dark grey upper surfaces with light grey undersurfaces, while "Hill Gray II" was a "wrap-around" medium grey and dark grey finish. By 1987, USAF aircraft assigned to air-defence and multiple operations were beginning to appear in "Hill Gray II". Earlier schemes had involved a separate colour for the aircraft undersides but this new finish was applied over the whole airframe.

FERRIS SCHEMES

Given the number of colour schemes which have been tried, abandoned and, in some cases, retried, it is hard to avoid the conclusion that camouflage is at least in part a matter of fashion. As a limited number of colours and ideas are regularly changed, little effort seems to be going into novel alternatives. The "dazzle" experiments of the early 1940s have not really been pursued. One of the few individuals to explore the unusual has been US aviation artist Chris Ferris.

Camouflage has been a subject of great interest to Ferris. One of his paintings of

a pale blue F-15 against a grey sky background was specifically intended to point out the folly of that aircraft's initial finish. Both the F-14 and the F-15 have been tested in a camouflage scheme devised by Ferris with upper surfaces finished in a medium blue whose jagged edges are vaguely reminiscent of "dazzle" camouflage.

In the late 1970s, a complex "dazzle" paint scheme was devised for Lockheed's Have Blue stealth demonstrator aircraft. This was intended to make it hard for a distant observer to determine the aircraft's shape. It worked so well that, when the first photograph of a Have Blue prototype was released, details

Above: The USN went visually stealthy in 1983 with an all-over grey scheme, plus low-visibility national markings.

Right: Aviation artist Chris Ferris devised this novel paint scheme for the F-4 Phantom, but it was never adopted for service.

Below: F-14s test another Ferris paint scheme. More recent experience suggests that luminescence is more important that colour.

of the aircraft's shape were hard to discern, particularly around the rear of the fuselage.

Ferris considers than an all-over grey would have been better in Vietnam than the three-tone treatment which was actually used. Canada seems to have taken his point; today's CF-18 Hornet fleet is camouflaged in a dull non-specular grey, while the tone used for the national insignia and other markings offers little contrast. One neat touch of deceptive camouflage is the false canopy painted on the underside, a feature intended to encourage tactical errors by the opposition during air combat manoeuvres.

The importance of camouflage was demonstrated

during the 1991 Gulf War, where the use by Iraq of optically aimed anti-aircraft guns and shoulder-launched SAMs made it important that aircraft operating by day should avoid detection. During the air campaign, almost 25 per cent of US aircraft casualties were A-10 close-support aircraft, 20 of which were hit during the war. None was damaged or shot down while operating at night.

The aircraft still had the dark green paint scheme originally devised to conceal them from above when flying low-level operations in northern Europe, and some pilots believed that this colouring made the A-10 stand out in the desert against both sand and sky. At night, the dark paint scheme probably helped conceal the aircraft, or at the best did not make it stand out.

Some A-10 units began to paint their aircraft the same light grey colour scheme used by most other USAF aircraft, but were later ordered by the Air Force Component, Central Command (CENTAF) to change them back to dark green. However, a postwar USAF aircraft-survivability study concluded that the concerns over the A-10 paint scheme were "valid" and recommended that, in the future, paint schemes should match the environment

in which the aircraft were being required to operate.

SMOKE AND LIGHT

Some effort has been expended on active optical camouflage – the use of lights and sensors to adjust the luminance of the airframe to match the background. Work on what were nicknamed "Yehudi lights" started in the USA after the Second World War. Various models of piston-engined aircraft including the B-24 Liberator and SBD Dauntless naval bomber were fitted with an experimental arrangement of lamps built into the wing leading edge. "Yehudi lights" are also reported to have been tested in the engine inlets of some F-4 Phantoms during the Vietnam War. Studies have shown that at longer ranges it is more important to match the luminance than the actual shade of colour.

Most modern jet engines are virtually smokeless, but this was not the case 30 or 40 years ago. Early-model B-52 bombers and KC-135 tankers tended to lift off from the runway amidst dense clouds of smoke which would send today's environmental pressure groups scampering for their protest banners. Jet fighters of the 1950s and 1960s were almost as bad, and this could be a major weakness in air combat. Experience in the skies over North Vietnam soon taught the USAF and USN that engine smoke could effectively pinpoint their fighters.

Smoke emission was to remain a bugbear of the Phantom throughout the Vietnam War. Smoke output peaked sharply when the engine was run at full military power. To avoid this effect

during combat operations, pilots would sometimes run with one engine on afterburner and the other throttled back. This resulted in the same total thrust as two engines at full military power, while the close spacing of the Phantom's engine bays minimised the effects of thrust asymmetry.

TRAILS

Contrails are another unwanted phenomenon which can betray an aircraft's position. More accurately known as "condensation trails", these are formed at altitude by the condensation or even freezing of the water vapour created as a by-product when jet fuel is burned.

During trials in 1962 of the first Teledyne Ryan Firebee reconnaissance drones (a programme which will be described in a later chapter), test interceptions by USAF and USN fighters showed how

easily contrails could guide an attacker, so work was started in that year on a "no-con" system. This involved two QC-2C drones equipped with a system which injected a chemical agent into the exhaust. It was not very successful; the best method of eliminating contrails proved to be giving the drone the ceiling performance needed to fly above the altitudes at which contrails form.

Details of anti-contrail measures are scarce. Like the 1962 experiments, most are thought to involve the use of chemical additives in the exhaust. These alter the size of the water droplets created in the air.

AIRFIELDS

Since a combat aircraft spends most of its time on the ground, where it is vulnerable to sneak attack, low-visibility aircraft ideally require low-visibility airbases. Application of camouflage to the airfield from which military aircraft operate was a Second World War development. One of the first experiments in heavily camouflaging military bases was conducted in the United

Above: **Smoke pours from the engines of an F-4C. Combat experience in Vietnam showed that smoke trails could betray an aircraft.**

Below: **Good camouflage discipline is essential when deploying V/STOL fighters such as these Royal Air Force GR3s off-base.**

Bottom: **Lockheed's Burbank plant vanishes under protective camouflage in the early 1940s. Fake "trees" help maintain the illusion.**

Below: **Almost two decades after the Six Day War, aircraft could still be found parked in unprotected lines during major exercises.**

States. In 1940 Brigadier
General Thomas M. Robins,
then assistant chief of the US
Army's Corps of Engineers,
was responsible for building a
new airfield at Windsor Locks,
Connecticut. To illustrate
what camouflage could do,
Robins worked with Lt
Colonel John Bragdon to
build the new base to conform
to the principles of visual
deception rather than the
formal arrangements which
the conventional military
mind would regard as neat
and tidy.

Airfield buildings were
positioned among existing
buildings present at the site.
The latter, like the natural
vegetation, were left in place
wherever possible. Roads
followed normal ground
contours rather than taking
direct routes, fuel tanks were
buried and barracks were
built to resemble the tobacco-
drying sheds common on
nearby farms. To break up the
outlines of the field's three
runways, their surfaces were
painted to match the shape
and colour of nearby fields
and to create the illusion of
being crossed by many paths
or roads.

HIDDEN FACTORIES

Other efforts saw the
camouflage treatment of US
aircraft factories on the west
coast. The most famous
instance was Lockheed-Vega's
Burbank works which was
exposed to the full talents of
Hollywood's special-effects
men. The entire site,
including buildings and
parking lots, disappeared
under a giant camouflage
shelter which incorporated
fake houses, gardens, roads
and even parked cars. To
maintain the illusion, the
positions of the "cars" were
regularly changed, while the
"houses" even had fake
"washing" hung out to dry
once a week. An idea of the
cost and complexity of the
illusion can be gleaned from
the fact that the bill for its
removal after the war came to
$200,000. A similar scheme
saw Boeing's vital Seattle
plant disappear under a fake
camouflage "town".

Researchers in the USA
have investigated methods of
applying an up to date version
of such techniques to NATO's
highly-vulnerable air bases in
Western Europe. The aim is to
fool not just the human eye
but also infra-red and radar
sensors. Some of the
techniques being studied were
revealed in 1985 when the
London newspaper *Sunday
Times* reported that the US
Government was funding
secret trials in the UK of
methods of reducing the
visibility of airfields. The
report linked this work with
the development of US stealth
aircraft. "If all goes according
to plan, invisible NATO
aircraft could be landing at
invisible airfields all over
Europe within a decade",
wrote defence correspondent
James Adams.

Some of the techniques
used were a re-run of the
1940s work. Trees were
planted to break up the
outline of buildings and
perimeter fences, while all
concrete surfaces, including
the runways, were treated
with a chemical solution
intended to give them an IR
signature similar to that of the
surrounding grass.

The article also described how
the Royal Air Force base selected
for the tests had been equipped
with water sprinklers which
would be used to douse hangars
and other major facilities with
water if the airfield was about to
be attacked. This would reduce
the IR signature of the genuine
targets, while heaters inside
inflatable decoy hangars would
create alternative realistic visual
and thermal targets.

As radar-invisible stealth
aircraft enter service in
growing numbers, air defences
will place increasing reliance
on alternative sensors. These
will include long-range electro-
optical television systems
mounted on interceptors and
SAM fire-control units in
addition to the more traditional
"Mark 1 eyeball". Far from
having been made obsolete, the
visual countermeasures
described in this chapter are
likely to grow in importance as
the effectiveness of radar and
thermal sensors are degraded.

RADAR AND RADAR CROSS-SECTION

To the Latin-speaking inhabitants of Dark Ages northwestern France, the region was the end of the known world. Looking out over the often angry sea which stretched to the horizon and beyond, they named it "Finis Terre" – the End of the Land. In the centuries that followed, this peninsula thrusting out into the Atlantic Ocean became a strategic position which required fortification, so the 16th century French castle builder Vauban erected a fort to guard the shore against naval threats, particularly the growing maritime power of the British Navy.

In most countries, a fort of this age would be a tourist attraction, complete with ticket office and tea room, but this one is guarded by barbed wire, and off limits to tourists. Its ramparts are now protected against a threat the like of which its builder could never have dreamed.

The upper part of the stone battlements are now covered with blankets of thick rubber-like material. Known to the electronics industry as Radar Absorbent Material (usually abbreviated to RAM), the coating is designed to absorb radar energy, ensuring that the old fort does not reflect the radar energy radiated by the nearby Mengam electronic-warfare test site run by electronics giant Thomson-CSF.

Inaccessible though Vauban's battlements may be, they are a good starting off point for a study of the most secretive of 20th Century military technologies – "stealth" – the art of making aircraft, missiles and other military systems invisible to radar. Let us return for a moment to the threat against which Vauban's fortress was designed, the traditional sailing ship armed with broadside-firing cannon. As will have been seen by anybody who has watched old movies, the standard naval cannon (or at least the Hollywood version) fired a spherical cannonball about 8 inches (20cm) in diameter.

How big would such a cannonball have looked to a radar at Vauban's fortress, had it been so equipped in Napoleonic times. The most obvious answer is of course the

Above: **Most radars operate at microwave frequencies, and must have a direct line of sight to the target. If over the** **horizon, the latter will be masked by terrain, so raising the antenna improves long-range coverage.**

area of a circle of 8 inches (20cm) in diameter. To save the reader from reaching for a pocket calculator while muttering the schoolboy formula "Pi times R squared", the area in question is 1.34 square feet (0.125 sq m).

Substitute a metal plate 14in (35.3cm) square, and you'd have the same physical cross-section, but the radar cross-section could be anything from less than a tenth of a square metre to several hundred square metres, depending on the frequency of the radar. For any given frequency, that radar cross-section would be at its maximum when the plate was positioned at right angles to the radar beam. Tilt it, and the radar reflectivity will fall dramatically. The position of the edge of the

plate with respect to the radar beam also influences the plate's radar cross-section. Welcome to the strange world of stealth, a universe where nothing is quite what it seems even before the electronic wizards have begun practising their super-secret electronic trickery.

RADAR WAVES

The key to understanding stealth is to understand how radar works and in particular how radar signals are reflected from aircraft structures. The following "crash course" on these subjects will strike a radar or stealth engineer as grossly oversimplified but it will attempt to cover in a single

chapter subjects to which a stealth technology textbook would devote 400 pages, while at the same time steering clear of the sort of mathematics and numerical analysis which would satisfy only the expert.

A radar wave is a form of electromagnetic radiation, as are the lower frequencies used for radio and TV and the higher frequencies such as infra-red energy and visible light. The basic theory of such waves was first described in the 19th Century by Clerk Maxwell who predicted their properties long before the technology needed to prove him right became available. The early pioneers of radio were starting from a blank sheet of paper; they were trying to find a method of creating and detecting waves whose existence had been foreseen by Maxwell.

An electromagnetic wave consists of two components – an electric field and a magnetic field – positioned at right angles to one another and whose values rapidly fluctuate in strength, rising to a peak, falling away to zero, then rising to a peak in the opposite direction before falling back towards zero. The entire process then repeats over and over again. The whole electromagnetic wave travels (engineers would say "propagates") in a direction at right angles to the electric and magnetic fields. Think of the latter as the vanes on a dart or arrow; the direction of propagation will then be along the length of the shaft.

FREQUENCY

In any book on radio or radar, let alone stealth technology, the terms "frequency" and "wavelength" are unavoidable. Both describe methods of measuring the rate of this cyclic variation. "Frequency" is a measurement of the number of times this cycle occurs in every second. Until the 1960s, it was expressed in cycles, kilocycles (thousand of cycles), megacycles (millions of cycles) or even gigacycles (thousands of millions of cycles) per second. The self-explanatory term "cycles per second" was replaced by the totally artificial term "Hertz" during the 1960s (after the German physicist Heinrich Hertz, 1857-94) in the interests of international standardisation, so in this book we refer to megahertz (MHz) and gigahertz (GHz).

"Wavelength" is an older concept. The wave propagates at 90 degrees to its electric and magnetic fields. The wavelength is the distance between two successive peaks in either of these fields. It's a useful measurement, being directly related to the physical size of components such as antenna elements – which is why it was widely used in the early days of radio. The two are directly inter-related. Increase the frequency and the wavelength is reduced. Decrease the frequency and the wavelength increases.

RADAR BEAMS

As the reader is probably aware, radar sets illuminate their target with a beam of high-frequency radar energy and detect the resulting reflections. A good analogy is the Second World War searchlight. Lost in the night sky, a bomber was virtually invisible from the ground. Once caught in the beam of a searchlight, it became visible and could be engaged by anti-aircraft gunfire.

Only two countermeasures were available to aid the aircraft, one passive and the other active. For most of the war, all air arms engaging in

Right: **Above the main antenna of this Thomson-CSF TRS-22XX radar is an upper unit for the interrogation of aircraft-mounted civil or IFF transponder systems.**

Below: **As frequency rises, wavelength falls, as do the dimensions of antenna feeds and waveguides.**

Wavelengths

Frequency	Wavelength
100kHZ	3,000m
1MHz	300m
10MHz	30m
100MHz	3m
1GHz	20cm
10GHz	3cm
100GHz	3mm
velocity of light = 300×10^6m/s approx	

Right: **The wavelength of a signal is the distance between successive peaks. The higher the frequency, the shorter the wavelength.**

Below: **An electromagnetic wave has two components at right angles – an electric field (shown in blue), and a magnetic field (shown in red).**

Waveforms

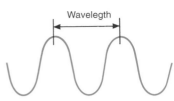

Wavelegth

Magnetic and Electric Components of a Wave

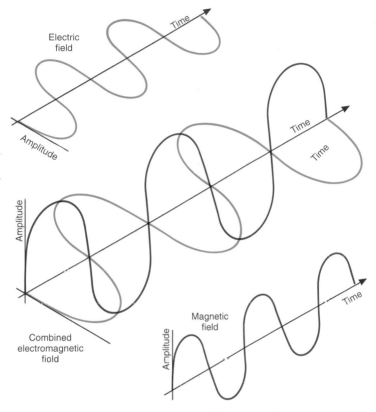

Electric field

Time

Amplitude

Amplitude

Time

Time

Combined electromagnetic fiold

Magnetic field

Amplitude

Time

night bombing painted the underside of their aircraft black, so as to minimise the amount of light reflected should they be caught momentarily in a searchlight beam. If caught and followed by the beam, the aircraft's only hope was to manoeuvre violently in the hope of slipping out of the narrow beam of light. If successful, once outside of the beam it was once more cloaked in darkness.

Both measures were partially countered by having several searchlights concentrate their beams onto any target detected by one of their number. Aircrew dreaded being "coned" by a group of searchlights. The cluster of beams interesecting on the coned aircraft illuminated a large volume of sky in the aircraft's immediate vicinity, while the additional light from every beam joining the cone increased the light level illuminating the aircraft, and thus the amount reflected back to the ground for the AA gunners to see.

REFLECTIONS

When British scientists started work on radar in 1935, they realised the importance of target reflectivity. If the new method of aircraft detection (then known as Radio Location) was to work effectively, it was essential that the reflection be as strong as possible. The illuminating signal would have to be as powerful as possible, given the state of radar technology as it existed then, while the frequency used would have to be one which the aircraft would reflect strongly.

Use of the word "reflect" simplifies a more complex process. The radar energy does not just bounce the way a squash ball does off the court wall. When an electromagnetic wave meets an electrical conductor, such as a wire, it creates within that conductor electrical and magnetic currents at the same frequency. That is how a radio antenna works – the electromagnetic wave from the distant transmitter induces a tiny current within the antenna which the radio receiver then amplifies. At the transmitter, the process works in reverse. The transmitter feeds an electrical current of the appropriate frequency into the antenna. This current creates an electromagnetic wave which the radiates outwards from the antenna. The process

Reflection of Radar Energy

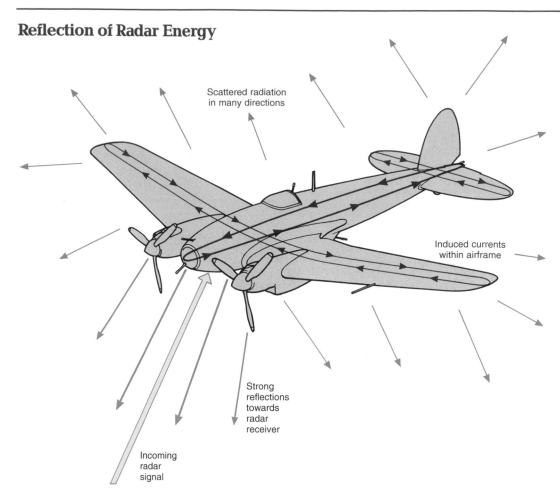

Scattered radiation
in many directions

Induced currents
within airframe

Strong
reflections
towards
radar
receiver

Incoming
radar
signal

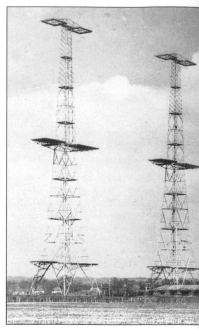

Left: The scientists and
engineers who developed the
first radars just before the
Second World War found it
difficult if not impossible to
predict how a radar wave
would reflect from an
aircraft. It seemed to scatter
in all directions. No simple
theory could explain what was
happening.

works both ways – a current
in a conductor can create an
electromagnetic wave, and an
electromagnetic wave can
create a current in a
conductor.

This is the central principle
of the phenomenon which
causes an aircraft or any
other target to reflect radio
energy. When the radar wave
hits the target, it induces
electric and magnetic
currents within that object.
By the act of flowing, these
currents in turn cause an
electromagnetic wave to be
created. It is this latter wave
which the radar sees as a
reflected echo.

From work on antenna
(aerial) design, the engineers
who developed Britain's first
radars already knew that a
wire whose length
corresponded to half the
wavelength of the radio signal
would re-radiate strongly.
Assuming that the wing of a
metal aircraft would behave in
the same way as a simple wire,
this suggested that the
optimum frequency would be
that which had a wavelength
twice the length of the wing
of a typical bomber of the
period.

At that time the latest
generation of German
bombers was beginning flight
tests and the equivalent
British types were about to

Above: The first British "Chain Home" early-warning radar stations were based on short-wave and television broadcasting technology.

Below left: On 26th February 1935, Sir Robert Watson-Watt used this primitive receiver to make the first detection of an aircraft target.

fly; so a good idea of the dimensions of wingspans of likely targets was available.

Although a follow-on generation of heavier bombers with wingspans of around 100ft (30m) or more could already be envisaged, the radar engineers decided to regard 80ft (25m) as a good compromise value, fixing the frequency of their equipment at 6MHz, where the wavelength would be 50m.

CHAIN HOME

Unfortunately, these frequencies proved unreliable due to ionospheric refraction. Wavelengths/frequencies of 26m/11.5MHz and eventually 13m/23MHz were both tried, before the latter was found satisfactory and was adopted as the basis for the pioneering "Chain Home" radar network.

The use of 23MHz for "Chain Home" had been unduly conservative from a theoretical viewpoint. From the practical point of view, it was nearly ideal, since the power transmitters and sensitive receivers required could be developed using the experience gained by short-wave radio equipment. The amateur radio enthusiasts who had steadily reduced operating wavelengths (increased frequencies) from

80m (3.75MHz) to 40m (7.5MHz) then to 20m (14MHz) during the inter-war era of radio experimentation were also to provide a valuable pool of trained manpower able to help with the task of keeping the network of "Chain Home" stations operational around the clock during the early stages of the war.

During the war, engineers in Britain and Germany found that further increases in operating frequency had little effect on target detectability. Since increased frequency (shorter wavelength) allowed a narrower beam to be obtained from a given size of antenna, the use of ever higher frequencies became the key to both improved accuracy and resolution and of ways of producing compact yet effective sets for airborne and

Below: Early research into radar reflectivity showed that the apparent echoing area – known as the radar cross-section (RCS) and

calculated as an imaginary sphere – varied widely with changing aspect angle. A small change in angle could affect the observed RCS.

Variation in RCS with Angle

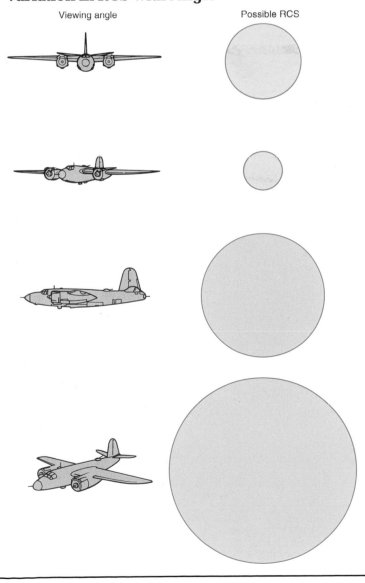

Viewing angle   Possible RCS

other applications in which space and weight were at a premium.

Soon after the war, security restrictions on the massive amount of research and development which had been invested in radar technology were relaxed, allowing the publication of several textbooks, culminating in the classic *Radiation Laboratory* series, a collection of definitive textbooks prepared by the Radiation Laboratory of the Massachusetts Institute of Technology to record the contemporary state of the art.

CROSS-SECTION

Reading these and other early radar textbooks books shows how far the engineers of the early 1940s had progressed in studying the complex processes by which radar energy is reflected by an aircraft. "It is essential to realise that the cross-section of a given target will depend not only on the wavelength, but also upon the angle from which the target is viewed by the radar", wrote E.M. Purcell in the 1947 *Radiation Laboratory* volume on radar systems engineering. "The fluctuation of [radar cross-section] with 'target aspect' as it is called, is due to the interference of reflected waves from different parts of the target .... Only for certain special cases can [radar cross-section] be calculated rigorously; for most targets [it] has to be inferred from the radar data."

To define the radar cross-section of a target, the radar engineer calculates the size of a sphere which would reflect the same amount of radar energy as the aircraft he has measured. The RCS in square metres is then the area of a circle of the same diameter as this imaginary sphere.

A Taylorcraft light aircraft had an RCS of 170sq ft (16m²), Purcell and collaborator A.J.F. Siegert reported, while a B-17 bomber had an RCS of 800sq ft (74m²). (Since those early days, RCS has by convention been measured in metric terms, so the corresponding imperial/US units will no longer be given in the text which follows.)

"Only a rough estimate of the cross-section of such targets as aircraft or ships can be obtained by calculation", they warned. "Even if one could carry through the calculation for the actual target (usually one has to be content with considering a simplified model) the comparison of calculated and observed cross-section would be extremely difficult because of the strong dependence of the cross-section on aspect."

RCS VARIATIONS

To illustrate this, they reported on tests made using a B-26 bomber. In many cases, the level of radar energy reflected could vary by as much as 15dB when the viewing angle was changed by only a third of a degree.

The decibel (dB) is a unit of measurement much used in electronics. It is often found in technical articles on anything from hi-fi to electronic warfare. The key to understanding it is to realise that it describes a ratio between two values and that it is calculated logarithmically and not arithmetically. An increase of 3dB amounts to an arithmetic doubling, for example, while an increase of 10dB represents a tenfold increase.

What Purcell and Siegert were saying in "scientific shorthand" was that a third of a degree change in viewing angle could affect the measured RCS of the B-26 by a factor of up to 32. Post-war research has shown that in practice the RCS of real-world targets can fluctuate by up to 80dB (up to a million).

One factor influencing RCS was propeller position, they reported, while the effect of propeller rotation both increased and modulated the radar return. Tests had shown that shutting down the starboard engine of the test B-26 reduced RCS in the sector from 2 to 5 o'clock by a massive amount. Much research in the 1950s and 1960s was devoted to studying the exact mechanisms by which electromagnetic beams were reflected by objects of various shapes and sizes.

Much of the results remain classified to this day but the little information which has leaked suggests that, although the individual phenomena which caused reflection from different types of basic shape were becoming better understood, the problem of calculating and predicting RCS remained close to unsolvable.

Two factors resulted in the eventual breakthrough. One was the Vietnam War, where US military aircraft and their crews had been exposed to radar-directed air-defences.

The other was the development of the supercomputer. These giant and incredibly fast machines

Variation in RCS with Propeller Position

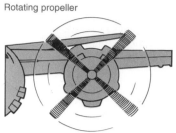

Rotating propeller

Widely varing RCS

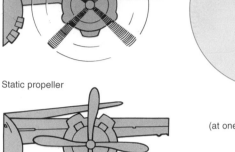

Static propeller

Static RCS
(at one angle and frequency)

Above: **Wartime researchers trying to understand RCS even found that stopping and starting an engine and its associated propeller could markedly affect the radar cross-section of a bomber.**

Right: **In the 1930s, UK radar designers tried to match wavelength with the wingspan of typical bombers.**

had been developed for two basic applications – codebreaking and computer simulation of the intricate processes and reactions at the heart of a nuclear or thermo-nuclear explosion. As soon as enough of these costly machines had been built to satisfy at least partially the needs of the codebreakers and nuclear weapon designers, radar engineers applied their massive capability to those thorny problems of RCS prediction.

To understand the different ways in which an aircraft or missile reflects radar energy, a good starting point is the principle stated earlier in this chapter. "When the radar wave hits the target, it induces electric and magnetic currents within that object. By the act of flowing, these

Typical Wingspans of 1930s Bombers

Aircraft	First flight	Wingspan
Dornier Do 17	1934	59ft (18m)
Heinkel He111	1935	74ft (22.4m)
Armstrong Whitworth Whitley	1936	84ft (25.6m)
Bristol Blenheim	1936	56ft (17.1m)

Above: **The development of radar-guided AA weapons such as the SA-2 Guideline created new interest in methods of reducing RCS.**

Right: **A radar wave which strikes a flat metal plate such as a fin reflects in much the same way as a light beam reflects from a mirror. Like a**

transmitted beam, this reflected energy forms a main beam, flanked by several smaller beams known as sidelobes.

currents in turn cause an electromagnetic wave to be created. It is this latter wave which the radar sees as a reflected echo."

This is what radar and stealth engineers call the scattering process, the newly created wave being known as the "scattered field". Stealth technology is the art of controlling that scattering so as to minimise the amount of energy returned to the radar.

The wavelength of a radar wave can have three possible relationships with the dimensions of the target – it can be much bigger, roughly the same size or much smaller. In each case, a different type of scattering will take place.

SCATTERING

If the wavelength is much larger than the dimensions of the target, all parts of the target are illuminated by the same part of the wave and the result is what is known as Rayleigh scattering. Under such conditions, only gross size and shape of the target are important and RCS is roughly proportional to target size. Since a frequency of around 100MHz is the lowest normally used for radar, the longest military significant wavelength which a target will receive is thus around 3m. In most cases, this will be smaller than the target, so Rayleigh scattering is of little importance, although it could be significant when predicting the RCS of small details such as gun muzzles, vents, grilles and protrusions.

In cases where the wavelength is close to the target dimensions, resonant scattering is observed. This, it

Diffraction

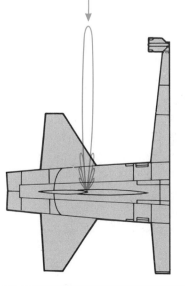

Scattered waves creep around tubular structure

Scattering from conical point

Scattering from sharp edge

Scattering from sharp corners

Above: Radar waves grazing a circular structure can creep around its circumference, while waves striking a conical point, a sharp edge such as a leading edge, or a corner are scattered by a process known as diffraction.

may be remembered, is what the British tried to achieve with the original choice of "Chain Home" operating frequency. Target behaviour under such resonant and near-resonant cases (known as the Mie region) is the most difficult to predict. The phase of the incident wave changes several times along the length of the target. Overall geometry of the target is important, since every part of the target affects every other part. Resonance may occur between specular reflected waves and creeping waves. The resulting Mie-region RCS is very dependent on aspect angle and can fluctuate massively.

When the wavelength is very much smaller than the target, interactions between the latter's different parts are minimal and the target can be treated as a collection of independent scattering centres. The incoming wave acts in a manner similar to light and the laws of optics, so stealth engineers use geometric optics (GO) to help them predict the RCS of a target.

The smallest target for most radars will be a jet fighter or a cruise missile. A light fighter is normally about 45ft (14m) in length, while a modern cruise missile is often around 21ft (6.5m) in length. The radar signals directed against them will have wavelengths of between 0.75in and 10ft (2cm and 3m). In most cases, the target will be 10 or more wavelengths long, making high-frequency scattering the most important component of the overall RCS.

INTERACTIONS

With high-frequency scattering, every part of the target scatters energy independently of the rest of the structure. This in theory would make it relatively easy to estimate the effect of each and, by integration, the scattered field and thus the RCS of the entire target. In practice, the interaction between all the individual scatterers which make up a complex shape such as an aircraft is so complex as to require the use of powerful computers.

Just as a curved surface on an aircraft will exhibit a reflection in sunlight, that surface will have a similar radar reflection. This is termed specular reflection and is a strong component of RCS. When a radar wave is reflected from a flat surface – another form of specular

Reflection

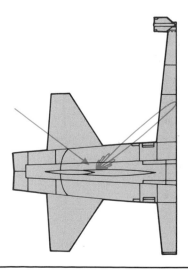

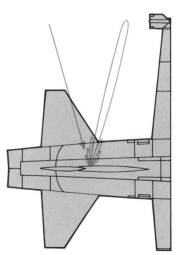

reflection – it behaves rather like a beam of light striking a mirror, or a squash ball bouncing off the walls of the squash court. The angle of incidence equals the angle of reflection. A simple example of this is when a child "skips" a stone across the surface of a pond. The stone descends towards the water at a shallow grazing angle of 10 or 15 degrees (the angle of incidence) then after striking the water begins to rise at the same 10 to 15 degree angle (the angle of reflection).

The reflected energy does not confine itself to a single beam or lobe. Diffraction results in the formation of sidelobes which send smaller amounts of energy off in a number of directions slightly displaced from the axis of the main lobe.

DIFFRACTION

This simple theory breaks down completely when dealing with such discontinuities as edges, tips and corners or changes in slope or curvature. Here the re-radiated field is the result of a process known as diffraction. It depends on the shape of the feature in question, the direction from which it is being illuminated, the position of the observer and the polarisation of the radar wave. To calculate the result, engineers rely on the geometric theory of diffraction (GTD).

Below: **Aircraft fuselages, external stores and even the metal skin of the wing or fins can all provide a habitat for travelling waves.**

Typical Radar Wavelengths

Frequency	Application	Wavelength
150MHz	Long-range surveillance	6.5ft (2m)
2GHz	Surveillance	6in (15cm)
10GHz	Tracking	1.2in (3cm)

Surface waves of electric and magnetic current flowing along the structure of an aircraft or missile in response to the arrival of radar energy pose further problems for the stealth designer. These surface waves come in several forms. Rounded targets such as cylinders or spheres suffer from creeping waves. As its name suggests, the creeping wave flows around the skin of a target. Starting from the point where the radar wave just grazes the edge of the curved surface (known as the "shadow boundary"), the currents creep round onto the

Above: **A combat aircraft is likely to be illuminated by many different radars, and a wide range of wavelengths.**

Right: **Radar waves grazing a long metallic structure such as this MiG-21 fuselage and its external tanks induce travelling waves in the skin.**

Below: **Travelling waves re-radiate radar energy away from the radar. On reaching a discontinuity or the end of the structure, they are reflected, and now add this energy to the total RCS observed by the receiver.**

Travelling Waves

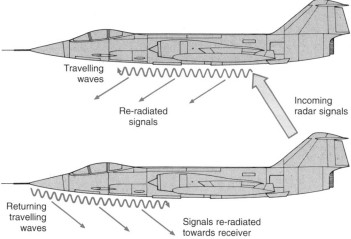

Travelling waves

Re-radiated signals

Incoming radar signals

Returning travelling waves

Signals re-radiated towards receiver

side not illuminated by the radar, then back towards the opposite edge. Once at the opposite edge, they then re-radiate energy back towards the radar. If the object around which they are creeping is more than 10 or 15 wavelengths in diameter, they are of little importance.

TRAVELLING WAVES

Much more troublesome are what are known as travelling waves which affect long slim objects such as missile airframes, fuel tanks and underwing stores, or even the entire fuselage of a slender aircraft such as the F-104 or TR-1. Radar energy striking such a target at low angles of incidence, that is to say close to head on, create what engineers call a surface travelling wave. This is an electric and magnetic current which heads down the length of the target object.

As it does so, it will emit its own electromagnetic field, a signal which heads in the same general direction as the illuminating radar signal. The principle of "angle of incidence equals the angle of reflection" still applies. Since this reflected signal is directed away from the illuminating radar, it adds nothing to the target RCS and is of no immediate concern to the stealth designer.

The problem comes when the travelling wave reaches the far end of the object along which it is flowing. Having nowhere to go, it is reflected back up along the body, still emitting its own

electromagnetic field. Unfortunately, this time the reflected energy is directed back towards the illuminating radar, adding to the target's overall RCS.

In the case of an aircraft fuselage illuminated from the forward sector, similar surface waves will be set up. As these travel backwards along the fuselage, they may meet discontinuities such as seams, gaps, changes in surface material or sudden changes in shape.

In terms of traditional aircraft engineering, such features are common and pose no problems. For example, mid-1960s vintage MiG-21s were notorious for large gaps between individual fuselage panels. On a stealth aircraft, such surface discontinuities must be eliminated. If the surface wave cannot continue along its route, it will reflect backwards along the fuselage as did the travelling wave, adding its own unwanted contribution to aircraft RCS. All discontinuities such as edges, gaps and corners are good scatterers of radar energy.

When an aircraft is illuminated from the rear sector, fuselage travelling waves can become a major problem. Moving forward along the fuselage, they eventually arrive at the nose, where they are reflected back down the fuselage, adding to the rearward RCS.

As we have already seen, the largest RCS component is specular reflection. On a typical aircraft, creeping and

travelling waves will account for around 1m² of the total. As RCS-reduction measures reduce specular reflection, these lesser sources become more important, so must be treated.

DIHEDRALS

A major headache for the stealth designer is the dihedral, a radar-reflective area created whenever two metallic surfaces are positioned at 90 degrees to

one another. An incoming radar signal entering the right angle formed by two such surfaces will carry out a "double-bounce" manoeuvre, the geometry of which ensures that the signal will be returned in exactly the same direction as the incoming. To see a simple analogy, drive a ball towards the corner of a pool table. It will bounce off one edge of the table, then off the adjacent edge, and emerge heading back towards the player.

To continue the analogy, if you sawed the corner off the pool table leaving a 12in (30cm) wide gap in place of the pocket, then drove the ball back towards the corner (but not directly into the gap) it would still carry out a similar bounce manoeuvre from the sides and re-emerge. This illustrates the fact that the two surfaces of a corner reflector need not meet; they only need be at 90 degrees with respect to one another.

CORNERS

Armed with this knowledge, the reader should have no difficulty is identifying radar-reflective corner reflectors on a modern warplane. Horizontal stabilisers are often at right angles to the vertical fin, underwing pylons are at right angles to the wing lower surface, cruciform wings and fins of missiles and bombs fit the bill nicely, while common features such as wing fences and stiffening ribs add their share of 90 degree corners.

Let three surfaces meet at 90 degrees and an even more dangerous triple-bounce manoeuvre is possible, returning a strong radar signal over a wide range of aspect angles. This junction of three surfaces is called a

Typical Dihedral Reflector

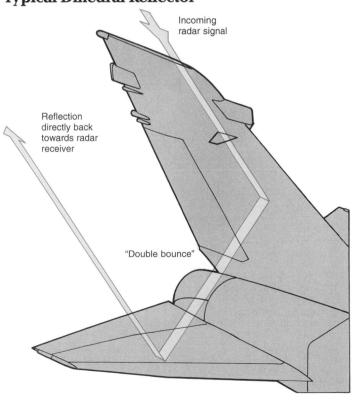

Incoming radar signal

Reflection directly back towards radar receiver

"Double bounce"

Left: **Two surfaces at 90 degrees can turn a radar signal through 180 degrees, providing a strong echo. Three surfaces meeting at right angles are even more effective at enhancing the reflection.**

corner reflector. In some non-aerospace applications corner reflectors are deliberately created. For example metal corner reflectors a few feet (less than a metre) in size are often fitted to the masts of sailing boats to help coastguard radar detect them.

No aircraft has such an external feature but canopies are transparent to radar waves and cockpits contain many box-like objects and 90 degree corners. Accidental creation of a corner reflector is only too easy.

To see a corner reflector in action, watch when driving at night for the reflective "cats eyes" often used as road markers. These are designed to catch the light from the car's headlamps, returning it directly to the driver. The more powerful the headlamps, the brighter the "cat's eyes" will shine. That is how a corner reflector behaves when seen by a radar.

CAVITIES

The corner reflector is just one of the features which the stealth designer terms a "re-entrant structure" – an object which traps and strongly reflects radar energy. Substitute the word "cavity" for "re-entrant structure", pick up a photo of your favourite warplane and you'll begin to take a jaundiced view of intakes, jet pipes, suck-in doors, air scoops and other vents, gun muzzles and other common features. All are prominent radar targets.

Bear in mind the fact that radomes, canopies and other transparencies are also radar-transparent and a new set of re-entrant structures can be found. The cockpit and any electro-optical (EO) fairings are prime candidates, while

Above: **Hidden from sight under nose radomes, radar antennas are designed to handle 'friendly' signals, but also add to RCS.**

Below: **Count the 90 degree angles on this Tornado interceptor and its weapons – each will add its share to the total radar signature.**

Left: **This Grumman A-6 Intruder has a typical collection of exposed cavities, inlets, vents and grilles – all highly reflective.**

work. Unfortunately for the stealth engineer they are not; when one is peaking in the positive direction, others are approaching their peak or dying away to zero, while yet more are doing the same thing in the negative direction. In engineering parlance, they are "out of phase" with one another. To complicate matters further, the polarisation of each individual return may be changed by the reflection process, while the reflectivity of each individual scatterer will vary with frequency, each member of the hierarchy of basic shapes is behaving in a different frequency-related manner.

The summation of all the individual reflections from a complex target is made even more chaotic by the effect of changes in viewing angle. Two individual reflections which are in phase to the observer (and thus boosting each other's strength) will be out of phase if the observer moves, while further movement will bring them back in phase, then out of phase again, and so on. Signals which are out of phase with each other will interfere with one another. If they are ot opposite phase, one will tend to cancel out the other – a process known as destructive interference. Take into account the fact that literally hundreds of signals are involved, then it is little wonder that the total fluctuates violently.

Such then are the complex and intractable rules of radar reflection. Given their compexity, it is little wonder

that as late as 1981, in *IEEE Transactions on Antennas and Propagation*, Edward M. Kennaugh was to describe how "As measurement capabilities improved, investigation of the variation of RCS with these parameters [target aspect, radar frequency and wave polarisation] provided the radar analyst with a plethora of data, but few insights into this relation." Despite his pessimism, enough was understood to allow engineers to devise methods of reducing RCS, creating design rules which would make stealth aircraft possible.

The breakthrough had come in the mid-1960s, when Pyotr Ufmitsev, then the chief scientist at the Moscow Institute for Radio Engineering, made a study of the equations devised by Clerk Maxwell and subsequently refined by the German physicist Arnold Johannes Sommerfield. From these, he devised a workable theoretical method of calculating RCS.

The computer technology of the time could not accurately compute the RCS of a collection of curved surfaces, but could tackle a series of flat surfaces. Since the design of an aircraft requires the use of curved surfaces, Ufmitsev found that the Soviet aircraft designers of the time were not interested in his theory, which was finally published in unclassified form under the title "Method of Edge Waves in the Physical Theory of Diffraction". The key to creating a stealth aircraft now existed, yet was to be ignored for almost a decade.

Below: **One of the biggest radar-reflective cavities on any aircraft is the cockpit and its cluttered consoles. This is a MiG-29 Fulcrum.**

behind the radome lurks an ideal reflector in the shape of the radar antenna, particularly if the latter is of the traditional paraboloid "dish" type. On some aircraft, the radar antenna is deliberately slewed to an extreme angle when the radar is not being used, so as to reduce its contribution to the head-on RCS.

RCS CALCULATIONS

In the Middle Ages, students of the occult drew up long lists of demons and spirits, solemnly documenting their relative positions and powers in a sort of satanic hierarchy.

Stealth engineers have their own version of the "Hierarchy of Hell", with the three-surface corner reflector cast in the rôle of the major villain. Such lists detail all the common geometric shapes in order of descending radar reflectivity. Directly beneath the three-surface corner reflector is its two-surface cousin, followed by the flat plate, cylinder, sphere, straight edge, curved edge, cone, followed by various types of curvature. It may seem at first sight about as pointless as the listing drawn up by their mediaeval predecessors, but it is in fact a list of many of the basic shapes into which a larger and more complex target may be broken down.

In theory at least, all you have to do is add up the RCS from a dozen or so major shapes, plus dozens if not hundreds of smaller ones to get the RCS of the complete aircraft. In practice, all these individual returns interfere with one another.

Remember how the components of an electromagnetic wave continually swing from positive to negative and back again? If all the hundreds of individual reflected signals were all in step with one another (engineers would say "in phase" with one another), such simple addition would

DESIGNING A STEALTH AIRCRAFT

Creation of a stealth aircraft or missile requires that the visual, radar, thermal and acoustic signatures be reduced. There are other more exotic signatures, some of which have potential as the basis for anti-stealth sensors, but these are the most important.

To achieve a militarily significant reduction in RCS, three techniques may be used: (1) avoid design features which will create strong reflections in the direction of the radar; (2) absorb rather than reflect the incoming radar energy; (3) mask or cancel out any remaining reflections;

No single approach will provide enough RCS reduction. The first and second of these techniques are already used in different degrees by existing stealth aircraft and missiles; the third could be in use already and will certainly play a significant role in future aircraft designs.

Earlier we used the analogy of comparing a radar system with a searchlight. In one respect, this analogy was badly flawed – the searchlight illuminated its victim so that other air-defence weapons could detect the reflected light. Once the powerful beam had lit the target aircraft, the reflected light could be seen by anti-aircraft gunners on the ground and even by the crews of any friendly nightfighters operating within visual range.

REFLECTIONS

In the case of almost all present-day radars, the sensor which is looking for the reflected echo uses the same antenna as was used to send out the illuminating pulse. Only the reflected energy which returns directly to the radar is usable. Energy which is redirected in other directions will do nothing to betray the target.

Careful control of aircraft shape plays a vital part in reducing RCS at microwave frequencies by directing the scattered signal away from the radar which is trying to receive it. On early stealth aircraft, including the Lockheed F-117A, it was the

main RCS-reduction measure.

For shaping to be useful as an RCS-reducing measure, it must be done when the aircraft is first designed, and compromises must be avoided. For this reason, little can be done to retrofit stealth onto an existing aircraft – the best the designer can hope to achieve is to delay detectability. The end result is not a stealth aircraft.

To avoid directing reflected energy back to the hostile radar, the stealth designer tries to observe a series of rules. One of the most important is to avoid the use of large flat vertical surfaces. No attempt was made when designing the B-52 to keep RCS to a minimum, so that aircraft's slab sides and relatively straight lines make it a prominent radar target. If vertical fins or fuselage sides must be used, these should be canted inward. Canted fuselage sides may be seen on the Boeing AGM-86B ALCM and on Teledyne's Model 324 and 350 RPVs, while the same company's AQM-91A Compass Arrow RPV shows

Left: **This mid-1980s Lockheed AFT "artist's impression" shows two-dimensional afterburner nozzles.**

an example of inward-canted tail surfaces. Many early-1980s artists' impressions of stealth fighters also incorporated inward-tilted vertical fins.

Two approaches may be taken to eliminate reflections from the fuselage. The most obvious is to curve the fuselage surfaces, preferably in two dimensions – a technique used on the SR-71 and B-1 bomber. For best results, this curvature should be concave (inward); convex (outward) curvature would be reflective. The designer should avoid discontinuities such as corners and abrupt changes of shape/profile, blending and smoothing all wing/fin and surface junctions. This removes geometric discontinuities which would result in wave scattering.

FLAT CANOPY

There remain limits to what can be done with curvature, especially given the fact that most practical designs demand convex curves. An early morning walk along a fighter flight-line on a sunny day will show just how effectively curved surfaces such as fuselage sides and cockpit canopies can reflect the sunlight over a range of

aspect angles. Radar waves would also reflect in a similar manner.

The first aircraft to try to eliminate this problem in

optical terms was the US Army's Bell AH-1S Cobra. On the earlier AH-1G and AH-1J, the canopy used conventional rounded transparencies but

Left: **Features of the B-52 which create high RCS include the slab-sided fuselage, and the engine pods and pylons.**

Above: **Light glints from the curved fuselage of a Mirage 2000. Radar energy can be reflected in the same manner, increasing RCS.**

Above: The angular "flat-plate" canopy on this AH-1S uses faceting to reduce optical glint. A similar technique can also be employed to reduce RCS.

the version adopted for the -1S was of flat-panel design, consisting of seven surfaces. Each individual section reflected sunlight in one direction only, making the overall design less likely to betray the aircraft's position.

The wing leading edge can be a strong reflector in the forward sector. Given that the reflected energy from an incoming head-on radar signal will leave a wing leading edge at an angle equal to twice that of the leading-edge sweep angle at the point of "impact", increasing the sweep angle will increase the amount by which the reflected energy is shifted away from the forward sector, thus reducing the chances that it will be detected by the receiver of the head-on radar. At high angles of sweep, most of the reflected energy is deflected at angles away from the critical forward sector.

FACETING

On most aircraft, the leading and trailing edges are straight or near-straight, so the reflected energy will be concentrated over a narrow range of angles. This phenomenon was noticed by the Swedish Air Force, which realised that its Saab J35 Draken was a difficult radar target when seen head-on. The two sweep angles of its double-delta wing served to direct radar energy well away from the forward direction.

Since wing and horizontal leading/trailing edges are good radar reflectors, the angles used on the wing and stabiliser leading and trailing edges must either be kept common (scattering the radar energy in a few carefully-chosen directions) or made as different as possible (so as to "dump" the reflected energy in several pre-planned sectors).

As wing sweep is increased, the delta wing becomes more attractive but, by its long chord, will provide an opportunity for travelling waves to be set up. These can in turn be minimised by rounding the wingtips, minimising the reflective discontinuity which the travelling waves will meet when they reach the trailing edge of the wing.

These are the basic rules which defined the configuration of the first stealth aircraft. Both the Lockheed (XST/F-117A) and Northop (B-2) teams came up with the same solution in terms of wing planform – straight leading edges which would re-direct the radar energy well away from the frontal sector, plus a moderate sweep angle which would keep the chord short enough to avoid the worst effects of surface travelling waves. Lockheed opted for a faceted fuselage – probably the only practical configuration given mid-1970s technology – and

eliminated horizontal and vertical tail surfaces by adopting a "V" configuration. Faceting would have imposed a significant range penalty on a long-range bomber, so Northrop backed a combination of curvature and advanced RAM for its flying wing design and relied on a sophisticated flight control system which would allow the elimination of all vertical surfaces.

CAVITIES

Creation of a practical stealth aircraft or missile requires meticulous attention to detail if RCS is to be minimised. Cavities such as air intakes, known to stealth engineers as "re-entrant structures", have a high RCS. Prediction of the RCS of a cavity is difficult and depends on what is in the cavity. As a first order approximation, the stealth engineer can assume that the RCS will be similar to that of a flat plate of equivalent size.

A cavity must either be shielded in some manner so that the radar energy cannot enter, or must be treated with radar-absorbent material (RAM). The techniques used to create effective forms of RAM will be described later in this chapter. For the moment it should be noted that devising RAM to treat cavities is not easy, since

The RCS Effects of Wing Sweep Angle

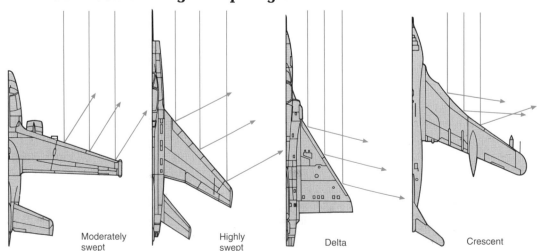

Moderately swept

Highly swept

Delta

Crescent

Left: The wing leading edge of an aircraft can be a strong radar reflector but increased sweep angles will direct radar reflections away from the critical head-on sector. Use of a changing sweep angle, such as on the crescent wing of the Handley Page Victor, can scatter the reflected energy over a wide range of angles.

the radar frequencies used for military purposes cover at between two and three orders of magnitude, and electromagnetic characteristics of the chosen material (such as permeability and dielectric constant) will vary considerably with frequency, as will the optimum thickness required.

The powerplant and its associated inlets and nozzles are large cavities, and can be a major contributor to RCS. The front and rear faces of the engine are the primary signature source, followed by the inlet edges, and any variable-geometry control surfaces used for adjusting airflow.

Many stealth configurations have engine inlets mounted above the wing or fuselage to keep them hidden from ground-based radars, but any aerodynamicist will warn of the possibility of airflow problems during high angle-of-attack manoeuvres. When radar energy strikes, the compressor or fan face of a jet engine effectively acts as a solid surface, preventing the wave from proceeding further. The most obvious way of reducing intake RCS would be to coat the first-stage blades with RAM. This would have the

Faceting on the F-117A

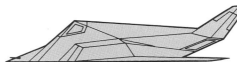

desired effect, but is not a practical solution – the absorbent material could not cope with the stresses caused by the high rotational speeds.

On a high-flying reconnaissance aircraft or maritime patrol aircraft, the threat may be primarily from below, allowing high-RCS features such as inlets and exhausts to be moved onto upper surfaces where they

Above: **The Lockheed F-117A Nighthawk stealth fighter makes extensive use of faceting in order to reduce RCS. Its shape remained secret until late in 1988.**

Below: **The huge inlets of the AV-8A (and other members of the Harrier family) will give radars a good view of the front face of the Pegasus turbofan engine.**

will be screened from below by the wing. On a low-level strike aircraft, the main threat may well prove to be look-down/shoot-down radars, forcing such reflective features onto the aircraft's underside.

In cases such as an air-superiority fighter where attack could come from above or below, shaping starts to get tricky. In his massive textbook *Radar Cross-Section Reduction* Eugene F. Knott poses the question "What rationale can be taken if all threat directions are equally likely?" His answer is not comforting – "It is a question that has not been satisfactorily answered."

Conventional ramp-type inlets often give a head-on observer a good view of the engine fan or compressor face, so are near-ideal radar reflectors. A quick look down the intake of a MiG-29 at the 1988 Farnborough air show gave me a good look at the front face of the powerful R-33 turbofan and the realisation that a reduced RCS was far from being a significant design goal when Belyakov and his team developed this agile and effective fighter aircraft.

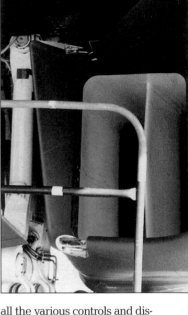

Above: **The inlets of the B-1A were designed for Mach 2 dash performance, so incorporated variable ramps intended to match the airflow to the engine.**

Intakes may be designed to use half-cone centre-bodies of the sort used on the Mirage fighter. Efficient and light, these would block much radiation, preventing it from reaching the engine. Further measures which would prevent radars from "seeing" the highly reflective front face of the jet engines include long sinuous serpentine or even zig-zag air trunking in which radar energy could be trapped inside the inlet, then bounced back and forth and damped by radar-absorbent material (RAM).

In the 1940s, the US National Advisory Committee for Aeronautics (NACA) developed flush inlets. Visible from a smaller range of angles than a conventional inlet, these could be a viable alternative to conventional designs. Tested in 1950 on the first of two experimental YF-93A prototypes, these were replaced on the second aircraft by conventional lateral intakes. The sole current application is on the McDonnell Douglas Harpoon anti-ship missile.

In the early 1960s, Teledyne Ryan reconnaissance drones were flown with wire-mesh screens over their prominent "shark's mouth" air inlets. This worked well against long-wavelength threats such as Soviet surveillance radars but would be difficult to implement against modern centimetric radars. To be effective, the mesh must be smaller than a small fraction of a wavelength. A quick look at the window of a microwave oven will show just how small a centimetric mesh must be.

Treatment of engine nozzles is also very important, and is complicated by high temperatures created by the efflux of a jet engine. The electromagnetic design requirements for radar-absorbent coatings are not different from those used for lower-temperature cavities such as inlets, but maintaining structural integrity is much more difficult.

The efflux from a jet engine will also have some level of radar reflectivity, and is dependent on maximum gas temperature. While the radar return from the efflux of an engine running in dry (military) power is insignificant, the rise in temperature which results from afterburning could result in strong radar reflection.

COCKPITS

One of the most troublesome cavities on an aircraft is the cockpit. Virtually as transparent to radar energy as it is to light, the canopy or windshield allows radar energy access to the cluttered and radar-reflective cockpit interior. The pilot's head and helmet, the ejection seat and all the various controls and displays in the cockpit all contribute a major share to the signature of the aircraft.

One way of preventing this is to use an external shape for the canopy which conforms to good low RCS design rules, then to metalise it with a coating which will have minimal effect of visibility, but will be "seen" by the radar as being an electrically conductive surface rather than a transparency – virtually an extension of the aircraft's skin.

Such coatings must pass at least 85 per cent of the visible energy and reflect virtually all of the radar energy. The techniques for doing this are well established. A thin layer of gold on the canopy transparency of the EA-6B

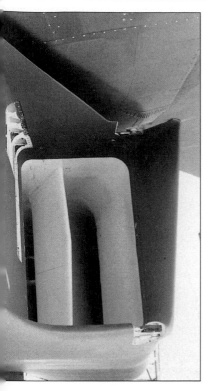

Above: **The B-1B is optimised for high-subsonic cruise, so the inlets were redesigned as simpler fixed-geometry units with engine-concealing anti-radar baffles.**

Below: **Side-fuselage flush intakes (seen here on the experimental North American YF-03 derivative of the F-86 Sabre) prevent radar from "seeing" the engine inlet.**

Right: **The antennas, equipment racks and LRUs within the radome of this Tornado IDS may act as hot spots when illuminated by enemy radar.**

Prowler protects the crew from the powerful signal emitted by the aircraft's jammers. Indium-tin is another possible canopy coating, and is reported to allow 98 per cent transmission of visible light.

For canopy-plating to be effective, the conductive film on the transparency must be electrically continuous with the fuselage. This implies the use of conductive seals such as the inflatable fabric-reinforced silicone rubber seals used on the Saab JAS-39 Gripen. Canopy profile should also be kept low in order to minimise scattering at the fuselage/canopy junction.

Since any form of radio or radar antenna is required to be an efficient receiver or radiator of electromagnetic energy, it is a difficult feature to incorporate into a stealth aircraft. On the F-117A, the radio system uses retractable antennas that can be extended when the pilot wishes to receive or transmit radio messages, but are kept retracted when the aircraft needs to be stealthy.

Radars are even more of a problem. Aircraft radomes are custom designed to match the operating frequency of the radar they cover, but are also transparent to a much wider band of frequencies, exposing the antenna to hostile radars.

A radar antenna makes two contributions to RCS. One is the scattering due to its structure, the other is more subtle, and due to its function-related shape. Radar energy arriving at a conventional paraboloidal "dish"

antenna will be gathered and focussed onto the antenna feed in exactly the same way as the echo return signal. Not being at the frequency for which the feed was designed, it will reflect, travelling back along the same route and being sent off on its unwanted way by the main reflector.

Flat planar-array antennas of the type used in more recent designs are less of a problem but measures must still be taken to reduce their RCS. The design used on the B-1B is deliberately canted downward to reduce its signature, relying on electronic beam steering to direct the radar energy ahead of the aircraft rather than in the direction the planar antenna is facing.

In the long run, the antenna must be concealed from hostile radars by mounting it within a special radome. One possibility for stealth aircraft would be to devise a "band-pass" radome transparent only to the relatively narrow band of frequencies used by the stealth aircraft's own radar. A more intriguing possibility is that of an electrically-switchable radome. This takes the band-pass concept a stage further by arranging for suitable electrical impulses to turn the band-pass characteristic off and on in much the same way that electrical impulses can be used to darken or extinguish

the characters on the LCD display on a digital watch. For most frequencies, and for even the band-pass frequency whenever the radar was not being used, the radome would be opaque.

Panels and doors also add their reflectivity to the total RCS of the aircraft. In a conventional aircraft the edges of such features are often at right angles to the direction of flight, a location which makes them reflect radar energy arriving from the forward sector. The solution is to sweep the panel edges, aligning those edges with other major edges on the aircraft. On stealth aircraft, door edges are either swept at a constant angle, or at several angles that combine to create a "sawtooth" edge.

TRAVELLING WAVES

Travelling waves and other surface waves flowing on the skin of an aircraft or missile can give rise to re-radiation of energy if they meet discontinuities such as seams, gaps between panels, changes in surface material or sudden changes in shape. In designing and building a stealth aircraft, care must therefore be taken to ensure that all gaps and seams are eliminated either by closing the gap with an electrically conducting material (the approach used on the B-1B) or by working to tight tolerances to eliminate gaps (as on the B-2).

Wing slats and flaps can create such gaps, particularly when used for manoeuvring. When an aircraft such as the F-14 Tomcat sets its wing geometry to the combat manoeuvring position, gaps exist between the wing, the slat and the flap. When the wing is illuminated by radar energy, such gaps will help reflect a signal. This is particularly true if the aircraft is illuminated from head-on or the rear quarter, when surface waves moving across the wing chord will meet one of those gaps.

A travelling wave flowing along a fuselage will eventually meet an unavoidable discontinuity – the point at which the structure physically ends, for example, at the tip of a radome or the end of a jetpipe or exhaust. The best way of dealing with it is to attenuate the wave before it reaches the end of the structure. This is often done by applying radar-absorbing material to the surface.

Stealth designers must also eliminate small exposed cavities such as gun muzzles, sensor windows or refuelling receptacles. Most features of this sort should be screened by small doors but the cannon muzzle would probably require a small frangible panel of metallised plastic.

Other conventional features which radar sees as scatter-inducing discontinuities are small fairings, protrusions, grilles, domes and wingtip fairings. If allowed to protrude, even rivets and

other fasteners can act as radar reflectors. Conventional airflow and pressure sensors can be strongly reflective. These must be designed for minimal radar signature and if necessary treated with RAM.

The move towards stealth technology in the former Soviet Union must be demanding a re-think by Russian engineers, who in the past have often resorted to external fairings as a means of accommodating features such as control surface bell-cranks which a Western designer would have buried within the airframe.

Probes and other protruding features will add to the aircraft's RCS, and designing low-observability versions is not easy. The Lockheed Have Blue stealth demonstration aircraft is reported to have used retractable probes that were extended for take-off and

Above: **The mechanism within the US-designed Mission Adaptive Wing (MAW) is classified, but this photo gives a good view of the unit's flexible upper skin.**

Below right: **Internal weapons carriage reduced the drag of the Convair F-102 Delta Dagger. On stealth aircraft, internal ordnance storage also reduces RCS.**

Below: **Unlike conventional leading edge slats and trailing edge flaps, the Mission Adaptive Wing leaves the upper and lower skin surface unbroken. Travelling waves flowing within the wing skin as the result of illumination by radar thus never meet gaps which would cause them to re-radiate energy and increase the apparent RCS.**

landing, but retracted when the aircraft's stealth qualities were being measured. While they were retracted, the aircraft derived speed information from its inertial navigation system.

F-117A project manager Alan Brown has noted that, "On an unstable, fly-by-wire aircraft, it is extremely important to have redundant sources of aerodynamic data. These must

Mission Adaptive Wing

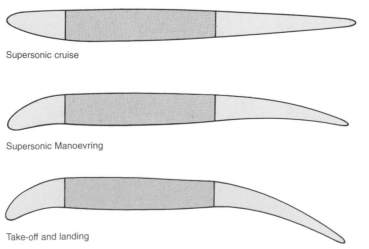

Supersonic cruise

Supersonic Manoevring

Take-off and landing

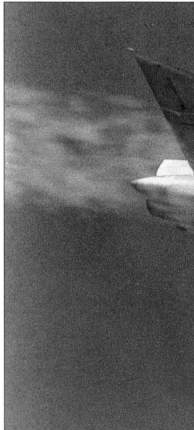

Above: **As part of the Advanced Fighter Technology Integration programme, this F-111 was used to flight test the variable camber Mission Adaptive Wing.**

be very accurate with respect to flow direction, and they must operate ice-free at all times. Static and total pressure probes have been used, but they clearly represent compromises with stealth requirements. Several quite different techniques are in various stages of development."

This need to keep the aircraft as clean as possible effectively rules out the use of traditional types of external stores such as missiles, bombs and equipment pods. External fuel tanks are less of a problem – they would be dropped before coming into range of a hostile radar just in the way that Korean War Sabres dropped tanks before tangling with agile MiGs.

All EW and EO systems must be carried internally, perhaps on interchangeable pallets, while ordnance must be carried in internal weapon bays or in semi-buried conformal locations. The latter might even be covered with expendable radar-absorbing fairings which could be dropped just before weapon release.

WEAPONS CARRIAGE

If any other type of underwing store is needed, it would have to be carried in a radar-absorbent container. A clue to how this may be done can be seen in surface-ship installations of the Harpoon anti-ship missile. This is mounted on the vessel in a cylindrical storage container/launcher. As the round leaves the tube at launch, its wings and fins unfold to their flight position. Delete the solid-fuel tandem booster (which would not be needed for air launch) and make the tube slightly greater in diameter to allow for radar-absorbent material, add streamlined nose and tail caps and you've got a stealthy air-launched Harpoon installation.

Missiles and small-sized bombs could probably be carried in a large underwing container treated with radar-absorbent material and fitted with "bomb doors" or frangible panels on the

Possible Stealth Weapons Carrier

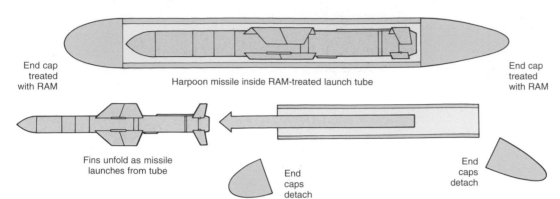

End cap treated with RAM

Harpoon missile inside RAM-treated launch tube

End cap treated with RAM

Fins unfold as missile launches from tube

End caps detach

End caps detach

underside – a stealthy version of the carriers currently used for light practice bombs.

To reduce the space which missiles take up in a weapon's bay or the sort of weapon carrier described above, folding or cropped wings and fins are likely to be used. One of the weapons due to arm the USAF's F-22 Advanced Tactical Fighter is the Raytheon AIM-120A Advanced Medium Range Air-to-Air Missile (AMRAAM). The AIM-120C5 version was the first to introduce cropped surfaces which would allow more missiles to be carried within the aircraft's internal weapons bays.

The exhaust plume from a rocket motor contains radar-reflective ionised gases, which may limit the degree of RCS reduction possible on a stealthy missile. An air-breathing powerplant such as a small turbofan would be more useful.

Moving all the ordnance into an internal bay, and eliminating traditional underwing sensor or EW pods, reduce RCS, but eat into the space available for internal fuel. The use of a weapons bay may also reduce the maximum weapon load, while elimination of external pods prevents the rapid updating of the aircraft by add-ons.

Imagine how slowly EW might have developed during the Vietnam War if all the vitally needed new jamming year had been internally mounted, rather than fielded as add-on underwing pods. The stealthy air force stands to lose this kind of fast-reaction capability. If a sudden requirement emerges for a new sensor or item of EW kit, someone is going to have to find space within an already tightly-packaged warplane.

COMPOSITES

The fact that stealth aircraft are made from composites has already taken a deep hold in aviation folklore. After all, composites are not metal and do not show up on radar.

Such, at least, is the popular theory. What may prove surprising is that the use of composites is not one of the most significant RCS-reduction measures. The wartime de Havilland Mosquito light bomber was made of wood but nobody ever suggested that it had stealth capabilities.

The sad truth is that building an aircraft from materials through which radar energy may pass simply gives the radar a good view of the aircraft's "innards" – in the case of the Mosquito, engines, fuel pumps, electrical wiring and the primitive avionics of the time. The Mosquito undoubtedly did have a lower RCS than a four engined Lancaster or Halifax but this was not militarily significant. The aircraft's survivability came from its high performance rather than any reduction in RCS.

On most stealth aircraft, the outer surfaces are coated with a metallic paint, so that the radar cannot penetrate the composite materials and enter the interior.

The rôle played by composites in reducing RCS is a more subtle one. Carbon is a poor conductor of electricity, being widely used in the manufacture of resistors used by the electronics industry. Epoxy resin is an insulator. As a result, the electrical conductivity of composite materials is low. Radar energy arriving at a composite panel or structure has a hard job setting up the electrical and magnetic currents which re-radiate the energy and form troublesome creeping and travelling waves.

By 1981, Northrop had more than 30 funded contracts worth close to $50 million to develop advanced composites technology. In the early 1980s, the company built experimental structures which were then subjected to a long-term study to investigate the effect of thermal "spikes", radiation

Above: **Many types of missile are already fitted with folding wings and fins so that they can be fired from tubular storage/launch tubes. If the tube and its end caps were to be treated with RAM, stealth aircraft could carry such weapons as low-RCS external stores.**

Right: **The de Havilland Mosquito light bomber was built from wood but this had surprisingly little effect on the aircraft's RCS.**

Below: **Composite manufacturing techniques used on the B-2 were the result of Northrop R&D efforts in the early 1980s.**

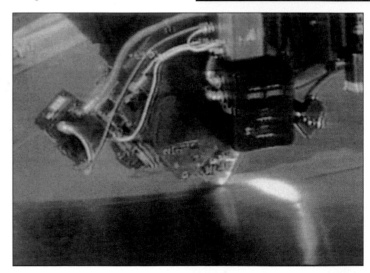

from nuclear explosions and laser energy.

RAM CONCEPTS

In the struggle to minimise RCS, a more useful ally will be reinforced carbon-carbon (RCC). This is created by baking and carbonising a matrix containing carbon fibres. As a material it is strong and exceptionally heat-resistant. Used in the manufacture of missile re-entry vehicles and the nose and wing leading edges of the US Space Shuttle, it could be

used to built low-RCS exhaust systems. To the stealth engineer, the importance of RCC is that it combines these physical virtues with another useful property – the ability to absorb radar energy.

Once the main reflection problems are identified, engineers can modify the design and employ special materials at vulnerable points. Reflections may be reduced by means of radar-absorbent materials – the radar equivalents of the black finish used on the undersides of Second World War night bombers.

There are two broad classes of RAM – resonant and broadband. Resonant absorbers are designed for use at a specific frequency but maintain some effectiveness over a range of frequencies on either side of this nominal operating point. Broadband RAM maintains its effectiveness over a much wider range of frequencies.

The simplest type of resonant RAM is the sandwich-type absorber. This operates on the same principle as the blue- or brown-tinged antireflection optical coatings applied to the lenses of cameras, optical instruments and even spectacles. When the light strikes such a lens, a portion is reflected by the coating. The remainder passes through the coating and strikes the front face of the lens. A portion is reflected, while the remainder enters the lens.

RESONANT ABSORBER

There are now two reflections to consider. Careful choice of coating material ensures that the amounts reflected by the coating and the glass are similar. The coating is arranged to have a thickness equal to one quarter of a wavelength of visible light. As a result, the reflection from the glass surface has travelled an extra distance totalling half a wavelength by the time that it re-emerges from the coating and meets the reflection from the front surface of the coating. That vital half-wavelength difference makes the two waves of light out of phase with one another. As one wave rises above zero, the other falls below zero by an equal and opposite amount. One is the exact opposite of the other and the two cancel each other out, a process known as destructive interference. In theory, all of the reflection should vanish, but the cancellation is never perfect, so some minimal reflection remains.

The earliest resonant RAM materials used the same principle. The Salisbury Screen consisted of a thin sheet of resistive material held at a quarter wavelength distance ahead of a metal backing plate by a low dielectric spacer. Dielectric materials have the property of resisting an electric current, while allowing electrostatic or electromagnetic forces to pass freely. In the Salisbury Screen, this often takes the form of a specially-designed foam or honeycomb material. Another type of absorber known as a Dallenbach Layer consists of a quarter-wavelength thick slab of electrically lossy material applied to a metal backing plate. Exposing a radar signal to a slab of lossy material is rather like exposing a marathon runner to a strong headwind. The slab does not conduct electrical currents, but does have the ability to dissipate a significant portion of any electric energy to which it is exposed. A radar wave arriving at the front surface of the lossy material meets a change in electrical impedance which gives rise to the front-surface reflection.

Principles of Resonant RAM

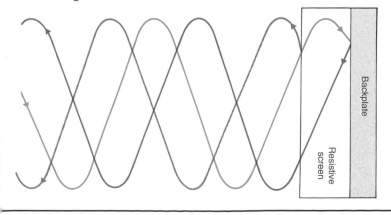

Left: **The Salisbury Screen is the simplest type of resonant RAM. A resistive screen is positioned in front of the back plate. The resistivity of the screen is such that 50 per cent of the incoming radar wave (shown in blue) is reflected from the screen surface, while the remainder passes through to reflect from the back plate. If these two surfaces are positioned quarter of a wavelength apart, the reflections from the screen (mauve) and back plate (red) cancel one another.**

Below: Rockwell engineers applied RAM to key areas of the B-1B in the effort to significantly reduce RCS. The wing root area was a source of reflections and required careful redesign. A thin dark strip of RAM is visible on the wing of this aircraft in construction.

Above: Small dark patches on the unpainted skin of this B-1B around the nose-mounted control vane indicate the presence of RAM.

Right: RAM made from pyramid-shaped elements lines the walls of this anechoic test chamber at the University of Eindhoven.

Had dielectric RAM been the sole solution, stealth technology might never have left the laboratory. Luckily a second type of RAM has been developed which proved much easier to apply to many types of aircraft structure. Known as magnetic RAM, this is based on magnetic material such as compounds of iron, ferrites (ceramic compounds of ferromagnetic materials) or carbonyl iron. These materials are often embedded in sheets of natural or synthetic rubber which can easily be glued into position.

A resonant absorber based on magnetic materials works in much the same way as its dielectrically-loaded counterpart, combining destructive interference with attenuation. Here the energy is dissipated as the magnetic dipoles within the material move in response to the impinging radar wave. The amount of lossy material and binder is selected in order to provide the optimum electromagnetic characteristics for the range of frequencies which the designer is trying to counter.

Most readers who own a cassette recorder or video recorder will be familiar with the brand name TDK. The

Although widely used for many applications such as damping the radar returns from buildings at airports or harbours (applications in which a single or at most a few frequencies need to be countered at minimal cost), interference absorbers are narrow-band and physically bulky, so are not very useful for applications such as stealth aircraft.

DIELECTRIC RAM

In more practical types of resonant (narrow-band) absorber, two effects are used to soak up the incoming radar energy – destructive interference between the reflections from the surface and the backing, and attenuation of the wave by the dielectric material. This type of material is known as a dielectrically-loaded absorber.

The goal of the RAM designer is to create a material the front surface of which will admit a radar wave rather than reflect it. Once within the RAM, the radar wave should then be absorbed, dissipating its energy in the form of heat. For decades, component manufacturers have fabricated electrical resistors from carbon, so it is hardly surprising that the same material should form the basis of many types of RAM. When radar waves strike such a RAM, its limited conductivity causes losses, as does the effort which the molecules must make while attempting to follow the alternating fields. This is known as "lossy dielectric" RAM.

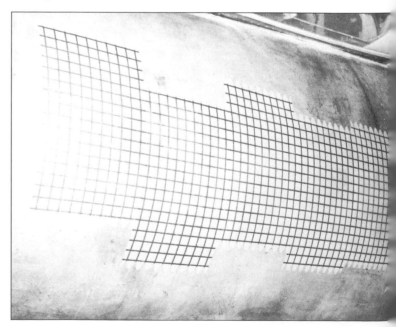

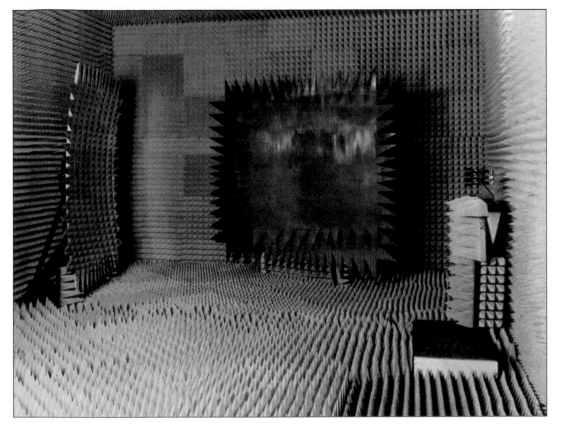

company is the world's largest manufacturer of magnetic recording tape. It owes this lead to Doctor Yogoro Kato of Tokyo Industrial University, who passed the patents for the newly invented ferrite to a venture capitalist in 1932. This co-operation resulted in the founding of TDK.

FERRITE ABSORBER

In the 1970s, the company teamed with NEC to study methods of reducing the metal contamination of water discharged by Japanese steel mills. Having learned how to precipitate this metal waste as

low-grade ferrite, they tried to find a commercial application for what was essentially a waste product.

An application which suggested itself was the creation of RAM. By mixing magnetic material with an epoxy liquid, NEC tried to develop a paint which could be applied to the structure of metal bridges to reduce their reflectivity as seen by radar. A 1979 trial proved disappointing; the paint coating applied to the bridge did absorb a limited amount of radar energy but not over a wide enough range of frequencies.

Narrow-band absorbers can be designed to operate at any frequency but, for any practical stealth applications, a broader coverage is needed. One way of accomplishing this is to make a multilayer absorber, each layer of which is designed to resonate at a different frequency. One simple example is the multilayer Salisbury Screen. The addition of extra resistive sheets and spacers broadens the range of frequencies on either side of the nominal design frequency. For best results, the resistivity of each sheet is arranged to be lower than the one ahead of it, so

that the incoming wave meets sheets of decreasing resistivity. This type of screen, known as a Jaumann absorber, can have two, three, four or even six layers. Since all layers are spaced by the same amount, the total thickness of the screen is increased accordingly. Its bulk makes it unsuitable for most airframe applications.

One early practical application of the Jaumann absorber was a RAM developed during the Second World War by the German Navy for the treatment of submarines. It consisted of seven layers of carbon-impregnated paper, each of increasing conductivity, separated by layers of foam plastic dielectric. It was effective at the 3cm and 10cm frequency band, but was 2.5in (6.35cm) thick and rigid. As a result, it was never deployed on operational U-boats.

PYRAMID ABSORBER

Once again, a more practical solution can be found based on dielectrically-loated and magnetically-loaded materials. What the ideal RAM should do is to gradually match the impedance of the air to that of the metal aircraft skin. If this were achievable, the incoming radar wave would never meet a change in impedance sharp enough to cause a reflection.

First attempts at creating graded material involved dipping mats of curled animal hair into a conductive mixture of carbon and neoprene. The mixture clung to the hair but, as the newly-dipped mats were laid horizontally to dry, the mixture tended to flow downwards, creating a rough and ready dielectric gradient. The resulting material was largely used in the laboratory and on the walls of the first anechoic (reflection-free) radio test chambers developed for indoor antenna testing.

A more practical method of grading the dielectric is to mould the material into a pyramid the apex of which is pointed in the direction of the radar wave. As the wave moves forward and thus down the axis of the pyramid, it exposes itself to more of the dielectric material. This technique is ideal for use in the construction of anechoic chambers, whose pyramid-studded walls are a conspicuous feature of modern photographs showing indoor antenna or RCS tests. The dielectric used here is carbon-loaded foam.

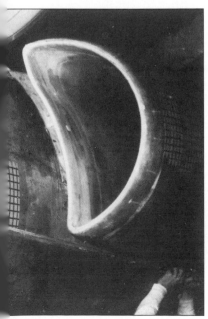

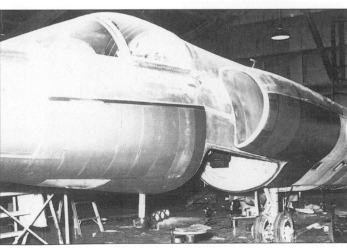

Left and Below: **In his book** *Dragon Lady,* **author Chris Pocock revealed how U-2 aircraft were fitted with panels of radar-absorbing**

Salisbury Screen (fuselage sides below and ahead of the cockpit) and Eccosorb (below the inlets) during late-1950s stealth experiments.

A pyramidal absorber of this classical type is impractical for aircraft use, except in a two-dimensional form buried within wing/fin leading or trailing edges. This type of material was used in the wings of the Lockheed SR-71 and can be clearly seen in some photographs of aircraft under construction.

Pyramidal or hair-mat RAM may be satisfactory for laboratory use, or for the treatment of large structures, but is far too bulky for most aerospace applications. When creating more practical designs, the RAM designer achieves the desired dielectric grading by forming the material from layers of dielectric. If a limited number of radar bands must be countered, a multilayer narrow-band RAM may have one of its layers designed to cope with one band and a second to deal with the other.

RAM PRODUCTS

Wide-band RAMs are normally created by adding a carbon-loaded plastic material to the base such as polyurethane foam. This creates the required "lossy dielectric". The thicker the material, the better the absorption. Maximum values of 90 to 99.9 per cent are possible.

MAGNETIC ABSORBER

Very little information has been released on the characteristics of ferrite paint – often referred to as "iron ball" paint in press reports of stealth technology. Advanced Absorber Products' AAP-021 is a polyurethane-cased sprayable coating, a heavy grey liquid which dries tack free in 40 minutes and hardens in 12 to 24 hours. Its RAM properties depend on the thickness to which it is applied. A 0.03in (0.76mm) coat will reduce the reflected energy by an amount increasing from 3dB at 6GHz to 13dB at 18GHz.

Being based on iron-like material, magnetic RAM is heavy. It also has a tendency to oxidise, a process which degrades its effectiveness. Oxidation is particularly severe at temperatures of more than 900°F (500°C),

creating problems when hypersonic aircraft or ballistic missile re-entry vehicles are being considered for RAM treatment.

Offsetting these disadvantages are the fact that it is thin and that it maintains its effectiveness down to sub-gigahertz frequencies. A Salisbury Screen intended to operate at 100MHz would be 29in (75cm) thick; even a dielectric absorber would be many inches thick. A magnetic RAM able to operate at the same frequency might be only a tenth of the thickness of its dielectric counterpart. Different magnetic materials have their peak efficiency at various frequencies but by layering them one on top of another a broader-band absorber will be created. Ferrite paint may also act as an electrical bonding agent between panels.

Magnetic RAM is most

Above: **The composite wings of Japan's F-2 fighter make extensive use of locally developed radar-absorbing material.**

Below left: **The radar reflectivity of the ferrite paint used on the Lockheed TR-1 can be varied by changing its thickness.**

effective at lower frequencies, dielectric types at the highest frequencies. The logical approach is therefore to combine the two, creating hybrid RAMs effective over the highest possible range of frequencies.

A typical advanced multilayer RAM of the type in service in the late 1980s apparently consists of three layers. The outer and inner layers are partly radar reflective and act rather like a Salisbury Screen. The central layer, made from lossy dielectric material, is intended to help contain the energy reflected from the innermost layer for long enough for cancellation to occur. It also acts as a traditional lossy dielectric absorber.

CIRCUIT ANALOGUE

Another type of RAM can be created by replacing the resistive sheet used in Salisbury or Jaumann absorbers with one on which conductive material is arranged in geometric patterns such as thin strips, grids, crosses or more complex shapes. The result is known as a Circuit Analogue (CA) absorber. The material offers a higher performance within a given volume than simpler types of absorber but must be custom-designed for each application, a task normally handled by a powerful computer.

CA absorber technology is probably the principle behind one new method of producing stealthy canopies. The easiest way of creating a canopy for a

stealth aircraft was mentioned earlier – application of a thin film of gold or indium-tin to the transparent material. This conducting film keeps the radar energy out of the cockpit but will tend to reflect it. A more recent technique involves making the entire transparency absorb radar energy. This is done by embedding within it a network of thin wires cut to dipole (half-wavelength) size. When combined with an inner conductive layer, this treatment probably turns the entire transparency into a CA absorber.

Most RAM used in stealth aircraft falls into one of two categories – sheets or other off-the-shelf bulk materials for general use and custom-designed components made from RAM material. Although RAM solves many RCS problems, it also creates its own constraints. Its weight will reduce aircraft performance and its bulk may prove troublesome in volume-restricted applications such as missiles. Its purchase and machining and installation cost will make the aircraft more expensive, while its very presence may well create new servicing difficulties for

ground crews, increasing direct operating costs.

By combining RAM with rigid radar-transparent substances, it is possible to create Radar-Absorbent Structural (RAS) materials, one of the most classified forms of radar absorber. Little information has been published on materials of this type. RAS can also be created by taking a non-metallic honeycomb, treating its surface with carbon or other lossy materials, then bonding non-metallic skins to its front and back to create a rigid panel. Honeycomb sections can absorb low-frequency radar if the individual cells are at least one-tenth of a wavelength of the radar signal.

Early stealth aircraft made extensive use of RAM and RAS, and paid a penalty in substantial additional weight. Improvements in analysis and design tools have allowed a significant reduction in the amount of RAM carried by more recent designs such as the F-22 Raptor.

One intriguing but little-discussed possibility for reducing RCS is that of cancellation of the scattered signal by the transmission of a second signal of equal frequency and amplitude but of opposite phase. In theory, this could be achieved passively by creating a suitable reflector (such as an accurately-machined cavity of appropriate dimensions) designed to create the appropriate echo. In practice however, this technique (often referred to as "impedance loading") would only work at a single frequency for which the reflector had been designed, while each scattering source on the aircraft would require its own associated and matching reflector.

Circuit Analogue Absorbers

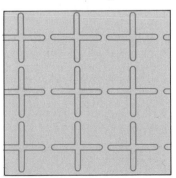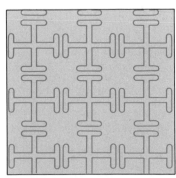

Above and above right: **By printing conductive geometric patterns on suitable base material, engineers can create Circuit Analogue (CA) RAM, a**

highly effective radar absorber, but one which must be custom-designed by computer to suit each new apsorption application.

CANCELLATION

The only realistic method of creating the waveform needed for cancellation would be by active means. Unfortunately, the technical problems are formidable. Aircraft-mounted sensors would have to measure the frequency, waveform, strength and direction of the signal to be countered. Complex signal processing equipment whose software contained detailed information on the aircraft's radar reflectivity at a wide range of angles and frequencies would have to predict how the incoming wave would reflect, then create and transmit a suitable cancellation signal.

Cancellation would not need to be 100 per cent to be militarily useful, while the task of matching the cancellation signal to the threat could be reduced in magnitude by reducing the threat sector and frequency range to be countered. Active-cancellation systems have been discussed in technical publications and it is possible that equipment of this type is being used on the Dassault-Breguet Rafale and the Northrop B-2 bomber.

Confirmation that France has developed active-cancellation techniques came at a conference on guided missiles held in London in April 1999 by SMi. During a presentation on stealth technology for missiles, Jean-Francois Gondet, senior technical adviser at Matra BAe Dynamics said that the techniques which the company has developed for minimising RCS included "active systems", but added that these were too highly classified to be discussed at an unclassified conference.

Also in the late 1990s came news of a new and novel technique for controlling RCS. Developed in Russia by the Keldysh Research Centre, it breaks the perceived theory held in the West that since shape has such a strong effect on RCS, little can be done to reduce the RCS of an existing aircraft. The Western view may be true when attempts are being made to reduce RCS by retrofitting RAM, but the Russian scheme creates an artificially generated plasma around the aircraft.

Two phenomena reduce the RCS of an aircraft protected by a plasma cloud, say the Russians. Radar energy tends to pass around a plasma cloud rather than penetrate it, and the energy that does penetrate interacts with the plasma-charged particles, and is partially

Above and below: **The B-2 programme made extensive use of computer-aided design and manufacturing (CAD/CAM) techniques. Computer screens** **linked to a 3D database replaced drawing boards, allowing the automatic manufacture of accurate components.**

absorbed. Western stealth techniques degrade the handling characteristics and agility of the aircraft, the Russians claim, while their system allows the designer greater freedom in terms of aerodynamic design. The hardware that must be added to the aircraft weighs less than 220lb (100kg), and consumes between 1 and 10kW of electrical power.

Three generations of plasma-protection system have been developed and tested by the Keldysh Research Centre. The first was a simple RCS-reduction system, while the second changed the frequency of the greatly attenuated reflected signal, and produced "some false signals" which helped to conceal the aircraft's location and speed. Progress with a further-improved third-generation system allowed the Russian government to clear

the first- and second-generation versions for export.

The effectiveness of plasma shielding has been demonstrated by ground and flight tests, say its developers. These have shown that the radar observability of an aircraft can be reduced by a factor of more than 100. The effectiveness of such a scheme depends on what the Russians define as "radar observability". A reduction in RCS of 100 would reduce the radar cross-section of a MiG-23 from around 64.5 sq ft (6 sq m) to around 0.6sq m. This is less of a reduction than that achieved by US stealth aircraft but, as we will see later in this chapter, would be enough to sharply degrade the effectiveness of radar-based defences.

Given present-day sensor technology, passive IR offers the only realistic option to radar for the long-range detection of aircraft targets.

With the growing use of IR sensors as a radar substitute, measures must be taken to reduce the thermal signature of a stealth aircraft.

The main sources of IR energy are hot metal components of the engine turbine and the exhaust nozzle, components which have been heated by the 1,800 – 2,300°F (1,000 – 1,300°C) efflux from the engine's combustors. The efflux leaving the tailpipe contributes relatively little – only some ten per cent of the total IR emission from a turbojet and even less from a turbofan.

If the engine uses an afterburner, the IR emission from the efflux can be increased by up to 50 times, causing it to rival or even eclipse that of the jetpipe. For this reason, all the first-generation of stealth aircraft – the XST, F-117A and B-2 – make use of non-afterburning engines.

The hot interior of the tailpipe is visible over a conical sector to the rear of the aircraft. From outside of this sector, an IR sensor will see only the outside surface of the nozzle, the temperature of which will be lower. The IR signature can be reduced by using the aircraft's aft fuselage and/or vertical tail surfaces to shield the jetpipes from view over as large a part of this sector as possible.

IR SCREENING

"Venetian blind" horizontal louvres arranged across the nozzle will restrict tailpipe visibility to a narrow range of vertical angles but would

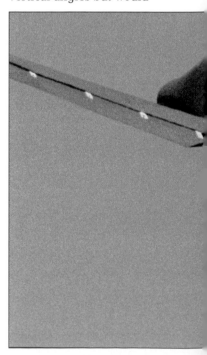

probably require cooling to ensure that they did not begin to rival the tailpipe in temperature.

Exhaust masking has been widely used by the designers of helicopters, but they have the advantage that much of the energy in the efflux has been removed by the turbine which drives the output shaft. On a jet-powered aircraft, the jet provides the basic propulsive force, so must be masked by aircraft structure over as wide a range of angles as possible. On the F-117A, YF-23, and B-2, the hot exhausts could not be seen from the lower hemisphere.

In much the same way that RAM has been developed to reduce radar reflectivity, materials have been devised to control IR reflectivity, but the critical dimensions such as thicknesses are now expressed in angstroms rather than in millimetres.

While a low level of IR emissivity may at first sight seem a valuable feature of the inner surface of a jet pipe or efflux duct surface, since it will reduce the emitted energy, it will also act as a good IR reflector, increasing the reflected energy that may be coming from a hotter internal region of the exhaust system. F-117A programme manager Alan Brown has stated that, "a careful optimization must be made to determine the preferred emissivity pattern inside a jet engine exhaust pipe. This pattern must be played against the frequency range available to [IR] detectors, which typically covers a band from one to 12 microns." In a late-1990s technical paper, he noted that, "Recently some interesting progress has been made in

Active Cancellation System

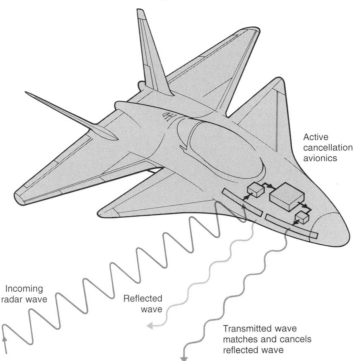

Active cancellation avionics

Incoming radar wave

Reflected wave

Transmitted wave matches and cancels reflected wave

directed energy, particularly for multiple bounce situations", but coyly added, "...that subject will not be discussed further here".

Metal layers are currently used in such materials, says Brown, but "the big push at present is in moving from metal layers in the films to metal oxides for radar cross-section compatibility. Getting the required performance as a function of frequency is not easy, and it is a significant feat to get down to an emissivity of 0.1, particularly over a sustained frequency range. Thus, the biggest practical ratio of emissivities is liable to be one order of magnitude."

Despite the traditional

Above: **Another method of reducing RCS is active cancellation. The incoming (strong blue) radar wave is sampled by a receiving antenna. Having predicted the aircraft's reflectivity at this frequency and angle, the avionics create and transmit a false echo (mauve), a signal designed to cancel out the genuine reflection (pale blue) from the aircraft's skin.**

Below: **In redesigning the B-1A to create today's B-1B, Rockwell reduced RCS by a factor of ten, but could do little to reduce the IR output from four afterburning GE F-101 turbofans.**

military preference for keeping everything from soldiers' boots to warships nicely clean and polished, the inside of military jetpipes is unlikely to satisfy a fastidious inspecting officer. The heat and carbon particles from jet efflux will soon dull the most carefully manufactured components. Jet fuel is a hydrocarbon, so tends to produce carbon when burned, though today's combat jets are virtually smoke-free compared with those of the 1950s and 1960s. In an engine efflux, carbon particles are comparatively harmless, adding little to the RCS of the exhaust gases, but on the inside of a jetpipe the build-up of carbon – a material with a very high IR emissivity – can create problems for the designer of a stealth aircraft, who will demand that the powerplant designer controls carbon output. "For the infrared coating to be effective, it is not sufficient to have a very low particulate ratio in the engine exhaust, but to have one that is essentially zero," says Alan Brown.

Having denied an enemy IR sensor sight of the hot engine aft section, the stealth aircraft designer must also reduce other sources of IR energy. An obvious target for treatment is now the exhaust plume. The efflux leaving the tailpipe contributes relatively little to the IR signature – only some ten per cent of the total IR emission from a turbojet, and even less from a turbofan.

If the engine uses an afterburner, the efflux emission can be increased by up to 50 times, causing it to rival or even eclipse that of the jetpipe. For this reason, all the first-generation of stealth aircraft – the Have Blue, F-117A and B-2 – use non-afterburning engines. To minimise the IR signature of the efflux, the latter must be cooled quickly by mixing the flow of hot gas from the core with cooler by-pass air. This is already done in a turbofan engine but it can be taken a stage further in a stealth design by using additional air to provide a cool shroud around the exhaust. Diverting a large flow of air through the engine bay and around the engine will also minimise the temperature rise in the structure of the rear fuselage.

Another way of reducing the IR signature is to replace the traditional circular exhaust nozzle with an elliptical or rectangular pattern. This would increase the perimeter of the plume, creating a wide "beaver-tail" of hot gases rather than a compact circular jet. It would increase the surface area of

Above: The tail surfaces of the Fairchild A-10 were designed to mask the engine exhausts from the seeker heads of IR-guided weapons.

the plume, increasing the rate at which the gases cooled, and would also reduce the band of heights from which an attacking fighter could observe a strong IR signature.

A two-dimensional rectangular nozzle of the type flight-tested on the F-15 STOL Demonstrator probably has a low IR and radar signature when the engine is running in dry thrust.

AIRFRAME HEAT

As the modern all-aspect IR missile demonstrates, the airframe is also a source of detectable IR energy. This heat comes from several sources – the engine, the avionics and the thermal effects of friction with the atmosphere at high speed.

As any designer of engine bays will testify, a jet engine runs hot. Nearby structure must either be built from titanium or other temperature-resistant alloys or be shielded from engine heat. Stealth aircraft are throught to have linings within the engine bay to prevent engine heat from spreading into the structure, warming the aft fuselage and increasing the aircraft's IR signature.

At present, most aircraft simply dump the heat gathered by the cockpit and avionics cooling systems but

Above and below: Two-dimensional vectored thrust nozzles have a rectangular outlet and a lower IR signature than conventional round nozzles. This experimental nozzle for the F100 turbofan was developed for use on the F-15 STOL demonstrator.

Right: The jet flap/lift concept tested in the early 1960s on the Hunting 126 research aircraft probably reduced the IR signature.

stealth aircraft will probably rely on closed-loop cooling systems. The heat could be dumped into the fuel, a technique pioneered in the SR-71 Blackbird, or radiated at frequencies not well transmitted by the atmosphere. Another component of the IR signature is reflected or re-radiated sunlight. This can be minimised by the use of suitable surface finishes.

ENGINE NOISE

Current stealth aircraft are subsonic. The levels of airframe heating induced by supersonic flight would make the aircraft an easy target for IR sensors, while the noise of a roaring afterburner would betray a covert reconnaissance or strike aircraft operating at medium or low altitude.

Several books discussing stealth technology have suggested that as a general rule, supersonic speeds and the use of afterburning are not compatible with low-observable operations. This had led their authors to question the wisdom of the hypersonic fighter or reconnaissance designs proposed by some aircraft companies, such as the Mach 5 methane-burning monster whose proposed configuration

was released by Lockheed in the early 1980s.

Such a view overlooks one of the odder aspects of flight at high Mach numbers. As aircraft speed builds up, increasing ram pressure at the engine inlet reduces efficiency, so efflux temperature begins to fall. By Mach 3 it can be lower than that of the same engine running at military (dry) thrust. Move to Mach 3.5 and the tailpipe emission will completely dominate that from the efflux.

One unavoidable factor associated with high supersonic speed is airframe heating due to atmospheric friction. This will be a major problem in creating any "Super Blackbird" type of aircraft. Working on the assumption that the possible threats to such aircraft will be SAMs or interceptors attempting "snap-up" missile attacks, it is possible to envisage partial solutions based on cooling systems which extract heat from the lower surface on the aircraft, re-radiating it upwards. Such a system would confound most present-day and future air defences but the Super Powers can afford to orbit space-based IR sensors such as the experimental US "Teal Ruby". These would find upward radiation from hypersonic aircraft an easy target.

COMPROMISES

Working with these basic rules for signature reduction, the designer must tackle the problem of creating a practical stealth aircraft or missile. The design of any aircraft it essentially a matter

of compromise between conflicting requirements. This is even more so when creating a stealth aircraft, since the designer must juggle a new set of rules and constraints over and above those of the past. The price paid for low RCS may be lower performance, reduced range or a lighter payload. In 1980, Lt Gen Kelly Burke, at that time USAF Deputy Chief of Staff for Research and Development, summed up the problem of developing a low RCS design: "You don't get any desirable feature without giving up some other desirable feature."

Even within the field of stealth technology, compromises will be called for. One disadvantage of shaping as an RCS-reduction measure is that reducing the returns in one direction involves increasing them in another. No matter how surfaces are angled, there will always be directions from which they are seen at normal incidence and where their reflectivity is high.

Before the designers can shape the aircraft, the authors of the operational requirement may have to indicate the approach to be followed. Should RCS be kept moderately low over a wide range of viewing angles, or does the user want the RCS from a certain critical sector to be kept as low as possible at the expense of "dumping" the enrgy in the form of strong reflections at other less important angles? Techniques such as operational analysis may help provide the answer here by allowing hypothetical aircraft using both approaches to RCS reduction

to be "flown" against the postulated enemy defences.

The powerplant and its associated inlets and nozzles create their own problems. Many stealth configurations have engine inlets mounted above the wing or fuselage to keep them hidden from ground-based radars but any aerodynamicist will warn of the possibility of airflow problems during high angle-of-attack manoeuvres. The sort of ventral air intake flight tested on the North American F-107 was not dropped just because it looked ugly.

When radar energy strikes the compressor or fan face of a jet engine it effectively acts as a solid surface, preventing the wave from proceeding further. The most obvious way of reducing intake RCS would be to coat the first-stage blades with RAM. This would have the desired effect but is not a practical solution – the absorbent material could not cope with the stresses caused by the high rotational speeds.

Moving all the ordnance into an internal bay and eliminating traditional underwing sensor or EW pods reduces RCS but eats into the space available for internal fuel. The use of a weapons bay may also reduce the maximum weapon load, while elimination of external pods prevents the rapid updating of the aircraft by add-ons.

HOT SPOTS

A major part of the design process is to identify at an early stage the main elements which contribute to the final RCS. To make the process of RCS reduction cost-effective, the stealth designer must identify these dominant scatterers, the features on the aircraft which make the greatest contribution to total RCS. These are known as "hot spots" or "flare spots". Stealth measures applied in these

Above: **This Lockheed Mach 5 concept would be a good IR target. Hypersonic stealth aircraft will have to 'dump' this unwanted thermal energy in safe directions.**

Below: **Thomson-CSF has studied the likely radar-reflectivity of the fan blades of M88 turbofan engine which were to be used in the production Rafale D and M.**

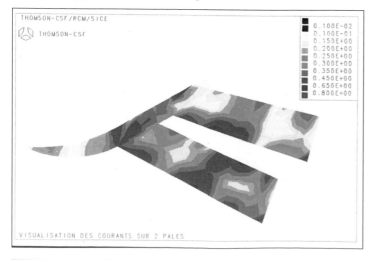

critical areas will make the largest overall difference to total RCS.

When an aircraft is viewed from the front, the largest contributor to RCS is likely to be the inlets. Being re-entrant structures, they tend to act like corner reflectors, efficiently trapping and re-radiating radar energy. Any cooling ducts or other inlets visible from the front will prove equally efficient radar reflectors. Another will be any forward-facing antennas in the nose radome of the aircraft or its missiles. If a radome is not fitted, a near-spherical metal nose may also act as an efficient scatterer, while travelling waves moving along the fuselage may add their own contribution. The cockpit is another cavity which may return strong echoes.

Moving away from the centre line, the wing leading edges play a major rôle in scattering. At broadside angles the fuselage sides, vertical fin, underwing stores and pod-mounted engines

become major sources. When radar waves strike wing and fin leading and trailing edges at near-grazing incidence, travelling waves can be set up, while further towards the rear sector radar returns from the wing and fin trailing edges will be observed. From behind the aircraft, the most important contributors will be the engine exhausts and any travelling waves set up along the fuselage.

RCS also varies with elevation angle. When an aircraft is viewed from the side and above, the wing/fuselage junction creates a radar-reflective 90 degree feature, while the right angle between the vertical fin and the horizontal stabiliser adds its own component. Radar waves arriving from above or below will also find the near-flat areas on the wings and horizontal control surfaces to be good radar targets.

Experience will allow designers to identify these features but their effect on overall RCS must be assessed. In the earliest stages of a

Above left: **Lockheed's experimental Q-Star may look crude, but this adapted sailplane proved the sound-reduction technology used on the low-noise YO-3A.**

Above: **The North American F-107A (an unsuccessful rival to Republic's F-105 Thunderchief) is the only jet fighter to have flown with a dorsal air intake.**

hypothetical design, this can only be done using RCS prediction codes, specialised computer software which makes use of a company or nation's accumulated RCS expertise. A Lockheed RCS prediction programme named Echo 1 provided the information needed to develop the Have Blue technology demonstrator and the F-117A.

By a process of analysis, the shape of the complete aircraft is broken down into simple parts – the plates, cylinders, edges, spheres and the like whose individual RCS is predictable. Then comes the task which only a supercomputer can realistically handle – synthesis of these into a highly-complex total RCS.

There is thus no neat or easy way to predict RCS and the magnitude of the task which the designer faces is dependant on the complexity of the shape he is considering.

It is thus no accident that one of the first applications which Thomson-CSF is applying to its RCS-prediction software suite is the design of stealthy re-entry vehicles. The sheer computer "number-crunching" power needed to carry out realistic RCS predictions was not available until the mid to late 1960s.

MEASUREMENTS

The next stage is to carry out measurements using an accurate model of either the whole aircraft or the areas of the aircraft identified as "hot spots". The latter can be tested at full-scale but, when the entire aircraft must be examined, the normal approach is to build an accurate scale model of the proposed design. This must either be made from metal or be electroplated or silver painted after construction so that its surface becomes electrically conductive. Unless a low electrical resistance is obtained all over the skin of the model, surface waves will not build up to the correct intensity.

In the 1960s and 1970s, most RCS testing was done at outdoor test ranges. These facilities consisted of a mounting able to hold the model and turn it to any direction required for the test. The radar transmitters used to illuminate the model and the receiver which sampled the returned signal were located at a fair distance away, at least 100ft (30m), and often 1,000ft (305m) or more. The radar beam directed at the target would at least partially illuminate the terrain. To reduce the effects of this, the ground between the transmitter site and the test position was carefully treated. One technique involved creating a berm, a vee-shaped raised area running from the transmitter to the test site.

Below: **The MiG-25 Foxbat was optimised for high-speed dash at Mach 2.8 and no attempt was made to minimise radar signature. Its huge inlets and abundance of right angled surfaces all help reflect radar energy.**

Non-Stealthy Features of MiG-25 Foxbat

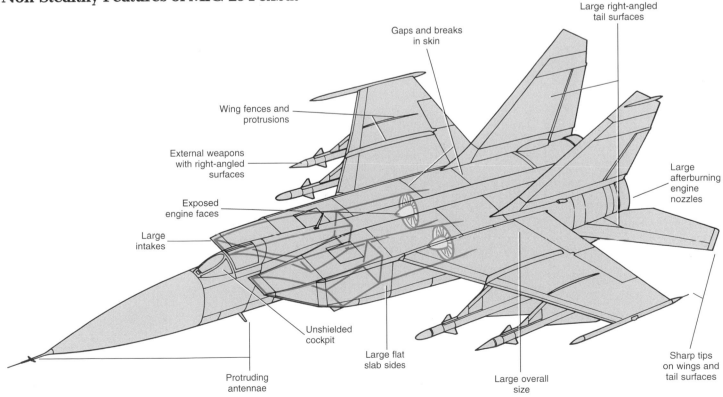

Gaps and breaks in skin

Large right-angled tail surfaces

Wing fences and protrusions

External weapons with right-angled surfaces

Exposed engine faces

Large intakes

Large afterburning engine nozzles

Unshielded cockpit

Large flat slab sides

Protruding antennae

Large overall size

Sharp tips on wings and tail surfaces

Another involved erecting a series of low lateral fences coated with RAM.

The problem with outdoor ranges is that their size makes them expensive to build and run, while the accuracy of the test results is affected by weather. There is also a risk that the security of the design of a new aircraft may be compromised. Given a photograph of a stealth aircraft, a low-observables expert can estimate its characteristics.

Indoor test ranges allow the radar cross-section of highly-classified stealth warplanes and missiles to be tested in complete secrecy and also eliminate the effects of weather on the measurements being made.

For the designer of such test facilities, the problem is to devise a way of creating the same conditions as an outdoor range. The most obvious technique is to line the walls of the test chamber with RAM, absorbing the beam once it has passed the target and maintaining the electronic "illusion" that the target is out of doors. This is normally done using the pyramidal type of RAM material described earlier. A radar signal directed into such a chamber will almost completely disappear when it meets the wall, with less than a fraction of one per cent being reflected.

If good results are to be achieved, the wave-front must be as flat as could be obtained from an antenna a long distance away. The most common technique is to direct the radar energy from the antenna not directly at the target but indirectly, via a specially designed reflector.

This collimates the energy, creating an evenly distributed signal identical to that from an antenna located a long distance away. An alternative but less common technique involves passing the radar beam through a collimating lens made of plastic but the manufacture of large enough lens structures has proved difficult.

At first, compact ranges were seen simply as convenient alternatives to outdoor ranges, useful largely for initial testing only but no substitute for definitive trials on a good outdoor range. Improvements in computers, range instrumentation and range design have now

Above: **This Lockheed concept of an ATF production line illustrates the computer-controlled technology needed when building the structure of future low-RCS fighters.**

Right: **The complex shape of the B-2 inlet follows a precisely calculated stealthy profile, development of which caused programme delays.**

Below: **The digital computer has revolutionised the science of RCS prediction. As this Thorn EMI polar diagram of an unidentified RPV shows, the measured RCS (red trace) is close to the forecast value (blue trace).**

reduced or even eliminated this performance gap. With the rise of stealth technology, most of the major US aircraft companies own both outdoor and indoor ranges.

RCS TESTING

Whether tested indoors or outdoors, the proposed design must be examined at varying radar frequencies. Whenever the wavelength being used is of the same order as the size of any feature on the aircraft, a resonance may occur, producing a larger radar echo. As different frequencies are tested, different-sized components on the aircraft will resonate when illuminated at the appropriate frequency. All the possible reflection mechanisms, such as specular reflections, edge diffraction, plus travelling and creeping waves are frequency-dependant, creating a mass of ever changing variables. To keep the magnitude of the task

RCS Measurement Plot

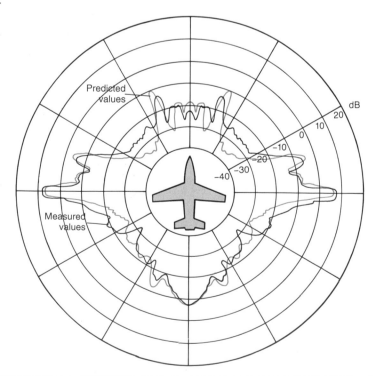

Indoor Test Chamber

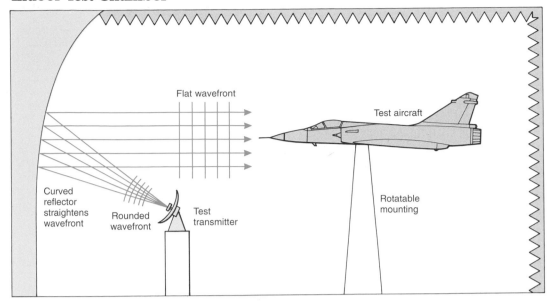

Flat wavefront

Test aircraft

Curved reflector straightens wavefront

Rounded wavefront

Test transmitter

Rotatable mounting

Above: Indoor RCS test ranges shield stealth designs from prying eyes, but the radar energy reaching the target must behave as if it had travelled a long distance. The most common scheme involves collimating the energy by means of a carefully shaped reflector, so that it presents a flat wavefront. The chamber is lined with RAM to absorb excess radar energy. within bounds, engineers will often confine their tests to the forward sector or any other direction in which RCS will be critical for the aircraft under investigation.

Many features of the proposed design can be checked with a simple plot of reflectivity versus range, repeated at different aspect angles. To get a really detailed radar "look" at a complex target requires more sophisticated test methods, usually involving synthetic aperture techniques.

The most normal use of synthetic aperture technology is in the creation of high-definition sideways-looking radars (SLRs). These obtain their near-photographic resolution by exploiting Doppler shift, the slight modification in signal frequencies caused by relative movement of the signal source and observer. (The classic example of Doppler shift is the apparent drop in pitch of the noise from a speeding train as it passes an observer standing on the railway platform.)

For RCS testing, instrumentation designers

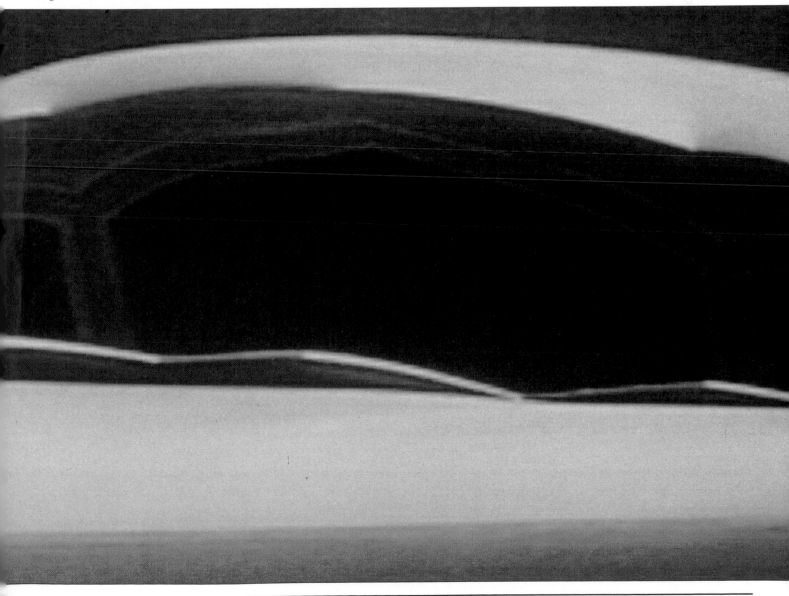

use inverse synthetic aperture radar (ISAR) technology. Instead of moving the radar, they move the target in order to create the Doppler effect. The target was normally rotated, so that its individual "hot spots" would display a Doppler shift, dependant on radar frequency, and any radial movement caused by their distance from the centre of rotation.

RADAR IMAGES

The end result of an ISAR test is a complex three-dimensional radar image whose basic co-ordinates are range and cross-range and where the third dimension (height) indicates reflectivity. This can be compared with the target and all sources of reflection swiftly located.

These tests allow the designers to identify all the high-reflective features of the proposed design – parts of the airframe which make an unduly large contribution to total RCS and whose physical size may have little relationship to their apparent radar size. A large airframe feature may contribute little to RCS while a small one may prove to be a major scatterer. These "hot spots" must either be eliminated from the design or be treated with RAM to reduce their reflectivity.

INDOOR TESTS

Once a prototype of the aircraft has been completed, it will undergo RCS testing to verify the results of the earlier tests with scale models. Until recently, this work had to be done at an outside test range, but can now be done in a secure manner thanks to a new generation of indoor test facilities – the designation "compact range" may seem almost a misnomer for a treated chamber able to swallow an entire fighter!

SECRECY

An advanced indoor range commissioned by Boeing in 1988 has a test chamber measuring 225ft × 112ft (68.6m × 34m) under an 80ft (24.4m) roof. This is large enough to test many types of aircraft, or half-scale models of larger designs. Targets under test can either be mounted on a radar-invisible pylon of ogival cross-section or be suspended on a system of cables which allows the "fly-by" RCS to be measured. High measurement accuracy

is a feature of the facility, as is the rigorous security demanded by "black" programmes. The foundations of one of the chamber's two test turntables are isolated from the rest of the base structure, while the support structure of the ceiling-mounted turntable is isolated from the walls by means of slip joints. In order to maintain strict "need to know" rules for models tested, a series of physically separated rooms for model storage and preparation are provided.

Once any remaining "hot spots" identified on the full scale aircraft or missile have been dealt with, the design can then be cleared for full production. All the test results and additional knowledge gathered during the development effort is then available for study, helping to refine the low-observable technologies, materials and techniques to be incorporated in the next generation of stealthy aircraft and missiles.

RCS REDUCTION

At first sight, the effects of reducing RCS do not seem particularly valuable. By inserting diminishing values of RCS into the radar range equation – a mathematical formula which defines the basic relationship between the various parameters of a radar and its range performance – it becomes obvious that a halving of RCS does not result in a halving of target detection range. Range varies with the fourth root of RCS, so halving the RCS reduces range by only 15 per cent.

It has been reported that the Folland Gnat lightweight fighter of the late 1950s could only be detected by radar when closer than the larger Hawker Hunter, but the difference is unlikely to have been significant. The smooth lines of the Avro (later Hawker Siddeley) Vulcan are also said to have made this aircraft a difficult radar target, although it probably did not translate into any great military advantage.

A key factor in determining the degradation in range caused by reducing RCS is the figure obtained by dividing the reduced RCS by the original figure. To determine the reduction in radar range, the result must be raised to the power 0.25.

$$\text{reduced radar range} = \left(\frac{\text{reduced RCS}}{\text{original RCS}}\right)^{0.25}$$

Assume that an aircraft has an RCS of 100sq metres – a value probably typical for a head-on B-52. Reducing RCS by 50 per cent reduces radar range to:

$$\left(\frac{\text{reduced RCS}}{\text{original RCS}}\right)^{0.25} = 0.5^{0.25} = 0.84$$

The B-1A is known to have an RCS one-tenth of that of the B-52, so the range resulting from this improvement is reduced to:

$$\left(10/100\right)^{0.25} = 0.56$$

A radar tracking a B-1A would thus have its range reduced by 44 per cent. If it could just detect a B-52 at a range of 100 miles or kilometers, it could only track a B-1A at 56 miles or kilometres. Substitute a B-1B (which has an RCS a tenth that of the B-1A and one hundredth of that of the B-52), and the range is reduced to:

$$\left(1/100\right)^{0.25} = 0.32$$

Radar range is thus reduced to 32 per cent. Reduce RCS by a further factor of ten by substituting an Advanced Tactical Fighter, and the range is reduced to 18 per cent.

In his 1985 book *Radar Cross-Section Lectures*, Professor Allen B. Fuhs pointed out that the degradation in real-life military situations may be much greater. For a tracking radar, the figures given above do apply, but in order for a target to be tracked it must first be acquired.

SEARCH RADAR

A ground-based or naval search radar tasked with locating an incoming target uses a moving radar beam to search a selected area in a time defined by the antenna scanning rate. According to Fuhs, the degradation in range resulting from reduced RCS is given by:

$$\left(\frac{\text{reduced RCS}}{\text{original RCS}}\right)^{0.5}$$

A reduction of RCS by a factor of 10 will cut detection range to 0.32, whereas reduction by factors of 100 and 1,000 will give detection ranges of a mere 0.10 and 0.03 of the original range, respectively.

A radar mounted on an aircraft has an even more difficult task, being required to search a volume of airspace in a given time. The formula for degradation now becomes:

$$\text{range reduction} = \left(\frac{\text{reduced RCS}}{\text{original RCS}}\right)^{0.75}$$

Reducing the RCS is now even more effective. Reduction factors of 10, 100 and 1,000 now give range reductions of 0.18, .03 and .006.

Briefing the press following the downing of an F-117A by the Yugoslavian air defences in March 1999, USAF Director

RCS	Reduced radar range		
	Tracking	Area search	Volume search
0.1	0.56	0.32	0.18
0.01	0.32	0.1	0.03
0.001	0.18	0.03	0.006
0.0001	0.1	0.01	0.001

Typical Missile Ranges

Missile	Max range (km)	Min range (km)	Min as % of Max (%)
Crotale	8.5	0.5	5.9
Roland	6.3	0.5	7.9
Rapier	7	0.5	7.1
Sea Sparrow	18	1	5.6
SA-6 Gainful	35	4	11.4
SA-5 Gammon	250	80	32
R-550 Magic	10+	0.3	2
AIM-7F Sparrow	50-100	0.6	0.6-1.2

Right: **Thanks to stealth technology, the RCS of an aircraft is no longer proportional to aircraft size. In this diagram, the aircraft are drawn to a constant scale, but RCS steadily reduces from that of the B-52 and Blackjack to that of the B-2 and F-117A stealth aircraft.**

Physical Size Compared to RCS

	B-52	100m²
	Blackjack	15m²
	FB-111	7m²
	F-4	6m²
	MiG-21	4m²
	MiG-29	3m²
	Rafale-D	2m²
	B-1B	0.75m²
	B-2	0.1m²
	F-117A	0.025m²

of Operational Requirements Maj. Gen. Bruce Carlson explained that, "It's not invisible. It never has been invisible. We know radars that can track our stealthy airplanes. They can sometimes find us. The key is that that zone of detectability or lethality is shrunk by orders of magnitude, but it's still not invisible. Our goal is that on the first day [of a war], we can, because we've shrunk those zones of lethality, find our way into the target area using good, detailed mission planning without being susceptible to enemy radars or their missiles or their airplanes."

RCS reduction will also blunt the effectiveness of SAM systems. Look up the performance of any anti-aircraft missile in a reference book, or even the manufacturer's brochure, and a maximum range figure will inevitably be quoted. Much more difficult to find is the missile's minimum range.

Immediately after leaving the launch rail, a round is not fully under the control of its guidance system, but must be brought on to the desired trajectory. This is particularly true in the case of SAMs, where the round will take an appreciable time to reach full flying speed. On some boost-slide weapons, the control fins are locked until the rocket motor has burned out, and only then does the weapon begin to guide.

For the sake of argument, let us invent a hypothetical "Missile X", a medium-range SAM with a maximum range of 25 miles (40km) and a minimum range of around 5 per cent of maximum – 1.25 miles (2km). In designing the range of the acquisition radar used to locate targets, the designer will have to allow some performance in hand, so as to ensure that by the time that the target is within range, it shall have been designated for attack, and the missile launcher will have slewed on to the correct bearing and be prepared for firing. The longer the range of the surveillance radar, the larger, heavier and costlier it will be, so the designer is not free to set any maximum range specification he likes. Let us assume that the radar is designed to detect a typical target at three times the maximum range of the missile –

75 miles (120km).

If the enemy introduces stealth technology, and reduces the RCS of a target by a factor of 100 (the sort of improvement which the B-1B shows over the B-52), then the maximum range of the acquisition radar falls – according to the equations given by Fuhs – to only a tenth of its design value. Instead of detecting the target at 75 miles (120km) range, the radar associated with "Missile X" will not achieve detection until 7.5 miles (12km).

By the time that the target is first detected, it will be well

within the missile's lethal envelope. Most of the weapon's 25 mile (40km) range will have been wasted, and the newly detected target will already be less than six miles (9km) from the system's minimum range.

JAMMING

Like ground clutter, the radar noise created by chaff or radar jamming will also help mask the low-RCS target. Reducing the aircraft's RCS also helps in the EW battle. It can reduce the amount of jamming power needed, allowing designers of

jamming equipment to reduce volume, weight and power consumption of their systems, or even to use new jamming techniques made practicable by the stealth aircraft's relative radar invisibility.

The small radar "size" of a stealth aircraft also makes it easier to shelter behind the protection of a stand-off jamming aircraft. The powerful signal from an aircraft such as the EF-111A was designed to mask a conventional fighter. It will be even more effective when screening the tiny radar target presented by a stealth aircraft.

EARLY STEALTH AIRCRAFT

About once a decade or so history throws up momentous events, the sort of thing which years later can lead to reminiscences along the lines of "I can remember where I was and what I was doing when I heard the news that...". For many readers of this book, these events are probably the assassination of President Kennedy or the shooting of John Lennon. For our parents or grandparents, it was Pearl Harbor, while a new generation will probably refer to the loss of the Space Shuttle *Challenger*.

These events are by definition memorable, but few can accurately date news of a different type – the new trend which may create major changes in some aspect of the world, but which arrives unbidden and unannounced. "Internet" may have become a household word by the late 1990s, for example, but who outside of a handful of computer enthusiasts could date its apparent birth?

Much the same applies to the first news of stealth technology. It seems to have crept into the public domain with virtually no publicity, a classic example of how first news of a major development can pass almost unnoticed. Legends die hard and aeronautical legends are no exception. An "official version" of the unveiling of stealth seems to have evolved and requires to be debunked before politically expedient claims become elevated to the status of history.

According to a number of 1980 pronouncements by US Government officials and even by President Carter, news of the programme had first leaked in August of that year. A subsequent official release of minimal information was depicted by the Democratic Party as a move intended to damp down future press leaks, while the Republican Party saw it as a blatant attempt by a shaky Administration to boost its image for the forthcoming US Presidential election.

Like many legends, it is neat, colourful and bears little relationship to reality. Reports of stealth technology had

been circulating for several years before the August 1980 incident. Casting my mind back over more than two decades, I cannot remember when I first heard of stealth. In much the same way as a police pathologist will give a spread of times of the likely moment of death for a murder victim, I can only reply "not before 30 June 1977 and not later than 27 May 1978".

In 1977, Friday was press day for the pages which contained regular news features in the British aviation magazine *Flight International*. On 30 June 1977, the day was going much like any other. The full quota of news stories had not yet been completed but the remaining shortages were nothing which a lunchtime visit to the nearby Rose and Crown public house was not helping to cure (a process known to staff reporters as "lubricating the fingertips"). Defence Editor Charles Gilson was working steadily on a large news story, while I was on the phone obtaining the regular weekly news report from the magazine's US correspondent.

At the end of a lengthy phone call and much notetaking, I realised that it was time to spoil Charles Gilson's entire day. "Carter has just cancelled the B-1", I explained. Under normal

circumstances, Gilson was the ideal boss, radiating a general air of calm in a profession noted for stress and frayed tempers. On this occasion, he reacted as if I had kicked him in the seat of the pants. "He's WHAT?", was his shocked response.

STEALTH APPEARS

Rapidly consigning most of

Below: **The single-seat configuration identifies this "US Air Force" aircraft as a CIA A-12, predecessor of the SR-71 Blackbird.**

the material we had written for that week's issue to oblivion and warning the production department that our news pages would be closing for press late, we started work on a massive two-page news story. Entitled "Rockwell B-1 cancelled", this explained President Carter's decision to abandon the swing-wing manned bomber programme in favour of deploying the new air-launched cruise missiles.

In the most important of my research files on which this book is based, a photocopy of the B-1 cancellation story is

Below: **When President Carter cancelled the B-1A bomber programme in 1977, the first XST stealth aircraft was already being built.**

the Fiscal Year 1977 US defence budget. The USAF announced for the first time that Lockheed was to develop and build the TR-1 variant of the U-2 family, while the Defense Research Projects Agency (DARPA) revealed that Lockheed had received a three-year development contract worth and estimated $90 million to develop and fly an undesignated new aircraft type. At the time, nobody seems to have realised the purpose of these unidentified aircraft. The first rumours of stealth technology were not to leak to the world's aviation press for sometime.

By the time that I reported the first crash of a stealth aircraft in the 27 May 1978 issue of *Flight International*, tales of radar-invisible aircraft were already in the public domain. Although the *Flight* story is only the second document in my own stealth files, the fact that I did not explain at great length within its half-page length exactly what a stealth aircraft was indicates that I was assuming that the reader was already familiar with the concept. My contemporary notes have long since vanished into *Flight* archives – I left the magazine 18 months later – but I can remember reading other (and almost certainly earlier) reports of the aircraft's existence.

WORLD WAR II STEALTH

The idea of stealth aircraft had been around for some time. During World War II German engineers also tried to apply RAM to an aircraft in order to reduce its detectability. The Gotha Go.229 jet-powered flying wing, ordered into production in

the first item. It's not there because of what it says but because of what it doesn't say. Nowhere in Charles Gilson's description of the reasons for the B-1 cancellation or my account of how cruise missiles would take over the Rockwell bomber's intended rôle does any mention of stealth technology or even the very idea of low observables appear. Obviously neither Charles Gilson nor I had heard of it, since it would have formed a natural part of our report. First news that Lockheed was working on new types of aircraft came in

early 1945 following flight trials of a prototype aircraft designated Horten Ho IX, would have been skinned with panels which sandwiched a core made of up charcoal, sawdust and a glue matrix between two sheets of plywood. None had been delivered by the time the war ended.

In March 1953 the USAF drew up a specification for a reconnaissance aircraft able to fly at heights far above those obtainable from existing types and interceptors. It proposed the creation of a subsonic single-seat aircraft with a radius of 1,500 miles (2,400km), and the ability to fly over its target at a height of 70,000ft (21,335m) or more while carrying a sensor payload weighing between 100 and 700lb (45-315kg). The resulting design was expected to combine the latest in turbojet engine technology with an airframe whose light construction and high aspect-ratio wings would be more reminiscent of sailplanes than combat aircraft.

The aircraft would be unarmed, so had to be difficult to detect, and hard to intercept. Both qualities were obtained largely by giving the aircraft a cruising height well above that of contemporary interceptors. The formal specification recognised that "the enemy will have limited methods of detection and/or interception of a vehicle of the required performance. The greatest opposition to the operation of this aircraft can be expected to be encountered from guided missiles."

Paragraph 2 (g) of the specification demanded that, "Consideration will be given in the design of the vehicle to minimising the detectability by enemy radar." The need to avoid emitting signals which an

enemy might detect was also appreciated. Navigation was to be by means of "a non-emanating system" while the sole item of communications equipment would be a simple short-range UHF radio. "No emanations from the aircraft will be permitted over enemy territory."

Although not invited to bid for the programme, Lockheed had learned of the new requirement. In May 1954, the company proposed a J73-engined CL-282 variant of its F-104 Starfighter. This was rejected in favour of the Bell Model 67 and Martin 294 designs. In November of the same year, an evaluation of updated Lockheed proposals led to a contract being placed for a small batch of aircraft. The Bell Model 67 (designated X-16) was cancelled, while the Martin design was to emerge as the long-span RB-57D.

The task of building the new spyplane was assigned to the Lockheed "Skunk Works". Based at Burbank, California, the Skunk Works is the stuff of which aeronautical legends are made – a project office where small, highly motivated design teams worked with a minimum of organisational constraints and even less paperwork to create advanced aircraft.

The Skunk Works is not the sort of establishment which looks good in company brochures. Even in the 1950s, when companies expected engineers to wear suits and ties, Skunk Works staff took advantage of the unit's isolation (it was off-limits to most Lockheed employees) to dress casually. According to a story in *The Washington Post*, when a Congressman visited the site in the early 1980s, "At Lockheed's Skunk Works, which resembled a slightly seedy industrial plant, the visitor ate stale doughnuts, drank coffee from a plastic foam cup, and was briefed by an engineer who tapped cigarette ashes into his cupped hand as he spoke."

Such informality might not impress visiting VIPs, but attracts talented design engineers the way wasps are attracted to a jar of jam. Focus that amount of raw talent with a bureaucracy-free environment, and advanced technology aircraft can be created with maximum speed and minimum cost.

The Skunk Works had been created in 1943 by Lockheed designer Clarence "Kelly" Johnson, by all accounts an

Left: **This Lockheed U-2R of the USAF's 9th Strategic Reconnaissance Wing is externally similar to today's Lockheed U-2S.**

irascible man with a penchant for "bawling out" or even firing employees whose work displeased him. Johnson was a brilliant engineer, famous as the designer of the Lockheed Constellation piston-engined airliner, the twin-engined P-38 fighter, and the F-80 Shooting Star jet fighter. When the reconnaissaance aircraft project started, Johnson was in his mid-40s, and was Lockheed's chief engineer.

Working in conditions of unparalleled secrecy, Johnson and his Skunk Works team built the first prototype in only eight months, rolling it out at the then-new Groom Lake AFB, Nevada, in mid-July 1955. A brief and unplanned hop during taxi trials on 29 July was followed by a first flight on 1 August . This first aircraft was designated U-2, with the production examples being U-2A. The "U for utility" designation was intended to conceal the aircraft's true role.

On 4 July 1956, the U-2 made its first overflight of the Soviet Union, with CIA pilot Harvey Stockman at the controls. From a base in West Germany, it flew across Poland and into Belorussia, passing over the city of Minsk before turning north to fly up to Leningrad (now St. Petersburg), then back to Germany. It became obvious that, despite its high operating altitude, it had been tracked by Soviet radars, and MiG fighters had made unsuccessful attempts to intercept it.

After around half a dozen overflights of Soviet territory, it was clear that the Soviet radar network was successfully detecting and tracking the U-2. Late in 1956 the CIA ordered a project known as Rainbow to find ways of reducing the aircraft's vulnerability. Kelly Johnson set his engineers to work in attempts to reduce the aircraft's radar signature.

As originally fielded, the U-2 flew with an all-black paint scheme designed to minimise its visibility at high altitudes. Its sole ally in avoiding radar detection was its small size – not much larger than a jet fighter – and its clean lines. At first sight, its long-span wings might seem like ideal radar reflectors, but in practice their vast span is so great that they resonate in the HF band rather than at radar frequencies.

The first approach involved stringing wire along the fuselage to scatter the radar energy arriving at the aircraft, but the resulting aerodynamic drag reduced cruising height by 7,000ft (2,135m). Radar-absorbent material (RAM) in the form of a Salisbury Screen was then added to the fuselage, but proved of limited effectiveness.

Finally, an early form of ferrite paint was applied. This reduced RCS by an order of magnitude

In July 1957 the first modified aircraft – known as a "dirty bird" – made a sortie into Russia in the Black Sea area. Recordings showed that the reduced RCS was not enough to prevent the aircraft being tracked, but reduced the U-2's operating altitude to 58,000ft (17,600m).

Given the limited amount of extra stealth which could be added to the aircraft, an electronic warfare unit known as the "Granger" was developed to confuse Russian surface-to-air missiles, and was installed in the tail section of the small U-2 fleet.

U-2 DOWNED

Lockheed and the CIA both realised that operations over the Soviet Union could not continue indefinitely. In the winter of 1959/60 Skunk Works engineer Bill Shroeder studied the likely effectiveness of the new Soviet S-75 (SA-2 "Guideline") SAM system which had begun to enter service. He concluded that the aircraft had less than a year of operating life left. On 1 May 1960, a U-2 flown by Francis Gary Powers was shot down near Sverdlovsk.

From analysis of photos of the wreckage issued by the Soviet Union, Kelly Johnson concluded that the aircraft had been hit from the rear, and it was later concluded that shock waves from a near miss had blown off the aircraft's tail. Johnson also suspected that the radar energy emitted by the "Granger" jammer may have helped the

Russians track Powers' U-2.

Johnson had already started work on a supersonic aircraft able to replace the U-2 and overfly current and future Soviet defences with impunity. Codenamed "Suntan", the CL-400 was intended to fly at even greater heights than the U-2, and to have a top speed of Mach 2.5. In appearance, the design which took shape on the Skunk Works drawing boards resembled a giant F-104. Around 300ft (90m) in length, it would have been powered by two wingtip-mounted Pratt & Whitney engines which burned liquid hydrogen rather than kerosene. The specification called for a range of 3,000 miles (4,800km), but this proved impossible to achieve, and the project was cancelled.

The earliest useful work on low-observable technology did not begin until the end of the 1950s. When drawing up plans from the spring of 1958 to the late summer of 1959 for a U-2 successor, Kelly Johnson's team at the Skunk Works investigated measures for RCS reduction. In the winter of 1958/59 the CIA concluded that a supersonic U-2 successor was feasible, and Lockheed and Convair were asked to propose suitable designs under a project codenamed "Gusto". Once again, Kelly and the Skunk Works engineers turned their talents to the task of creating a supersonic spyplane, but this time a design whose engines would burn some form of conventional jet fuel.

Above: **On the original photo of this SR-71, triangular RAM panels are clearly visible on the starboard wing leading edge and chine.**

A-12/SR-71 DESIGN

The initial design for what would eventually become the Lockheed SR-71 was the A-1, an aircraft designed to fly at Mach 3. However, President Eisenhower was not prepared to accept a solution based purely on high speed and high altitude – he demanded the lowest

possible radar cross-section. Low RCS had been a desirable quality in the U-2, but for the new aircraft it was mandatory.

As the A-1 design gave way to more refined offerings, Skunk Works engineers decided to fit radar-absorbing ferrite and plastic materials to all leading edges, and to make the vertical surfaces from radar-absorbing composites. The A-1 concept was followed by the A-2, then a series of further-refined layouts.

By May 1959, design A-11 had acquired fuselage chines, and a near-flat lower fuselage surface. These measures had reduced RCS by 90 per cent. By the summer of 1959 both teams had submitted designs. The Lockheed proposal was selected, and in August 1959 the company was given the go-ahead for the construction of the first prototype A-12, an aircraft which would incorporate low RCS features such as wing/body blending, built-in RAM, and radar-absorbing ferrite paint.

When designing the U-2, Lockheed had been able to take only limited RCS-reduction measures, but the A-12 took the entire art a massive step forward. As North American designers working on the XB-70 bomber and F-108 Rapier fighter had discovered, creating an aircraft able to cruise at Mach 3 was difficult enough, but in creating the A-12 the Skunk Works tackled the tasks of combining this level of performance with stealth.

Comparison of the A-12 with the similar-sized F-108 is instructive. The fighter had an angular appearance which bordered on ugliness, with a

Above: In an attempt to improve the effectiveness of the AGM-28 Hound Dog missile, the USAF ordered an RCS-reduction programme.

Below: Having proved a difficult radar target, Teledyne RPVs became useful recce platforms for the Vietnam War.

slab-sided forward fuselage, box-shaped rear fuselage, and wedge inlets – features that were highly radar reflective. The A-12 had rounded lines which made extensive use of wing/body blending, while its engines were fed by inlets whose conical centrebodies would help shield the compressor face from radar observation.

The plastic materials used in areas such as the wing leading edges, chines and elevons were developed by Lockheed, and took the form of a radar-absorbent plastic honeycomb designed to cope with temperatures of up to 600 deg F (315 deg C). On the A-12, it accounted for 20 per cent of the total wing area. It was not strong enough be used structurally in a Mach 3 design, so was added to the leading and trailing edge in the form of V-shaped sections. The Skunk Works is also reported to have flown experimental components such as all-plastic vertical fins.

The dark paint finish used to help radiate heat away from the aircraft gave rise to the unofficial designation "Blackbird". It was designed with two qualities in mind. It offered high heat emissivity, so helped to radiate friction-generated heat when the aircraft was cruising at Mach 3. It also incorporated the radar-absorbing "iron ball" pigment

Above: Soviet radars such as Fan Song and its associated SA-2 Guideline missile forced the USAF to study anti-radar measures.

used on the U-2 and TR-1.

The original A-12 was a single-seat reconnaissance aircraft built to meet the CIA requirement. When the strategic reconnaissance task was transferred to the USAF in 1960s, the two-seat SR-71 was developed to handle the task. A third YF-12A version was tested as a long-range interceptor in the mid-1960s, but was not adopted for operational service.

In November 1959 Lockheed started a long series of RCS tests of a full-scale model of the A-12. Trials were to continue for a year and a half before the results were deemed satisfactory. RCS of the A-12 and the follow-on SR-71 remain classified, but a reported figure of only 0.16sq ft (0.015 sq m) for the SR-71 seems highly optimistic for an early 1960s design.

"The SR-71 was an example of where we took the aerodynamic design and then added some radar absorbing material to the airplane to make it slightly stealthy," explained USAF Director of Operational Requirements, Maj. Gen. Bruce Carlson, during a 1999 press briefing on stealth technology. "We focused the low observable technology in the front quarter at certain frequencies on the radar spectrum, mostly in what we call the target tracking or X-band area. That's the area that SAMs normally do their target tracking in. There's a slight degradation in the capability of that SAM as that airplane is coming toward it." From the rear, RCS was essentially unaltered.

Low-observable technology was also seen as a method of improving the survivability of unmanned vehicles. In 1960, even before the jet-powered AGM-28A Hound Dog had become operational with SAC, North American was given a contract to reduce the RCS of the follow-on AGM-28B version.

RYAN DRONES

Early in 1960, Ryan Aeronautical proposed to the USAF the development of a reconnaissance version of the Ryan Q-2 Firebee target drone. The company had toyed with the idea of a reconnaissance drone in the mid-1950s but it was not until the growing deployment of Soviet SAMs in the late 1950s which threatened the future of U-2 operations that the USAF showed serious interest.

On 1 April of that year, a Soviet SA-2 Guideline missile downed the U-2 being flown by CIA man Francis Gary Powers. On 8 July, Ryan was given a $200,000 USAF contract to demonstrate the use of modified target drones for reconnaissance known as project "Red Wagon". One of the goals of this project would be to assess RCS reduction measures which might improve survivability without an extensive re-design.

A wire screen was fitted to mask the air intake from long-wavelength radars of the sort which the Soviet Union used for surveillance, blankets of RAM were fitted to the fuselage sides and the nose section was treated with what has been described as "non-conductive paint".

Test results were applied to a new stealthy design known as the Ryan Model 136. This featured a high aspect ratio unswept wing, a twin tail with inward canted verticals and a dorsal air inlet and engine installation. Work had barely started on the programme when Harold Brown (then director of Defense Research and Engineering) ordered the cancellation of "Red Wagon".

Ryan reworked its proposal, offering in the summer of 1961 a design optimised for operations along and close to the Warsaw Pact borders rather than overflight. Known as "Lucy Lee", this would have climbed from 65,000ft (19,800m) to 72,000ft (22,000m) as fuel burned off. Once more, stealth would be a feature, with the RCS being "reduced to a minimum using defraction (sic), transmission and absorption techniques". Once more, Brown declined to give the go-ahead.

Perhaps with the Brown "axe" in mind, the company had also submitted a

minimum-modification rework of the Q-2C drone as an air-launched platform for reconnaissance missions. Known as the 147A Fire Fly, this was given the go-ahead in early 1962 funded under the USAF "Big Safari" special reconnaissance programme.

The first 147A was a Q-2C modified to act as a testbed for the proposed navigation and guidance system. The remaining three were Q-2Cs with a fuselage stretch of 35in (89cm) which increased fuel capacity by 68 US gallons (257

Below: **SR-71 technology was taken a stage further in Lockheed's highly-classified D-21 reconnaissance RPV programme. It proved unsuccessful, and surviving examples were retired in the late 1970s.**

litres). Several had extended-span wings which the USAF obtained from a US Army Q-2 project. Flight trials started in April 1962 with the first camera-equipped sortie taking place on 27 April.

On 17 May, a 147A was flown from Tyndall AFB, Florida, to test the effectiveness of the RCS-reduction measures. The crews of the five F-106 Delta Dart interceptors sent to hunt down the 147A found it virtually impossible to obtain radar lock-on, even when vectored to the drone by GCI. Final interception was carried out as tail-chase pursuits following the drone's contrail, while eight Hughes GAR-3A (AIM-4F) Falcon semi-active radar missiles failed to down the Ryan aircraft.

Above: **Although a good radar target, the XB-70 cruised at speeds and heights beyond the reach of present-day SAMs.**

CUBA

During a test run over the Atlantic missile range on 5 August, Air Defense Command had launched interceptors to catch the drone. The result was embarassment all round. The fighters failed to locate the drone but an over-confident Ryan crew ran the tiny aircraft out of fuel, dropping it in the sea 65 miles (105km) off the coast. Another flight on 9 August saw the F-102 and F-106 interceptors obtaining only momentary radar glimpses of the drone and eventually pursuing a non-existent "target"

across Florida and into Georgia.

On 29 August, a U-2 aircraft returned from a sortie over Cuba with photos which showed the installation of SAM sites. Although the presence of ballistic missiles would not be detected until mid-October, this was the opening move of what was to become the Cuban Missile Crisis. Following the loss of a U-2 over Cuba, two 147A drones were rushed to Tyndall AFB. A drone-equipped aircraft had barely started engines to begin the first mission over Cuba when the order to cancel the flight was given. The 147A was not to see action but Ryan had demonstrated that the tiny craft was ready to go to war. The company was rewarded by a contract for the definitive big-winged 147B. Flight trials of this model started in May 1963 and missions were flown to test the effectivess of the

craft's RAM blankets. A year later, the 147B was rushed to southeast Asia to play its rôle in the early stages of the Vietnam War.

NEW BOMBERS

The year 1964 also saw the much-delayed first flight of the North American XB-70 bomber. Nobody watching the maiden flight on 21 September was under any illusion that the six-engined Mach 3 monster would ever see SAC service. The decision to make the programme a purely technological demonstration had been taken in 1960. In my opinion, it was a bad decision and one which would be paid in human lives in the skies over North Vietnam later in 1972. Many of the bomber crews who died over North Vietnam in the Linebacker II raids would be alive today had they been piloting 2,000mph (3,200km/h) B-70s rather than

elderly subsonic B-52s through the skies over Hanoi and other heavily-defended targets.

In its search for a new bomber during the early 1960s, the USAF had carried out studies of concepts such as the Advanced Manned Precision Strike System, the Low Altitude Manned Penetrator, the Strategic Low Altitude Bomber and the Extended Range Strategic Aircraft. By 1965, this work had focused on a concept known as the Advanced Manned Strategic Aircraft. A specification issued that year called for an aircraft able to fly at high subsonic speed at low level or at supersonic speed at high altitude and emphasised the need for RCS reduction. It was to result in the decision to build the Rockwell B-1.

Research into stealth technology really got into its stride in the early to mid-1970s. It was aimed at countering the development by the Soviet Union of jam-resistant high-power monopulse ground radars, and overcoming the performance of modern look-down/shoot-down that were radars able to observe targets flying within ground clutter.

HAVE BLUE

In the 1960s Dr Leo Windecker had designed and built an all-composite fibreglass light aircraft known as the AC-7 Eagle 1. This was a four-seat aircraft of conventional appearance, powered by a 285hp (213kW) piston engine. In 1963 he offered this to the USAF as a possible low-RCS research

aircraft but the concept fell on deaf ears. When he re-proposed the idea in 1972, the concept of low-observables was coming into vogue.

The prototype Eagle was lent to the USAF for RCS tests and Windecker Aviation was given a USAF contract to build the YE-5A, a modified Eagle with internal changes such as the addition of RAM. Delivered in 1973, this was tested by the USAF and Lockheed, being used in studies of the radar reflectivity of glass-fibre constructed airframes.

By 1975 the US Air Force's Foreign Technology Division had finally translated and republished Pyotr Ufmitsev's "Method of Edge Waves in the Physical Theory of Diffraction". Ignored in the Soviet Union, it immediately caught the eye of US mathematician Denys Overholser – an employee of the Skunk Works. He decided to bring it to the attention of the chief designer.

Kelly Johnson had retired, and been replaced in January 1975 by Ben R. Rich. Formerly Johnson's vice-president for advanced projects, Rich had joined the Skunk Works in 1954 to work on the U-2, so was a veteran of the CL-400 and A-11/SR-71 programmes. In his 1994 biography *Skunk Works*, Rich recalled how Overholser had "decided to drop by my office one April afternoon, and presented me with the Rosetta Stone breakthrough for stealth technology. The gift he handed me over a cup of decaf instant coffee would make an attack airplane so difficult to detect that it would be invulnerable against the most advanced radar systems yet invented, and survivable against even the most heavily defended targets in the world."

Reading Ufmitsev's paper, Overholser had realised that if an aircraft could be built whose surface was made up from flat triangular shapes, its RCS could be predicted. What can be predicted can be controlled. Rich gave him three months to convert Ufmitsev's theory into a practical RCS-prediction programme. In only five weeks, Overholser, assisted by retired Lockheed mathematician and radar expert named Bill Shroeder, had created the new "Echo 1" software and, in conjunction with a Skunk Works designer named Dick Scherrer, had used it to devise the optimum low-observable shape for an aircraft.

Left: **This P-50 Barlock radar is probably a US-built replica of the Soviet original, a novel research tool in the US anti-radar effort.**

The breakthrough had come at an ideal time. By the summer of 1975 the US Defense Advanced Research Projects Agency (DARPA) had become interested in the concept of stealth aircraft. It had awarded five US aircraft companies around $1 million each to conduct proof-of-concept studies, and planned to award the company which produced the most promising design a contract to build two flying technology demonstrators.

Unfortunately for Rich, Lockheed was not one of the five. Its earlier signature-reduction work had been highly classified, and the company's last successful fighters had been built during the Korean-war era. Although the existing DARPA funding for stealth studies had been entirely allocated to the existing five contractors, Lockheed was allowed the join the competition

HOPELESS DIAMOND

By May, Overholser and Scherrer had devised a design they called the "Hopeless Diamond". Shaped like an arrowhead, it promised to have an RCS a thousandth of that of the D-21 drone. Despite opposition from Kelly Johnson (who still served as a part-time consultant to the Skunk Works, and had dismissed the "Hopeless Diamond" as "crap"), Rich set up a team to explore the new configuration.

Kelly was prepared to wager 25 cents that the "Hopeless Diamond" would not match the low RCS of the D-21, but lost his money on 14 September when a comparative test conducted using models of the two designs showed that the RCS of the "Hopeless Diamond" was exactly as predicted – a thousandth of that of the D-21. These results were confirmed by later tests using a 1/10th scale model of the proposed aircraft.

By October, Lockheed and Northrop had been declared the finalists in the DARPA competition, and in March 1976 Lockheed tested a full-scale model of their proposed design at the USAF radar test range at White Sands, New Mexico. The "Hopeless Diamond" displayed an RCS around the size of a golf ball, and proved ten times less detectable that the rival Northrop design.

In April 1976, Lockheed was declared the winner, and given a $30 million contract to develop and manufacture two XST (Experimental Stealth Tactical) demonstrators. The project was codenamed "Have Blue". Construction of the first aircraft started in July 1976.

Early in 1977, President Carter's Defense Secretary Harold Brown and his advisors carried out a survey of all current research and development programmes in the hopes of identifying key areas which might yield useful operational advantages for the US military during the new Administration of President Carter. A similar technology survey in the early 1970s had resulted in the US cruise missile programmes, so Brown doubtless hoped that another potential breakthrough could be found. He rapidly identified low-observable technology as a likely candidate. Spending on stealth technology was already running at around $10 million a year, and it was becoming obvious that RCS reductions large enough to give real military advantage were within reach.

Under-Secretary for Defense William J Perry established an executive committee with himself as chairman. Known as Xcom, this included key military procurement officials with the clout needed to drive new technologies through the traditional DoD bureaucracy. From the autumn of 1977 onwards, Xcom studied stealth proposals from the services and industry. Those thought promising received massive funding; the others were weeded out. Funding was increased tenfold. The main beneficiaries were Have Blue and a Lockheed stealthy cruise missile codenamed Senior Prom.

At the same time, knowledge of the stealth effort was tightly controlled. In DoD parlance, stealth was classified as SAR – Special Access Required. Stealth was given what Perry would later describe as "extraordinary" security protection "even to the point of classifying the every VERY existence of the program". The long-term effectiveness of such secrecy was doubted. "In 1977 I told the [Defense] Secretary that with good luck we would conceal programme existence for two years," Perry would tell a House Armed Services Subcommittee in 1980.

Two Have Blue aircraft were built at a total cost of $37 million. Neither aircraft was given a USAF serial number, but were numbered 1001 and 1002 by Lockheed. The first would be used to evaluate the flying characteristics of the faceted airframe, and the second to explore the effectiveness of the RCS-reduction measures.

Have Blue was similar in general configuration to today's F-117, but was only 47ft 3in (11.58m) long, and 22ft 6in (6.71m) in wing span. Powered by a pair of non-afterburning General

***Above:* A military pilot who made an early unauthorised sighting of the F-117 described it as looking similar to the Martin Marietta X-24.**

Electric GE J85-4As turbojets, it had a maximum take-off weight of 12,000lb (5,400kg). The wing had a leading edge which was swept back at 72.5 degrees. Its control surfaces consisted of two inboard trailing edge elevons and four spoilers (two on top of the wing and two on the bottom). There were no flaps or speed brakes. The twin vertical tail surfaces angled inward about 30 degrees, and positioned just ahead of the engine exhausts.

Wherever possible existing hardware was used to save time and money. The cockpit instrumentation and ejector seat were from the Northrop F-5, the fly-by-wire system needed to "tame" the airframe's aerodynamic qualities was from the F-16, and the undercarriage was that of the Fairchild Republic A-10. When completed, both aircraft were given a complex "dazzle" camouflage paint scheme which made it hard for a distant observer to determine the aircraft's shape.

The first Have Blue was completed in November 1977, then flown by C-5 Galaxy to the "Ranch" airstrip at the Tonopah test range near Nellis AFB. Here it made its first flight

on 1 December 1977. Lockheed test pilot William M. "Bill" Park made the first flights, and was later joined by Lt. Col. Norman Kenneth "Ken" Dyson of the USAF.

Have Blue 1001 was to have a short life. The landing speed was around 160kt, and when touching down after a flight on 4 May, it hit the ground hard enough to damage the right main landing gear. Worried that the aircraft might skid off the runway, Bill Park increased engine power and climbed away, retracting the undercarriage. When he began a second approach, the damaged gear refused to lower. After several landing attempts, he climbed to 10,000ft (3,050m) and ejected just as the aircraft ran out of fuel. As he ejected, he hit his head and was knocked unconscious. Unable to control his parachute, he landed heavily enough to cause severe injury which was to force him to retire from flying. The aircraft was destroyed in the crash.

***Right:* While the B-2 was still under wraps, several analysts attempted artist's impressions. This concept by Bill Gunston was more sensible than many rival "designs", and boldly predicted the absence of vertical surfaces. Those ventral inlets would have been a poor stealth feature in a high-level bomber which is the B-2's main rôle.**

In his autumn 1980 testimony to the House Armed Services Subcommittee, Perry was to claim that, "We have kept its [stealth's] very existence secret for more than three years" rather than the two years he had predicted back in 1977. It has to be assumed that both he and the subcommittee did not closely read the newspapers and aviation press. Contrary to his claims, the secret had been well and truly "blown" two and a half years earlier by the loss of the first Have Blue.

At the time, the USAF did its best to conceal the loss of such a highly-classified aircraft. Reporting the loss of an unidentified aircraft operating from Nellis Air Force Base, the USAF declined to make any statement beyond the straight admission that an accident had occurred in which a pilot was slightly injured. A USAF spokesman would add only that, "for security reasons that is all the information available". Press reports gave the pilot's name as William Park, noting that he claimed to work for Lockheed. Admitted to a Los Angeles hospital, and treated for multiple fractures and concussion, he was discharged four days later.

At first, the aircraft was thought to be a Lockheed TR-1, but by late in the month sources were confirming that the incident involved a prototype stealth aircraft. This information led me to write a news story "Stealth Aircraft Lost in Nevada"

in *Flight International*'s 27 May issue.

The flight test programme resumed in June 1978 when Lt. Col. Ken Dyson made the first flight of the recently delivered 1002. Over the next year and a half, Dyson flew 65 test sorties, which assessed the ability of the aircraft to avoid detection by various types of radar. Trials are reported to have been made against ground and airborne radars, including the surveillance radar of the E-3 Sentry AWACS aircraft, and captured Soviet radar and missile systems. All of this development flying seems to have been conducted from the Groom Lake test facility at Nellis AFB, Nevada, although Eielson AFB in Arkansas was also linked to reports of stealth aircraft trials.

On 11 July 1979, Have Blue 1002 was lost at Tonopah Test Range during what was to have been its second-last scheduled test flight. One of its J85 engines caught fire, burning through the hydraulic lines and forcing Dyson to eject. Unlike Park, Dyson made a safe ejection and was uninjured, but the aircraft crashed. The wreckage of both Have Blues was secretly buried at Nellis AFB.

Despite the loss of both aircraft, the programme had been successful, demonstrating that the faceted fuselage had reduced RCS just as theory had predicted. It has also shown that maintaining a low RCS over a

period of operational use would not be easy. Great care had to be taken to seal all joints between doors and access panels and the aircraft's fuselage, and to make sure that the aircraft's external surfaces were completely smooth. Flight tests showed that even a fixing screw not fully tightened to bring its head flush with the skin was enough to sharply degrade the RCS. Maintaining the stealth characteristics of an operational stealth aircraft would require painstaking attention to detail, but could be achieved by a skilled ground crew.

The results of Have Blue trials gave the US the confidence to adopt the new technology for operational aircraft and missiles. By the autumn of 1980, several stealth-related programmes had been launched. US spending on the new technology rose by a further factor of 10, bringing it to 100 times its early-1977 level.

In the late 1970s and early 1980s, DARPA had conducted a series of cruise missile penetration evaluations. Intended to assess the weapon's ability to cope with Soviet defences, these tested the weapon's radar and IR signatures in the presence of background clutter and its ability to use terrain masking. The data gathered were used to predict the likely capability of future Soviet defence systems against small cruise

missile targets.

Work on the stealthy Senior Prom cruise missile had been under way at Lockheed since 1977 under a "black" project budgeted at $24 million. Senior Prom was designed to fly at low level, and by 1980 it was being test-flown from B-52 aircraft based at Edwards AFB. Senior Prom was never adopted for service. It was followed by DARPA's 1980 "Teal Dawn" programme to develop technology for stealth cruise missiles. At least one company – General Dynamics – is known to have flown test hardware as part of this programme.

SABER PENETRATOR

By this time the B-1 seemed likely to emulate the XB-70 in being reduced to a museum piece. As recounted earlier, President Carter announced in June 1977 that he would not approve production of the new bomber. Although convinced that conventional bombers were too vulnerable to modern air defences, behind the scenes he gave the go-ahead for studies of possible bombers based on low-observable technology. These were carried out under a secret programme code-named "Saber Penetrator".

By 1978 the Lockheed Skunk Works was beginning to turn its attention to a possible stealth bomber, and it is likely that similar studies were under way both at Northrop and elsewhere. With the help of two senior bomber pilots on loan from Strategic Air Command, the Skunk Works drew up proposals for a tactical bomber. Able to carry a 10,000lb (4,500kg) payload, it was in the performance class of the US Air Force's F-111. The result was a two-year study contract codenamed 'Senior Peg'.

A second contract codenamed "Senior Ice" was awarded to Northrop, which in 1975 had lost the competition to select a new lightweight fighter for the USAF, and had to take a back seat to McDonnell Douglas in the programme to convert the unsuccessful YF-17 into the carrier-capable F/A-18. Having subsequently lost the competition to build the Have Blue, and facing the problem that sales of its long-running F-5 series would soon end, the company launched a major effort to maintain its design capability by offering a new single-engined F-5 derivative on the fighter market, and an advanced stealthy bomber design to the US Air Force.

In his 1994 memoirs, Ben Rich claimed that Northrop may have

Early "Stealth Bomber" Concept

received the bomber study contract because by then the US Government wanted to compensate the company for the damage done to the sales prospects of the F-20 Tigershark by a withdrawal of a US licence to sell the latter aircraft to Taiwan, the most likely customer for the new fighter. His recollections may not be accurate – the 1978 study contracts were awarded around the time that the F-20 (then known as the F-5G) was being designed, and well before the Carter Administration effectively vetoed its sale to Taiwan.

Management of both "Senior Peg" and "Senior Ice" programmes was handled by the USAF's new Low-Observables Project Office, which was also managing the Senior Prom cruise missile project.

In the summer of 1980, a growing number of Executive and Congressional officials were briefed on the stealth bomber concept. At the same time, the political battle between President Carter and California Governor Ronald Reagan for the US Presidency began to hot up. Stealth was about to become a factor in the US election.

In its issue of 4 August 1980, *Aviation Week* quoted an unidentified Administration official as talking of "a growing perception that we have made a mistake in cancelling B-1" and reported that the House-

Below: **White nose markings on the B-1B may aid refuelling-boom operators but under some conditions may compromise camouflage.**

Top: **Dense clouds of smoke from eight Allison J35 turbojets made the take-off of Northrop's YB-49 flying wing far from stealthy!**

Above: **The experience needed to design flying wing bombers was obtained from the private-venture Northrop N-1M, which flew in 1940.**

Senate Authorization Conference Committee favoured the purchase of one or even two new types of bomber. Insistent that a new bomber be fielded by 1987, the committee suggested the building of 100 modified B-1s, followed by 100 new-technology bombers "using all new technology, particularly stealth technology to avoid radar detection".

A week later, the magazine carried an item headed "Bomber Biases". President Carter remained opposed to the B-1, the magazine reported, and was not convinced that the USAF was agreed on the need for a new bomber. Identifying one of the aircraft candidates as "the advanced stealth bomber", the story stated that "the White House intends to continue studies" of new bombers, adding that "Some Administration officials believe a delay in the studies will allow more time to perfect stealth technology".

LEAKS

In the September issue of *Armed Forces Journal International*, Benjamin F. Schemmer revealed that hundreds of millions of dollars were being spent on programmes to which only a few dozen US Government officials were privy to full details. "Several different types of aircraft have been built. Scores of flight test hours have been accumulated on several prototypes, although only a handful of pilots have flown the planes."

No one single technical trick was responsible for stealth, he explained, correctly identifying all the main techniques used for signature reduction – structural shaping, composites, IR shielding and surface treatment with RAM.

AFJI had known about "essential elements of the program for several years", claimed Schemmer, "but has not revealed them following a request by a senior Pentagon

official in mid-1978 that AFJI not print, on national security grounds, a story...about the first stealth test prototypes".

Acting in response to the growing number of stories, on 22 August Defense Secretary Harold Brown released some limited information on the classified programme. The United States had built aircraft which could not be intercepted by existing or projected Soviet air defences, he explained. He denied that the existence of stealth technology had been a factor in President Carter's decision to cancel the B-1 bomber but suggested that "any new bomber will use some elements of this technology".

Background information was presented by Perry, who explained how stealth was a "complex synthesis" of many techniques which were now classified at the "highest security level". In the three years since 1977 the USA had made "remarkable advances" in the new technology and was beginning to develop practical applications. A degree of stealth technology could be applied to existing aircraft, he explained, but stealth would be most effective when applied to a new design. The cost of a stealth aircraft would not be substantially different from that of conventional designs.

The Republican Party claimed that information of stealth technology had been improperly released by the Administration in order to boost its image on the sensitive topic of defence – Reagan was attacking the Democrats as being "soft" on defence issues. It was even suggested that the source of the leaks might have been none other than Defense Secretary Brown.

Two months later, Reagan won the Presidential election, bringing into power a new Administration determined to boost America's defence capability. The most obvious way of doing this was to exploit the new stealth technology.

FLYING WINGS

The year 1981 was to prove to be a key year for stealth.

In the summer of that year, Lockheed was given a secret contract to develop and manufacture a production aircraft based on the XST. The company also received the go-ahead to develop a stealthy cruise missile. In early 1981, Congress directed that a new bomber be developed for SAC but did not specify what form

this aircraft should take, simply ordering an initial operating capability (IOC) by 1987. A total of $300 million in development money was added to the 1981 defence budget, along with $75 million for long-lead procurement.

The USAF was ordered to decide by 15 March 1981 on the type of aircraft to be ordered. The obvious candidate was an advanced derivative of the B-1 but the USAF was pushing a stretched derivative of the FB-111A known as the FB-111H, while behind the scenes lurked the possibility of an all-new aircraft based on stealth technology.

Around the time the new Administration took office in early 1981, the USAF assigned the responsibility for stealth aircraft development to General Alt Slay, the head of Air Force Systems Command. Slay was not interested in having an F-111-sized stealth bomber, and ordered that work be re-focused on a strategic bomber.

A Request for Proposals on what was then known as the Advanced Technology Bomber (ATB) was issued in 1981. To bid for the task of building the new aircraft, Lockheed linked up with Rockwell to create a team combining massive expertise in stealth and bomber technology.

In a little-reported programme in the late 1970s, Northrop invested large amounts of company money in secretly developing expertise in low-observables technology. By 1981, it was ready to challenge Lockheed for the task of building the new bomber. Like Lockheed, the company teamed up with an established bomber design team, in this case Boeing.

In addition to its stealth expertise, Northrop also had extensive experience with flying wings, a configuration which potentially offered low RCS. The experimental N-1M had flown in 1940 and was followed by several examples of the NM-9 – one-third scale prototypes for the planned XB-35 bomber. The latter had a wing span of 172ft (52.4m) and was powered by four Pratt & Whitney Wasp Major engines driving contrarotating propellers mounted at the trailing edge of the wing. The first flights were on 25 June 1946 but, even before they had flown, the decision had been taken to rebuild both prototypes as jet bombers, redesignating them XB-49.

The first modified aircraft

took to the air in October 1947, powered by eight 4,000lb (1,815kg) thrust Allison J-35-A-15 engines, and was followed in January 1948 by the second example. The latter aircraft crashed in June 1948 following an in-flight structural failure. Although some pre-production YB-49 and YRB-49 aircraft were subsequently built, the USAF abandoned the flying wing concept in the early 1950s and none of the Northop bombers saw operational service.

Northrop was not the only company to see the potential of the flying-wing layout for a stealth bomber. In its late 1970s bomber studies, Boeing had looked at tailed and tailless delta designs. Like Northrop, Boeing wanted to exploit the fact that radar energy tends to diffract off flat horizontal surfaces, while long-chord wing sections of the type used in delta or flying wing designs are deep enough to allow the use of radar-absorbent structures, and internally-mounted RAM. Rockwell had also looked at flying wings during the same period, including a 77ft (23.5m) span design in the FB-111 performance class, but it is not clear whether a similar configuration was offered for the ATB competition.

At the Skunk Works, the team working under Ben Rich also concluded that the flying-wing was the best layout for a strategic-range stealth bomber, and his team produced a design which was so similar to that on the Northrop drawing boards that a visitor mistook a model of the Lockheed design displayed on Ben Rich's desk for that of the Northrop concept. The Lockheed design was smaller than that proposed by Northrop, however. Lockheed decided that the

lower cost of the smallest aircraft able to meet the requirement would be attractive to the customer, while Northrop opted to offer a design optimised for maximum range.

Like Have Blue, the new bomber was selected following competitive RCS tests. For Have Blue, full-scale models had been used, but the sheer size of the rival ATB designs required the use of quarter-scale models.

ADVANCED BOMBER

Attractive though the ATB might be, there seemed little chances of its being developed or fielded by the 1987 deadline imposed by Congress. In July 1981 US Air Force Secretary Verne Orr stated that a stealth bomber might take ten to twelve years to develop. Any attempts to field it earlier would involve "tremendous cost". In the decade or more which development of a stealth bomber would take, the Soviet Union might be able to develop new types of sensor other than radar and IR which could be used to detect stealth aircraft, providing a partial or even total countermeasure. The Air Force would prefer a B-1 available in 1986 rather than a stealth bomber in 1992, he suggested.

Reagan solved the bomber dilemma on 2 October 1981 by announcing that the B-1 would be restored to production status allowing a batch of 100 to be built. While these aircraft provided a low-risk boost to SAC's strength, a new advanced technology stealth bomber aircraft could be developed in great secrecy for service in the early 1990s.

Following the RCS model tests, Lockheed heard unofficially that its design had offered a lower RCS than the Northrop submission, so was

Above: **Heavy shadows and a dark matt finish hide the long wingspan of the B-2 as the first prototype rolls out from the hangar.**

surprised when it was informed in October that the Northrop design had been selected. The longer range and heavier payload of their design had tipped the scales in its favour. In his memoirs, Ben Rich says that the USAF told Lockheed that while the Skunk Works design had been stealthier than the Northrop aircraft, the latter aircraft's heavier payload would require fewer sorties to achieve the same result.

Later that month, the Northrop public relations department issued what was probably its shortest-ever press release. The entire text consisted of a mere 75 words: "LOS ANGELES – Oct. 20, 1981 – Mr. Thomas V. Jones, Chairman of the board of Northrop Corporation, confirmed today that Northrop has been notified by the Air Force of its selection as prime contractor to conduct initial research and development on advanced bomber concepts. This effort will have a material impact on Northrop. The key team members are Boeing, LTV/Vought and General Electric Aircraft Engine Group.

All details are classified, and no further comments will be made".

They meant what they said. In future press briefings for Northrop products, it was consistently made clear that this one subject would never be covered. With virtually all details of the new stealth fighter, stealth bomber and new cruise missile shrouded in a blanket of secrecy, the era of the "black" programme had arrived.

THE WORLD OF BLACK PROGRAMMES

One consequence of the build-up in US military strength during the eight-year Reagan Administration was a concentration on high-technology programmes such as the Strategic Defense Initiative ("Star Wars"). In parallel with this has been a growing tendency for much of the Pentagon's high-technology budget to disappear under a cloak of secrecy in what were dubbed "black" programmes.

"Black", that is to say, virtually invisible programmes are not new. The "Project Manhattan" effort to develop the atomic bomb during the Second World War was probably the first. Similar secret efforts saw the development of the U-2 spyplane and its A-12 successor, while the same category of high security has always shrouded the US reconnaissance satellite programme.

As their formal title of "Special Access Programs" (SAPs) indicates, "black" programmes use a rigorous system of security control, with information being provided only to carefully selected individuals. SAPs fall into two categories – unacknowledged and acknowledged. Projects often start life in the first category, and move to the second when their existence is finally revealed.

An unacknowledged SAP is one whose existence is classified as a "core secret". This is defined in USAF regulations as "any item, progress, strategy or element of information, the compromise of which would result in unrecoverable failure".

Having decided that outside knowledge of the existence of any "black" programme would undermine its military value, the US DoD set the stage for several forms of deliberate "disinformation" which makes denials that a specific programme exists of little value. For a start, an individual questioned by an outsider about a "black" programme may genuinely have no knowledge of that programme, even if that individual's position or rank suggests that he or she should. In 1977, General George Sylvester was commander of the USAF's Aeronautical Systems

Division and responsible for all USAF aircraft programmes. Despite this, he was not aware of the existence of the Have Blue aircraft.

If the questioned individual does have knowledge of the "black" programme, that person is by definition required to deny the programme's existence. The traditional "no comment" will not be enough to guard what has been classified as a "core secret".

In theory SAPs must report to four committees of the US Congress – the House National Security Committee, the Senate Armed Services Committee, and the defence subcommittees of the House and Senate Appropriations Committees. SAP briefings are conducted in closed, classified sessions, and in some cases are minimal. For the most highly classified SAPs, the need to conduct even this level of briefing can be waived by the Secretary of Defense.

Watertight secrecy may be good for security but, as the "black" cloak fell over a greater portion of the Pentagon budget, some critics questioned whether such classified military programmes were spending money wisely. Denied special security clearance, most members of Congress cannot even review the budgets of "black" programmes.

For a nation so committed to openness, democracy and

accountability as the United States, "black" programmes have introduced a new way of working. Secrecy covering stealth projects has been so tight that the USAF is reported to have filed false flight plans with civilian agencies when stealth aircraft were being flown, according to *Washington Post* sources in 1987. In the same year *Aviation Week* reported that the DoD had even instructed some contractors to falsify their records in order to conceal the fact that they were running "black" programmes.

SECRECY

In some cases, excessive secrecy was hampering procurement decisions. In 1987, Congress learned that one US service had recently attempted to start a major "black" development programme, unaware that a similar programme had been under way for several years as a "black" programme by another service. During the long-running lawsuit over the A-12 Avenger II programme (described later in this chapter), McDonnell Douglas and General Dynamics claimed that technology developed in other stealth programmes but denied to the A-12 team could have solved some of the problems that led to the project's cancellation.

Above: **Given its coat of "Iron Ball" paint in 1970, this was the last 100th Strategic Reconnaissance Wing U-2 to literally go "black".**

A few recent figures show the scale of current US "black" programmes. In Financial Year 2001 (FY01), the USAF plans to spend $4.96 billion on classified research and development programmes, a figure which accounts for almost 40 per cent of its total R&D budget. It will spend a further $7.4 billion on classified procurement programmes.

LOCKHEED F-117

To this day, the best-known "black" programme is the Lockheed F-117 stealth fighter. A secret contract awarded on 1 November 1978 covered development of the aircraft, and manufacture of a first batch of production examples – initially five, but soon expanded to 25. In parallel with this work, GE was given a contract to develop a non-afterburning version of the F404 to power the new aircraft. The FY82 defence budget is thought to have contained as much as $1 billion in "black" funding for the programme. The project was given the codename "Senior Trend". Some reports suggested that the aircraft's popular name was "Ghost" or "Specter", but it eventually received the name "Nighthawk".

Although the stealth fighter was often referred to as the F-19 during the early 1980s, the USAF has always insisted that the designation F-19 has never been assigned. The ostensible reason – the risk of confusion with the MiG-19 – is obvious nonsense; the designation F-21 was cheerfully assigned to the Kfir fighters leased from Israel for use in dissimilar combat training programmes. There were suggestions that the true designation might be "RF-19", or even AR-19 (Attack/Reconnaissance 19). Lockheed Martin now admits that "the designator 'F-19' was briefly reserved for the aircraft, but it was never officially applied".

The true designation "F-117A" first emerged in the winter of 1987/88. It reflects not the post-1962 system of aircraft designations, but the older USAF system which produced the fighter and bomber designations from before World War II until the era of the "Century-series" fighters such as the F-100 and F-104. It seems that the USAF applied "old-style" designations to various Soviet fighters which it had acquired for evaluation, and that when it needed a designation for what should have been the F-19, it took the next available "Century-series" number.

The first F-117 was completed in May 1981, and flew on 18 June. It confirmed the basic design of the aircraft, which was 70 per cent longer and 97 per cent greater in wingspan than the Have Blue, and had a maximum

Right: **This early impression by a Lockheed artist would have revealed the basic shape and faceting of the "F-117" that the DoD wanted kept secret.**

take-off weight four and a half times heavier.

The initial batch of five aircraft (780 to 784) was used for aerodynamics and propulsion tests. The only significant change found necessary was a stiffening and 15 per cent increase in size for the twin tails. This followed the loss of one tail surface on an aircraft during the initial test programme.

Aircraft 785 was the first production example, but crashed immediately after take-off on its first flight on 20 April 1982, injuring company test pilot Bob Riedenauer. An investigation showed that the wiring for the pitch and yaw controls had been reversed. The first aircraft to be handed over to the USAF was 786, which was delivered on 23 August 1982.

The first USAF squadron to operate the F-117A was the 4450th Tactical Group. Formed at Tonopah, Nevada, on 15 October 1979, it was equipped initially with 18 A-7D Corsair IIs until the first F-117A Arrived. Located at the edge of the Nevada test range, Tonopah had been renovated under a $295 million programme, and given a 12,000ft (3,660m) runway, and 54 single-aircraft hangars intended to keep the aircraft out of sight during the day.

Next F-117A unit to form was

P-Unit (which later became the 4451st Test Squadron) in June 1981. Q-Unit (later the 4452nd TS) began operations on 15 October 1982, while Z-Unit (later the 4453rd Test and Evaluation Squadron) was formed on 1 October 1985. The Group was transferred from the direct control of Tactical Air Command to Tactical Fighter Weapons Center at Nellis AFB in 1985.

The F-117A was a demanding assignment for the hand-picked aircrew selected to fly the new fighter. Pilots were required to have a minimum of 1,000 hours of flying time, mostly on fighters. Normal tour of duty was four years, later reduced to three. Families were not allowed on the base, but lived in or around Las Vegas. Personnel spent five-day duty periods at Tonopah, flying to and from the base in

specially chartered Boeing 727-200s of Key Airlines.

To maintain security, the new aircraft flew only at night. Hangar doors were not opened until half and hour after sunset, and only after the hangar lights had been extinguished. Ground movements were lit only by flashlights. There is no two-seat trainer version of the aircraft, so new aircrew joining the 4450th faced the daunting prospect of making their first flight in the type at night from a blacked-out airfield and without the benefit of a check ride. They were trained by Lockheed instructors using what has been described as (then) the most realistic flight simulator in USAF service. This

Below: **Lockheed Martin could not persuade the US Navy to order the proposed A/F-117X strike/attack aircraft.**

was developed in the mid-1980s by Link-Singer.

Early operating experience showed that after flying, pilots had to be indoors before sunrise. Seeing sunrise disturbed sleep patterns, and pilots trying to sleep having seen the dawn found it difficult to do so. Ben Rich has described the pilots' existence as being like that "at a vampire's convention as daybreak approached scurrying to their blacked-out rooms before they were caught by the sun."

These constraints proved a problem in the summer months. Flying could not get under way until around 9pm, often continuing until well after 3am, with aircraft sometimes flying two sorties per night – one starting before midnight, followed by another in the early morning hours. Anyone who has worked shifts will realise the havoc which changing time cycles can play on the human constitution. In this respect, pilots are no different to their ground-based counterparts, and fatigue became a recognised problem at Tonopah.

On 10 July 1986 the commanding officer of one squadron wrote a report stating that, "fatigue-induced burnout is getting worse with time. I believe we are on a collision course with a mishap." That night, Maj. Ross E. Mulhare took off in F-117A no. 792 to fly a training mission. At about 1.45am, the aircraft crashed on a hillside 15nm (28km) northeast of Bakersfield, California, killing its pilot. A year later, aircraft 815 flown by Maj. Michael C. Stewart struck the ground within the Nellis Range during another training mission. Both pilots had less than 80 hours of F-117A flight time, and were attempting demanding sorties on nights with little or no moonlight. An official USAF investigation concluded that both crashes could have resulted from pilot fatigue and disorientation.

Aircraft 804, last of the original production batch, was accepted on 20 June 1984, but by then a follow-on batch of 39 had started down the line, the first being handed over in August. One of these aircraft – 815 – crashed on 14 October 1987, almost two years after entering service.

Until its unveiling in late 1988, the F-117A didn't officially exist, but no-one was working hard at the pretence. During a press conference held on 26 September 1986 at Malmstrom Air Force Base in Montana, SAC commander General John T. Chain told reporters, "I've visited the factory. I've seen the airplane." He pronounced himself pleased with the aircraft's technical performance,

Above: Released on 20 April 1988, this artist's impression of the B-2 gave the world its first view of a USAF stealth aircraft. Some journalists were sceptical, but the drawing in fact proved reasonably accurate, apart from the missing engine exhausts.

citing the development of stealth aircraft and other new Air Force programmes as being partly responsible for the high morale in his command.

The first artist's impression of the B-2 bomber was released in April 1988, and many observers wondered why the existence of the older F-117A had not been released before. Air Force chief of staff General Larry D. Welch explained in May 1988 that the Air Force was more concerned about the Soviets seeing examples of early stealth technology than the B-2. The low RCS of the first stealth aircraft (he did not specifically describe this as the F-117A) depended almost exclusively on the aircraft's shape, he claimed, while the B-2 combined a variety of low-observable technologies. A good photograph the F-117A would have betrayed most of its secrets, thus explaining the extensive measures the USAF had taken to keep the type away from prying eyes.

From the mid-1980s onwards, there were rumours that the several F-117As had been flown by C-5 Galaxy to bases outside the USA. The UK was often mentioned as a destination, and

Right: 10 November 1988 – Assistant Secretary of Defense for Public Affairs J. Daniel Howard releases the first F-117A photo.

the 37th TFW's A-7s are known to have visited RAF Woodbridge. In a conversation with the author, the Soviet air attaché in London even claimed to have seen the Lockheed aircraft at a UK base. A diplomatic cocktail party didn't seem the best time to pursue such a delicate subject, but before I next had a chance to meet him, he had joined the long series of Soviet diplomats expelled by Prime Minister Margaret Thatcher during the mid to late 1980s.

Early in 1987, USAF and Pentagon seriously considered reducing the classification of the F-117A, a move which would make sense with the B-2 stealth bomber due to roll out in the following year, followed in the early 1990s by other stealthy designs such as the Navy's A-12 and the USAF's YF-22 and YF-23. If the Pentagon continued to try to hide stealth aircraft, "we're going to have to build a

roof over the Air Force", one defense specialist told *The Washington Post* in March of that year. Despite the pressure from Congress, nothing was done.

F-117 "OFFICIAL"

By early October 1988, the time finally seemed right to unveil the F-117A. With the B-2 due to be rolled out in the following month, continued high classification of an older design seemed illogical, while a court case in which some Lockheed employees were alleging damage to health from exposure to dangerous chemicals used in F-117A manufacture seemed likely to uncover more information about the aircraft.

On 4 October, all was ready for the big event. Press kits (complete with photo) were prepared, and Senator Chic Hecht of Nevada was ready to present a press briefing that afternoon. At the last moment

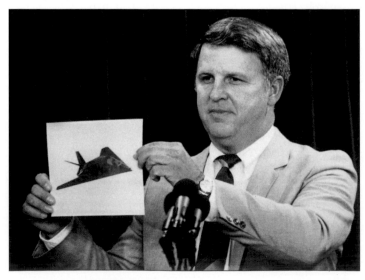

Above: **Clandestine photos of F-117A operating by day gave the world its first glimpse of the aircraft's planform.**

Below right: **How a stealthy advanced bomber apparently looked to a Lockheed Skunk Works artist working on the concept of a delta planform.**

the plan was scrapped, apparently after intense debate at what one newspaper report described as the "highest levels of the Defense Department and on Capitol Hill". One theory behind the sudden clampdown was that unveiling of the aircraft during a presidential election could be seen as a political ploy. "There was a bipartisan view that this was not the most auspicious time for this," one DoD source told the Associated Press, suggesting that the aircraft might be unveiled after the presidential election.

Although the *Washington Times* had managed to obtain a draft copy of the press release, publishing this on the morning of 4 October, the photo stayed under wraps until 10 November. Underexposed and heavily retouched, the picture finally released to the press was almost as uninformative as early-1960s photos of Soviet space exploits. But it did represent a landmark in the history of "black" programmes. No aircraft in aviation history had remained "under wraps" for so long.

By April 1989, the F-117A was operating by day, allowing the first clandestine photographs to be taken, revealing the aircraft's true appearance for the first time. The 4450th Tactical Group, was reclassified as the 37th TFW, its three squadrons becoming

the 415th TFS "Nightstalkers", 416th TFS "Ghostriders", and 417th TFS "Bandits". In October 1989, the 4450th was redesignated the 37th Tactical Fighter Wing, coming under the operational command of the 12th Air Force. At the same time, the unit phased out its A-7Ds, and used T-38s for the training role. In April 1990, the Defense Department announced that the total cost of developing and building the F-117A had been $6.26 billion, and the unit cost was $106.2 million.

Public debut of the aircraft came on 21 April 1990, when several aircraft visited Nellis

AFB to be viewed by the families of 37th personnel, and more than 200 reporters and photographers. The F-117A gave the United States unprecedented military capabilities, pilot Capt. Randall Peterson, told onlookers, but admitted that, "We're not allowed to discuss any capability. A lot of the information is still classified."

"I only wish I could tell you what this fighter can really do," said Ben Rich, who was visiting Nellis for the occasion. "The performance is awesome and the weapons system is unmatched anywhere in the world."

By July 1990 Lockheed had built a total of 64 F-117As – five pre-series aircraft plus 59 production examples. It had planned to build 100, but the aircraft's higher than anticipated costs had forced a cutback. Seven aircraft were delivered in 1982, eight a year from 1983 until 1985, seven in 1986, four in 1987 and three in 1988. The final example was 88-0843, handed over on 12 July 1990.

There is no chance of the F-117A returning to production. The USAF has all the Nighthawks it can afford, and the US Government is reluctant to export stealth technology to any but its closest allies. Britain is reported to have considered the F-117 as a possible replacement for the Hawker Siddeley Buccaneer light bomber, but the existence of the Tornado made this unlikely. "The F-117 production line has closed down," F-117 programme manager Paul Martin told *Flight International* in September 1990, ". . . any application of that airplane to the RAF's needs would be something that the [UK] MoD and the US Air Force would have to agree on."

B-2 BOMBER

The initial development contract for the larger and more sophisticated stealth bomber was worth $7,300 million. Based on the successful Senior Ice design, it was codenamed Senior CJ. The first five years of the programme were a technology-demonstration

Above: **Every line of those curves is dictated by stealth. The dark patches under the leading edge are for conformal radars.**

phase, which may have been timed to end in early 1985 just about the same time as B-1B production was running down. Had problems emerged with the flying-wing aircraft, a follow-on order for the B-1B or the proposed B-1C could have been placed.

Work on the technology needed for what would become the B-2 initially went faster than anticipated, proving more effective than planners had hoped when confronted by the technology used in current-generation Soviet radar systems and new threats still under development in Soviet laboratories.

The technology-demonstration phase of the programme may have included the airborne testing of a scaled-down prototype. Probably built to $\frac{1}{2}$ scale and powered by four non-afterburning F404s, this would provide RCS data,

information on stability and control of such an unconventional shape. Most sources agree that it flew sometime in 1982.

It is possible that this trials aircraft was rebuilt in the mid-1980s to become more representative of the proposed production configuration. One source told me in the spring of 1988 that the sub-scale aircraft had been flying for about 15 months, a date in complete disagreement with earlier accounts and which (if true) could only be explained by either a rebuilt, or even an all-new second test aircraft.

"From the outset, we stressed that the B-2 is on the leading edge of technology, and there were some very significant technical risks associated with the B-2", USAF Chief of Staff General Larry D. Welsh was to tell the British magazine *Defence* in early 1988. "We had some twelve risk areas we identified, and insisted on closure of each of those risk areas before we embarked on

full-scale development. Since we closed out that risk reduction effort, we really haven't had any surprises. Since that time, development has proceeded quite smoothly".

By 1983, the results obtained from early ATB development work were already better than had been anticipated, giving the USAF the confidence needed to press ahead with the new aircraft at the expence of any follow-on B-1B procurement.

PUBLICITY

At the Farnborough Air Show held every two years in England, the world's aerospace companies rent chalets which face the runways and flying displays. Best-positioned of these is Chalet A1, a coveted location hired years ago by the Northrop Corporation of the USA, whose booking was promptly renewed for each subsequent show. However, 1988 saw a break in this long-running scheme. Not only was

the US company not occupying its traditional site – it was not exhibiting at the show at all.

The reason for abandoning this prime piece of Farnborough real estate was not penny-pinching but the fact that the company was in the embarrassing position of being unable to discuss its latest products – all were highly-secret "black" programmes the end results of which would not be available for export in the foreseeable future.

Back in the days when Chalet A1 was Northrop territory, many aviation journalists – including the author – would *rendezvous* there on the first "press-only" day of the show. The object of this exercise was to meet the company's chief designer Lee Begin. Most companies are nervous about letting their head of advanced projects mix with journalists but Northrop allowed Begin to "hold court" with a small audience of experienced defence journalists with whom a

mutual rapport had been established over the years.

At these sessions, Begin would talk about his company's projects – sometimes on the record and sometimes as unpublishable background – with a degree of freedom which would have induced apoplexy in the Public Relations departments of lesser corporations. That was the way he worked – the journalists he trusted were given extensive briefings but they in turn accepted the restrictions which he sometimes imposed as the price of gaining access to a man who was helping shape the future of aviation. I do not know of any occasion where anyone let him down.

CONFIGURATION

At the 1983 Paris Air Show, Begin showed me sketches of some of his future concepts for jet fighters – concepts which still remained "under wraps" (and unreported by me) five years later. When I asked if I could have copies of his sketches, he

laughed, but declined. "The public relations department would lose their lunch if they even knew you'd seen them! But I think you'll find this interesting." Reaching into his briefcase, he handed me a copy of a recent paper he had written on the history of Northrop "Flying Wing" aircraft.

I was puzzled. Lee knew that my interest in 1940s and early 1950s aviation history was minimal. Why did he think I would find his paper of interest? Not until several weeks later did the long-delayed penny finally drop – the only conceivable reason why Begin would be spending his valuable time dusting off Flying Wing History had to be that the same configuration was being used for the then highly-secret Northrop Advanced Technology Bomber.

When first planned, the Northrop aircraft was designed to be an approximate match for the Soviet Tu-26 Backfire. Specified to cruise at Mach 0.8 over ranges of up to 5,000nm (9,250km) – a distance equal to the Soviet aircraft's range – the ATB was to weigh 280,000lb (127,000kg) at take-off and carry a payload og 10,000lb (4,500kg). During the early 1980s, the design was scaled up several times until it was in the same general range and payload class as the B-1B. In early 1984, the B-2 was reported to weigh around 400,000lb (181,400kg) at take-off and to carry a maximum internal weapon load of approximately 40,000lb (18,100kg).

Work on the B-2 was handled in a former Ford Motor Co. auto-assembly plant in Pico Rivera, California. By 1986, a full-scale engineering mock-up had been built at Pico Rivera. This allowed the basic design to be frozen, with the last significant changes being added in 1986. Early in the programme, the decision was made to build the prototypes using production tooling. This was probably done for two reasons. For a start, transition from prototype to production aircraft would be made easier. Less obvious is the fact that the use of production tooling would allow engineers to maintain close tolerances when assembling the aircraft's structure and skin.

At a meeting of Northrop shareholders held in May 1988, company chairman Thomas Jones described how the tooling "can be adjusted to accuracies of within one thousandth of an inch. The end result is a system that allows every major

structural assembly of the B-2, regardless of complexity, to fit together exactly as designed." What Jones did not tell the meeting was that the reason for these exacting tolerances was related to the aircraft's stealth characteristics. The electrical discontinuity created by small gaps can scatter electro-magnetic energy. On the B-1B, small gaps in the skin were closed by adhesive tape, but a more sophisticated solution was required for the less-observable B-2.

On 19 November 1987, the USAF awarded Northrop a $2,000 million production contract for the B-2, a move which was not cleared for public release until 26 January 1988. On that date, the Air Force confirmed that production funding would be granted to Northrop and to the main sub-contractors – Boeing, LTV and General Electric – but spokesman Captain Jay DeFrank would not identify the rôles of these companies, give the number of bombers which the money would buy nor even say whether a firm, fixed-price contract or some other type had been awarded. Nor would the Air Force comment on reports that the date of the first flight had slipped.

NEW METHODS

For a long time, the date of the aircraft's roll-out and first flight remained classified. These were widely expected to take place in late 1987 but the date came and went. Delivery to Northrop's new final-assembly facility at Palmdale airport, California, of the first set of B-2 wings did not take place until August 1987 when they were flown in by a Lockheed C-5 Galaxy.

The USAF was not disturbed by the slippage to early 1988, having foreseen the possibility of delays. General Thomas McMullen, then head of the USAF's Aeronautical Systems Division (ASD) had explained a year earlier that the new bomber had "met challenges, and there are more to come, but they are straightforward engineering issues. That is not to say that there are no risks; there is certainly a schedule risk, and some technical risks".

Early in January 1988 the Los Angeles Times quoted two unidentified Northrop employees involved in the programme and Wall Street securities analysts as saying that the bomber's first test-flight had been delayed by four months and was not expected until August of that year. Northrop sources had

declined to discuss the reasons for the slippage, the newspaper said. The Washington Post suggested that the slippage might delay initial operational capability (IOC) "perhaps more than a year" due to unspecified "technical and production problems".

It seems that one area of difficulty lay in the inlets. By April 1988, the prototype had not yet received its engines. Installation of the powerplant was reported not to be imminent. Aviation Week suggested that a "major redesign of the inlet and powerplant mounting structure" was likely and could be implemented on the fourth full-scale development aircraft.

Some of the difficulties may have sprung from the aircraft's massive use of composites, as engineering staff learned to adapt conventional tooling and metal-orientated production and assembly methods to the new materials. For this reason, "holes drilled in composite materials sometimes come out oblong-shaped", Aviation Week reported in early 1988. Despite the use of production-type tooling, installation of components on the prototype was largely a matter of labour-intensive hand fitting.

One unfortunate side effect of the high degree of compartmentalisation demanded for security reasons was that sub-contractors whose equipment had to work together were not able to communicate with each other. Only after delivery did incompatibility problems emerge, forcing time consuming and expensive modification and redesign work. Technical drawings were in many cases being reworked rather than confirmed.

PROBLEMS

Problems were also reported with the aircraft's windscreen – part of the load-bearing structure – and with cracking of the composite leading edges. The B-2 is the first large and heavy aircraft to use large areas of composite honeycomb, so such problems were always a possibility as designers and assemblers learned how to handle and fabricate components made in the new material.

The short timescale may also have resulted in sub-assemblies being shipped to the Palmdale final-assembly plant before all testing had been completed, causing unplanned trouble-shooting and modification work on the assembled aircraft. "Ship One is literally crawling with people", an unidentified observer told *Aviation Week* in April 1988, "and most of them aren't Northrop people, because they can't even get on the airplane".

Below: **Shrouded in white plastic and rubber mats, production B-2s take shape on the Northrop line. Black screens cover all inlets, plus the leading edges on the rear two aircraft.**

Despite highly-publicised programme-management problems at Northrop, Under Secretary of Defense for Strategic and Theater Nuclear Forces Dr Lawrence Woodruff told the House Armed Services Commettee in the spring of 1988 that the programme was "progressing well" but insisted that, in response of Congressional concerns, the USAF has set up "an initiative for maintaining cost, contractor performance and management discipline within the B-2 program" and that Northrop was assessing

"the condition of its own management system".

News that Boeing was hiring extra staff for the Palmdale final assembly plant, while Northrop was apparently laying off hundreds of staff from its Pico Rivera facility, led to speculation that Boeing had been secretly given an increased rôle in the management of the programme. This was strongly denied by Northrop which issued a USAF-approved statement emphasising that no changes in programme management had been made

or were planned. Boeing's hiring of staff was directly due to that company's work as a sub-contractor to Northrop, the statement indicated.

B-2 REVEALED

On 20 April 1988, The USAF released an artist's impression of the B-2 and confirmed that the prototype would fly in the autumn. "The first flight of the Advanced Technology Bomber, or B-2, is currently scheduled, for this fall", the service said. The bomber would take off from the final

B-2 Advanced Technology Bomber

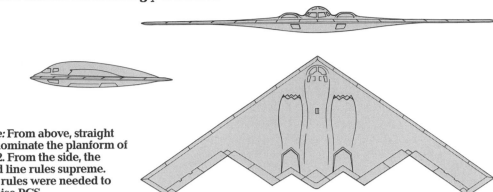

assembly facility at Air Force Plant 42 in Palmdale then land at the Air Force Flight Test Center at Edwards AFB, where flight testing would be carried out. "The initial flight of the B-2 will highlight the return of the flying wing design to military aviation", it was stated. No date was given for the maiden flight, however, and the service refused to give further details of the aircraft's size, crew number, weapons load, performance or cost.

The drawing which provided few details of its

Above: **From above, straight lines dominate the planform of the B-2. From the side, the curved line rules supreme. These rules were needed to minimise RCS.**

construction aside from its general shape was not totally accurate; the USAF admitted that several details had either been omitted or altered. The science-fiction shape created some scepticism but, during an interview with *Defence* magazine, USAF Chief of Staff General Larry Welch insisted that the drawing was generally accurate. "There are a few details that are obscured for security reasons. You will note that there are no exhausts in the picture."

According to the USAF, the shape of the new bomber had been declassified because the prototype would soon "be outside doing things and people will see it". Some saw the sudden de-classification as a public-relations ruse, an unexpected move designed to defuse growing Congressional demands for greater access to information on the growing number of major "black" programmes.

Roll-out had been expected in September 1988, leading to a first flight in October or November, but these dates could not be met. On 12th November, the long-awaited roll-out finally took place. The audience was given only a frontal view of the new bomber, but a light aircraft which overflew the rollout ceremony provided *Aviation Week* with an unauthorised view of the hidden rear section.

For the next eight months, the B-2 became the world's best known and most criticised "hangar queen". Technical problems delayed the maiden flight until 17 July 1989.

CRUISE MISSILES

The B-2 may have been developed in near-total secrecy, but the security blackout around America's stealth cruise missile work has been even tighter. Despite late-1970s claims that existing cruise missiles such as

the ALCM and Tomahawk were virtually unstoppable, by the early 1980s Pentagon planners feared that growing Soviet EW expertise might allow them to interfere with the radar elements of the TERCOM guidance system and that cruise missiles – particularly the GLCM – were becoming vulnerable to S-300 (SA-10) attack.

During the development of Tomahawk and the ALCM, tests had been carried out to measure the weapons' radar, IR and visual signatures. As a result of this work, RCS, IR output and luminosity were all reduced. It was now clear that this was not enough. In the short term, the USAF hoped to counter the SA-10 and interceptor threats by modifying its cruise missile fleet, adding an on-board active ECM system based on work carried out in an extensive programme codenamed "Have Rust".

A three-year development programme was envisaged, allowing deployment in the mid-1980s. ALCMs would have to be modified but GLCM rounds would be delivered complete with the EW sub-system when these weapons were deployed in the early 1980s. The status of the cruise missile EW programme remains highly classified. One source told me in 1988 that the scheme had not gone ahead in the form originally planned but confirmed that some improvements had been made to the weapons.

In July 1982 the USAF completed a study of possible next-generation cruise missiles and concluded that development of an improved model using the latest technologies could counter the sort of air defence system which the Soviet Union was expected to field in the 1990s. Just as the AGM-86 and BGM-109 had exploited mid-1970s breakthroughs in technology such as miniature electronics and small low-consumption turbofan engines, the new weapon would use the improved guidance systems and better engines of the 1980s, coupling these with stealth technology.

The idea of a low-RCS cruise missile was not new. In testimony before the Senate Armed Services Committee in 1977 John B. Walsh, DoD Deputy Director of Space and Stretegic Systems described how studies had been carried out into ways of reducing missile RCS.

A formal requirement for a new cruise missile was drawn up that same month and the programme was approved by President Reagan in August. A request for proposals was issued to industry in September. Technology for a new cruise missile was already in hand, thanks to programmes such as DARPA's little-publicised Teal Dawn. This had explored areas such as airframe shaping, RAM and advanced propulsion. All designs to be evaluated would use the same engine, the Williams International F112 turbofan which entered full-scale development in July 1982. The IOC date for the new missile was targeted for 1986, a goal which some saw as unrealistic even in 1982. It was in fact to prove hopelessly optimistic.

COMPETITION

Boeing, Lockheed and General Dynamics all competed for the task of building the new missile. Having developed the ALCM-A and -B, Boeing was obviously in a good position to win the new programme and, given the fact that ALCM production was being cut back, had the strongest incentive to do so. Unfortunately, Boeing faced severe competition. Lockheed had the useful experience gained from its own stealth cruise missile programme, while General Dynamics had worked on Teal Dawn and so was clearly in a good position to bid for the new weapon.

At the time, General Dynamics was somewhat under a cloud, the results of quality-control problems with the Tomahawk. Working in the company's favour was the fact that its Teal Dawn experience would give it the head start needed to match the ambitious timescale of the new missile. From the first, the company seems to have set the pace, while its rivals had to embark on redesigns of their submissions.

The initial Boeing

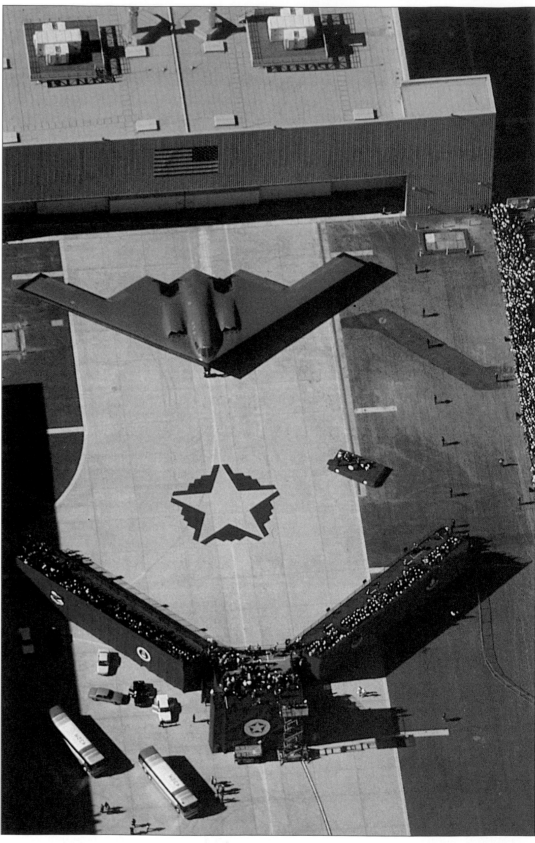

submission was a development of the AGM-86 design but the company soon realised that this could not provide the performance needed to gain the new contract. By late 1982, the company was reported to be frantically working on a higher-risk concept able to take greater advantage of the latest stealth developments.

Boeing was "scrambling to come up with a new aeronautical design", a DoD official told *Aviation Week* in November of that year.

Like Boeing, Lockheed redesigned its entry. The first design offered was stealthy but proved aerodynamically unstable. It also required external carriage, a feature not desirable in a world of

Above: **Security breach or public relations ploy? A light aircraft overflew the B-2 rollout and revealed the novel shape of the exhausts.**

low-RCS warplanes.

Progress was swift enough to allow the USAF to scale down its ALCM procurement. The Air Force had planned to buy 3,418 ALCMs but, in

Top: In the course of development, ALCM-B was modified to reduce its RCS, a move dictated by advances in Soviet air defences.

Above: As the B-2 lifts off the runway, the huge main undercarriage doors probably act as vertical stabilising surfaces.

Below: The pyramid-shaped absorbers which line the walls of this test chamber allow accurate RCS measurements to be taken of the Matra Apache.

February 1983, announced that production of the ALCM-B would end after the FY83 buy, bringing the total number of rounds delivered to only 1,499. The planned ALCM-C would not be built.

AGM-129

On 15 April 1983, General Dynamics was announced winner of the Advanced Cruise Missile (ACM) competition. It was given a fixed-price contract which covered full-scale development of the AGM-129 and contained options on the first two production lots. Such was the new programme's high classification that the Air Force would not release details of the total value of the contract, the number of rounds to be procured or the programme schedule. Unofficial estimates suggested that the unit cost of the new missile would be about $3 million, with the entire ACM programme costing about $7,000 million.

The targets set for the ACM were ambitious. In addition to being stealthier than the

current ALCM, it was required to have better guidance, a lower terrain-following altitude and a longer range, probably around 2,300 miles (3,700km). After launch, the new missile was expected to fly up to 1,000 miles (1,600km) farther than current cruise missiles, travelling around, rather than through, Soviet air defences.

As in the case on manned stealth aircraft, reducing the RCS involved careful shaping. The AGM-129A has a flattened body shape with a wedge-shaped nose, forward swept-wings, a folding vertical fin and folding horizontal tailplane surfaces. The air inlet for the Williams International F112-WR-100 turbofan engine is under the missile body just behind the wings, and the exhaust forms part of the missile's flat-wedge tail assembly.

By April 1988, the programme was reported to be at least three years behind schedule and likely to cost an additional $2,000 million. A report issued by House Armed Services Committee Chairman Les Aspin described the ACM programme as a

"procurement disaster", citing deficiencies in quality control and inept supervision by the Air Force and the manufacturer. Aspin blamed the delays and cost over-runs on what he described as mismanagement by General Dynamics and the USAF. "The highly classified Advanced Cruise Missile is the worst system I reviewed", he stated.

The report was vague as to the exact nature of the ACM's problems, noting simply that the project was "protected in nearly all interesting details by high classification".

Problems seem to have arisen in several areas. Quality control problems at General Dynamics had been responsible for the initial one-year slippage. In 1987 a total of 44 critical components in the missile were singled out for quality control checks, while the company accepted Air Force recommendations for ground testing the missile prior to beginning flight tests. In the spring of 1988 General Welch spoke of unspecified "design and manufacturing concerns" which would require further testing.

DEPLOYMENT

Early flight trials seem to have high-lighted other problems. The weapon's low-RCS shape seems to have had an adverse effect on its flying characteristics, while other problems emerged with the missile's computer software. In June 1988, SAC commander General John Chain told an Air Force Association symposium that the programme "...is not coming along as quickly or as well as I would like". Deputy Chief of Staff, Plans and Operations, Lt.Gen. Michael Dugan expained that the results of early flight trials had been erratic, having included "a couple of flights that didn't do especially well". Work was under way to identify and correct the problems, he stated, but "testing has not been completed yet, so how it will all sort out, I just don't know".

The AGM-129A finally became operational in 1991. By the early 1990s, the USAF

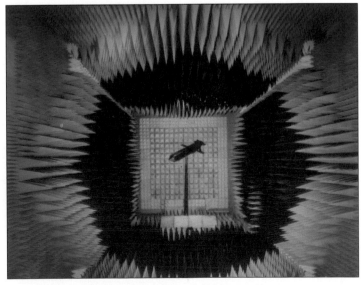

expected to deploy 1,500 ACMs, which would have made up around half of the service's cruise missile strength. Although McDonnell Douglas was awarded a contract in 1987 to qualify it as a second source producer of ACM, in 1992 procurement was scaled back to only 460 rounds, and production ended in 1993. The AGM-129A was designed for use on the B-52H, B-1B, and B-2A, but it is understood that only 48 B-52H were equipped with the weapon. A scheme to modify a small batch by replacing the 200kT range W80 nuclear warhead with a conventional HE payload was proposed in 1998, but was not adopted.

Stealth is also an important feature of more recent air-to-surface weapons. In the late 1990s, the USAF drew up plans for a 1,000nm (1,800km) range stealthy Long-Range Cruise Missile (LRCM), a concept which has attracted interest from the UK, raising the possibility of a joint development programme. The resulting weapon would use stealth to penetrate hostile defences, but could improve its survivability by using very-low-altitude terrain-following flight, or even active countermeasures. It is expected to have a datalink permitting in-flight target updates, plus some form of terminal-guidance seeker, and a warhead able to deal with very deeply buried or hardened targets.

Some degree of stealth technology is also being built into tactical missiles due to enter service in the current decade. These include the Lockheed Martin AGM-158 Joint Air-to-Surface Stand-off Missile (JASSM),

the Franco-German Matra BAe Dynamics Storm Shadow (known as SCALP EG in French Air Force service), and the Norwegian Kongsberg Nytt Sjomalsmissile (NSM) anti-ship missile.

Once the Norwegian weapon has been launched, the lugs on

its upper surface retract. A cover then closes over them to maintain the weapon's low radar signature. The entire nose section is roll-stabilised with respect to the missile airframe. As the missile banks to turn, the nose section counter-rotates so

that its stealth-configured nose remains at the optimum angle for low detectability.

NEW FIGHTERS

By 1976, the USAF was planning to incorporate stealth technology in its next-generation fighter. First studies for what would become the Advanced Tactical Fighter (ATF) were begun in 1969-70, and by 1975 a tentative plan had been drawn up to test prototypes in 1977-81. Lack of money doomed these original plans, but by 1976 stealth technology was promising enough to persuade the USAF to begin the Have Blue programme, and to add a low-observability requirement to the specification for its F-15 replacement.

In 1981 the USAF issued to industry a request for information on possible ATF

Left: **Under the watchful eye of a chase aircraft, the stealthy Lockheed Martin Joint Air-to-Surface Stand-Off Missile (JASSM) flies a test mission.**

Right: **Wing/body blending, outward-canted tail fins, and inlets under the wing were low-RCS features of this Rockwell ATF proposal.**

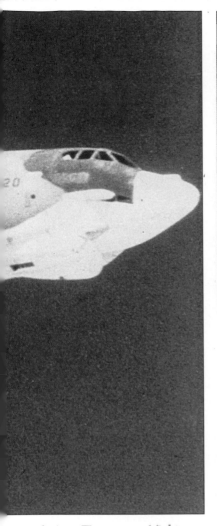

Left: General Dynamics AGM-129 Advanced Cruise Missile (seen here being carried by a B-52 trials aircraft) is stealthy with more range than ALCM. Following the end of the Cold War, orders were cut back to only 460 examples.

Above: A Have Blue prototype. Very small, and with less faceting than the definitive F-117A, it differs mainly in the inward canted fins and rudders, which actually increased the infra-red signature.

Below: The incredibly high sweep of the Have Blue prototypes is seen here, as is the fact that the under-side is faceted, unlike the F-117, which is completely flat. Handling was extremely difficult, with high sink rates at low speeds.

designs. The proposed fighter had to be able to handle air-to-air and air-to-ground missions, and was intended to have the performance needed to evade Soviet air defences, allowing the aircraft to fly deep inside Eastern Europe in order to attack Warsaw Pact fighters and air bases. To achieve this, it was to combine advanced low-observables technology with the ability to supercruise (fly at supersonic speeds without afterburning).

The ATF was required to give pilots a first-look, first-shot, first-kill capability through the use of reduced observables and advanced sensors. Its avionics suite was to be a highly

integrated system that would allow the pilot to concentrate on the mission, rather than on managing the sensors, as in current fighters. Other demands were for higher reliability, maintainability, and sortie generation rates than were available from the F-15.

In October 1985 the USAF asked contractors to submit proposals for a fighter able to enter service in the mid-1990s as the eventual replacement for its F-15 Eagle and F-16 Fighting Falcon. Bids were to be submitted by December of that

year, and would lead to between two and four companies or teams being selected to take part in a three-year study intended to balance the performance and cost of the new fighter against its operational requirements. Choice of a contractor to develop, flight-test and produce ATF would be made in early 1989, with the plane making its first flight in late 1991 and entering service in the mid-1990s.

By July 1986, the USAF decided to restructure the programme. Instead of flying a single selected design in late 1991, it would now select two rival concepts to be flown as competitive prototypes, an arrangement which the service last used in the mid-1970s YF-16/YF-17 Lightweight Fighter competition. On 31 October 1986 it announced that Lockheed and Northrop had been selected for this demonstration/validation phase of the programme.

In April 1987, the US Air Force Systems Command awarded two industrial teams contracts worth $691 million covering a 50-month development programme. Each company was to produce two prototypes and a ground-based avionics testbed. A target date of October 1989 was set for the first flights of the Lockheed YF-22 and the Northrop YF-23. Lockheed teamed with General Dynamics (Fort Worth) and Boeing Military Airplanes to produce its two YF-22 prototypes.

One of the first activities carried out by both teams was a study of possible methods of risk

Below: **By 1986 the appearance of the Lockheed ATF had changed greatly. Laterally raked intakes appeared, much smaller canards were now located high and aft of the cockpit, and the fins were much more steeply canted.**

Right: **An artist's impression of the Lockheed ATF contender released in 1985 shows a chined nose similar to that of the SR-71, a fairly orthodox delta wing with canard foreplanes, and vectoring engine nozzles.**

reduction, and alternative technologies. This was ordered as part of a larger Systems Requirement Review carried out by the Air Force. On 11 October 1989 the evaluation phase of the programme was extended by six months.

Powerplant development was running ahead of that of the airframe, a wise policy in any aircraft programme. In October 1983, General Electric and Pratt & Whitney were given $200 million contracts covering the development and ground testing of rival designs of Joint Advanced Fighter Engine (JAFE). Pratt & Whitney's engine was the PW5000, designated XF119 by the US DoD. This ran for the first time in late 1986. Rival design from General Electric was the GE37. Designated XF120, this variable bypass design began bench tests in mid-1987. In early 1988, both teams received contracts worth close to $342 million for the development of flightworthy "YF" engines. One YF-22 and one YF-23 was to be powered by

the YF119, the other example of each by the YF120.

The task of producing the ATF radar was given to Westinghouse, teamed with Texas Instruments. In April 1987, the team won this vital contract for both the YF-22 and the YF-23, a blow to rival radar giant Hughes Aircraft, which had teamed with General Electric to bid for the ATF radar.

YF-22 AND YF-23 DESIGNS

Lockheed and Northrop produced very different designs. The Lockheed YF-22 had a trapezoidal wing and twin tails, and bore a vague resemblance to the F-15. The need for stealth dictated the use of a forward fuselage that was diamond-

Right: **Were the Lockheed artist's ATF impressions of 1985 and 1986 deliberate disinformation? The YF-22 seen here shows no sign of a tail-less canard delta; only the thrust-vectoring nozzles remain.**

Below: The losing ATF contender was the Northrop/McDonnell Douglas YF-23. A more radical design than the YF-22, its outstanding features were the trapezoidal wing planform and steeply canted ruddervators .

shaped in cross-section, and large flat fuselage sides. The inlet ducts were curved inwards and upwards, shielding the front faces of the twin engines from direct illumination by hostile radars.

The Northrop/McDonnell Douglas YF-23 was about 7ft (2.1m) longer than the YF-22, and had a more "science-fiction" appearance. It was more slender than the Lockheed aircraft, and had a diamond-shaped wing, and all-flying twin tail surfaces canted 50 degrees outwards in a "V" configuration. The wing leading edge was swept back at 40 degrees, while the trailing edge was swept forward at the same angle. Every line in the

Above: **With its rounded lines and outward-canted V-tail, Northrop's YF-23 looked like something out of science fiction.**

aircraft's planform was parallel to one or the other of the wing leading edges, a measure intended to concentrate the radar returns from the aircraft into a few well-defined directions. As on the YF-22, the inlet ducts were curved in two dimensions to shield the front faces of the engines. The engine efflux was released into trench-shaped cut-outs in the rear fuselage. This helped cool the hot exhaust gases, reducing the aircraft's IR signature.

Below: **On the YF-23, all straight edges were positioned at one of a handful of predetermined angles, a measure intended to reduce RCS.**

One significant difference between the two designs was that the YF-22 had two-dimensional engine nozzles which could be vectored 20 degrees up or down at any power setting. Northrop opted to rely on aerodynamic control surfaces, believing that thrust-vectoring would compromise stealth, particularly in the rearward sector.

During the flight-test programme, Northrop's YF-23 achieved its early milestones

Above: **This futuristic shape formed the basis of several "stealth fighter" construction kits, but was only an advertising artwork used by EW manufactuer Loral.**

ahead of Lockheed's YF-22. The first YF-23 was powered by P&W engines, and was rolled out at Edwards AFB on 22 June 1990. It flew for the first time on 27 August 1990, with test pilot Paul Metz at the controls, in a sortie which lasted for 20 minutes.

The first YF-22 was rolled out on 29 August 1990. Powered by GE YF120 engines, it flew for the first time on 29 September 1990, with Lockheed test pilot Dave Ferguson at the controls. The

Below: Not much stealth technology is visible in this Grumman advanced fighter proposal of the early 1980s. The inlets would be good radar targets.

second YF-22 was powered by P&W YF119 engines and flew on 30 October 1990, with Lockheed test pilot Tom Morgenfeld at the controls. Neither carried any radar or cannon, but both were able to carry and launch Sidewinder and AMRAAM missiles. The second YF-23 was powered by GE engines, and flew on 26 October.

Both aircraft demonstrated "supercruise" capability. The first YF-23 "supercruised" on its fifth flight, and achieved its highest recorded supercruise of Mach 1.43 on 14 November. The GE-powered YF-22 had an optimum supercruise speed of Mach 1.58, slightly faster than the Mach 1.43 of the P&W-powered example. With afterburning, both YF-22 aircraft could exceed Mach 2 at 50,000ft (15,250m).

On 15 November, the GE-powered YF-22 demonstrated thrust-vectoring for the first time. The concept proved successful; trials showed that the YF-22 could achieve supersonic roll and pitch rates in excess of those that can be achieved by a conventional fighter at subsonic speeds.

The YF-23 demonstrated a maximum speed of Mach 1.8, manoeuvred at up to 7 g, and reached a maximum angle of attack of 25 degrees. Like the YF-22, the YF-23 had no radar or cannon. During the flight-test programme, it did not fire missiles.

While an intensive programme of competitive flight tests was under way at the Air Force Flight Test Center at Edwards AFB, California, in late 1990, in November of that year the USAF requested both teams to submit final engineering and manufacturing development (EMD) proposals, which they did on 2 January 1991.

YF-22 SELECTED

On 23 April 1991, the USAF announced that it had selected the F-22 powered by the F119 engine. The reasons for the choice remain classified, but the USAF seems to have favoured the manoeuvrability provided by thrust vectoring over the extra stealth offered by the rival design. Perhaps with memories of the engine problems it had suffered with the F100-powered F-15 and F-16, it had opted for the more conservative engine design.

One factor which may have steered the USAF away from the YF-23 was the design of its weapon bays. To maintain a low RCS, both teams relied on internal bays to keep non-stealthy ordnance hidden from hostile radars. However, the Northrop design would have carried two Joint Direct Attack Munitions-sized weapons stored one above the other behind a single set of weapons-bay doors. If the first weapon could not be released for any reason, the second could not be used.

An engineering and manufacturing development (EMD) contract was awarded on 2 August 1991 for 11 prototypes (including two tandem-seat F-22Bs) plus one static and one fatigue test airframes. Pratt & Whitney was given an EMD contract for the engine. The combined value of both contracts was $10.91 billion ($9.55 billion for the airframe and $1.36 billion for engines). Subsequent contract changes, including three Congressional budget cuts and subsequent revision of the programme schedule have increased the contract values to a total of $18.6 billion.

As a result of these changes, the number of prototypes was reduced to nine, and the two-seat model was eliminated. All prototypes will be the single-seat F-22A version. Under the EMD contract, the F-22 team will complete the design of the aircraft, produce production tooling, and build and test nine flightworthy aircraft and two ground test articles.

The Critical Design Review (CDR) of the F-22 and the Initial Production Readiness Review (IPRR) of the F119 engine were completed in February 1995. These showed that fabrication and assembly of the EMD aircraft could begin.

The Pratt & Whitney-powered number two prototype had not been retired at the end of the

demonstration and validation (dem/val) phase of the programme. It returned to flying status on 30 October 1991. The other prototype was stripped of its GE engines and used for EMD systems mock-up tests. It is now on display at the USAF Museum in Dayton, Ohio.

Construction of the first components for the first EMD aircraft (91-4001) began in the winter of 1993. The production configuration resembled the YF-22, but had a wing sweep of 42 degrees rather than the 48 degrees of the YF-22. The vertical stabilisers were reduced in size by approximately 20 per cent. The original YF-22 surfaces had been sized to avoid potential spin problems. Since none materialised, the size was reduced to reduce drag and weight.

To improve pilot visibility, the canopy was moved forward 7in (18cm) and the air inlets moved 14in (35.5cm) to the rear. Changes to the shape of the wing trailing edges and the horizontal stabilisers reduced the aircraft's RCS, improved the aerodynamics, and added structural strength.

Aircraft 4001 was rolled out on 9 April 1997 during a ceremony at which the name Raptor was announced for the new fighter. The planned May 1997 first flight date was to slip, apparently due to fuel leaks and other hardware-related problems. The first flight finally took place on 7 September 1997 from Dobbins ARB in Marietta, Georgia, with F-22 Chief Test Pilot Paul Metz at the controls.

As more aircraft joined the test fleet, the scope of testing gradually expanded. Aircraft 4002 flew on 29 June 1998 and was used to expanding the flight-test envelope, demonstrating a 26 degree angle-of-attack. It was also used for testing weapon separations from the internal bay.

First flown on 6 March 2000, aircraft 4003 was the first to have an internal structure that is fully representative of the production aircraft, and was used to perform demonstrations to 100 per cent of the planned load factors. It also was earmarked to make the first AMRAAM launch trials.

Aircraft 4004 was the first to have a full suite of avionics and software. It started life with Block 1.1 software (Block 0 had been used for initial F-22 flight tests), but was upgraded to Block 1.2 before its first flight. It flew for the first time on 15 November 2000, and initial reports from the test pilot and instrumented data indicate that the AN/APG-77 radar began tracking multiple targets almost immediately after the aircraft left the runway.

Full radar functionality required the use of Block 3.0 avionics software, which flew for the first time on 5 January 2001 during the first flight of aircraft 4005. The Block 3.0 software provided functions such as radar processing and sensor fusion, electronic warfare and countermeasures, communication, navigation and identification, and pilot/vehicle interface. "Flying Raptor 4005 with the Block 3.0 (software) represented the program's current most technically demanding challenge," said F-22 System programme director Brig. Gen. Jay Jabour,

Right: **From this angle, features such as the single-piece transparency to the cockpit, including the sawtooth leading edge, the chined nose and trapezpoidal intakes raked laterally and vertically, are clearly seen.**

"This successful flight, in addition to our other recent achievements, demonstrates the program is ready for low-rate production."

Aircraft 4004 through 4009 will fulfil a number of functions – testing of the Communications, Navigation, and Identification (CNI) system, electronic warfare, radar integration with missiles and the M61A2 cannon, JDAM releases, and low-observables testing. The entire flight-test programme is expected to last for 4,337 flying hours and 2,409 sorties. Less than half will be used for airframe and systems testing; the greater part is for mission avionics testing.

Below: **The F-117A is a subsonic attack aircraft, but the F-22 will combine stealth with supersonic performance and high agility.**

Bottom: **From some angles, the Lockheed Martin F-22 has a passing resemblance to the F-15 Eagle which it is due to replace.**

NAVAL STEALTH

The next US "stealthy" aircraft programme – the US Navy's A-12 Advanced Tactical Aircraft (ATA) – was to have a less happy history. First reported in 1985, this was to have been a subsonic all-weather aircraft able to carry out all-weather or night deep interdiction missions.

Development of the new aircraft was ordered in 1983, with the intention that Initial Operational Capability (IOC) would be achieved no later than 1994. Only two industrial teams responded to the Navy's Request For Proposals – General Dynamics teamed with McDonnell Douglas, and Northrop teamed with Grumman and LTV. With the collapse of the T-46 programme, Fairchild was out of the military aircraft business, while Boeing, Lockheed and Rockwell seem to have opted not to bid.

When drawing up its fighter proposals under the ATF programme, GD had studied several designs, one of which was a flying wing configuration nicknamed "Sneaky Pete". Although rejected by the USAF, the design was to form the basis of GD's ATA submission.

In November 1984, both teams were awarded concept-formulation contracts, which were followed in June 1986 by Demonstration Validation (dem/val) contracts. The two teams are reported to have favoured competitive prototyping, but this proved unaffordable.

Proposals for the full-scale engineering development and manufacture of the first eight aircraft were requested in 1987. By late that year it had become obvious that the USN could not support both the A-12 (at that time still known simply as the ATA) and the new F404-engined Grumman A-6F Intruder. Work on the A-6F was stopped. This decision has probably increased the urgency of the A-12 programme. The basic Intruder has been in service since the 1960s, and the planned fielding of the A-6F in 1989 would have modernised the Navy's strike power pending the later arrival of the A-12.

Grumman might have hoped to recoup its losses on the A-6F (unofficially estimated as at least $150 million) by winning a share of the ATA work. This was not to happen. In a surprise move in late December, the Northrop/Grumman/LTV team (which was widely tipped to win the ATA competition) declined to submit "best and final" bids for the task of developing the new aircraft.

On 24 December 1987, a mere

four days after Northrop's virtual withdrawal from the competition, the Navy pronounced the General Dynamics/McDonnell Douglas team winners of the contract to develop the new aircraft. Full-Scale Development began in January 1988 under a contract which covered eight flight-test aircraft and five ground test airframes. The first flight was expected in June 1990.

The A-12 Avenger II was due to replace the US Navy's A-6E fleet in the mid to late 1990s, and a total buy of around 450 seemed likely. The USMC hoped to obtain 60 A-12 aircraft as replacements for the A-6E. Under an MoU signed in April 1986 between the USAF and USN, the Air Force would consider the A-12 as a potential replacement for the F-111 and, in the longer term, for the F-15E. Initial A-12 deliveries would be to the USN, with the USAF getting its first A-12s around 1998. The UK was also seen as a possible purchaser, with the A-12 a potential replacement for the Panavia Tornado.

Like earlier USN types adopted by the USAF, the A-12 would be modified by the USAF to match Air Force requirements, and make it better suited to land-based operations. By 1988, discussions between the two services had not thrown up any problems in this area.

The aircraft that took shape was a delta flying wing with a span of 70ft 3in (21.41m) – 36ft 3.25in (11.06m) with the wing folded – and a length of 37ft 3in (11.35m). Empty weight was 39,000lb (17,700kg), rising to

80,000lb (36,300kg) gross. Powered by two General Electric F412-400 non-afterburning turbofan engines, each developing approximately 13,000lb (5,900kg) of thrust, it was expected to achieve a speed of 580mph (930kmh) at sea level, and a combat radius of 920 miles (1,470km). The ordnance would be carried in internal weapon bays to minimise drag and RCS.

The GE F412 turbofan was derived from the F404-GE-400 used in the F/A-18 Hornet. It had a lower pressure ratio than the fighter engine, plus an improved two-stage low-pressure turbine based on that of the GE F110 engine of the F-15 and F-16, and a redesigned high-pressure turbine. Avionics would include a Westinghouse AN/APQ-183 multimode radar, Martin Marietta navigational FLIR, General Electric Infrared Search and Track System (IRST), and a Honeywell digital flight-control system.

In December 1989, a Major Aircraft Review (MAR) of four US combat aircraft programmes slowed the production rate, cut the proposed aircraft for the USMC, and slipped the planned USAF purchase by more than five years. It was still anticipated that the aircraft would fly by early 1991 and that full-scale development program would be completed within planned budget.

Unfortunately, the contractors were faced with structural and cost overrun problems and, despite the Navy asserting that it was satisfied with the aircraft at the Critical Design Review, the programme was cancelled on 7 January 1991.

Above: **When the first edition of *Stealth Warplanes* was written, the shape of the planned A-12 Advanced Tactical Aircraft (ATA) was still classified. Our artist's impression of the aircraft approaching a tanker drogue (reproduced here) probably caused amusement among members of the General Dynamics/McDonnell Douglas team who were building the real thing, but was intended to show the reader some of the technologies applicable to a stealthy strike aircraft.**

Right: **In reality, the A-12 was a pure delta, a planform which would have focussed any radar energy reflected from the aircraft into a small number of harmless directions. Unexpected growth in weight and cost led to cancellation, leaving the US Navy without a dedicated strike aircraft.**

In a further attempt to develop a new attack aircraft, in 1991 the USN started the AX programme, which called for a strike aircraft to meet a less ambitious specification which required lower range/payload performance and less stealth. Described by one observer as "A-12 lite", the programme – later redesignated AFX – would have entered service first with the Navy as a replacement for ageing carrier-based A-6Es, and later with the US Air Force as a replacement for F-111, F-117, and F-15E. While still in its concept-design stage, it was cancelled in September 1993. Since then, the USN has planned to rely on the

F/A-18E/F Super Hornet for its fighter and strike capabilities.

Low-observable technology is also being built into conventional aircraft. The RCS of the F/A-18C/D was lower than that of the original F/A-18A/B model, while an improvement of approximately the same order of magnitude will be introduced by the F/A-18E/F.

In the summer of 1995 the US Joint Technical Co-ordinating Group on Aircraft Survivability (JTCG/AS) reported in its Aircraft Survivability Newsletter that this built-in stealth plus the aircraft's advanced EW suite "make the E/F a formidable combatant that is extremely difficult for enemy systems to acquire and track."

TACIT BLUE

During the early and mid-1990s, there were persistent rumours of a "black" stealth aircraft with a large fuselage whose bulky shape earned it the nickname of "Shamu" among the "stealth-watching" community. (The real-life Shamu was a killer whale exhibited at a US theme park, and the very idea of a whale-shaped stealth aircraft seemed bizarre.) Some artists' impressions showed an aircraft which looked a bit like a scaled-down version of the Boeing Stratocruiser propeller-driven airliner of the 1950s.

On 30 April 1996, the USAF finally lifted a cloak of secrecy from Tacit Blue, a technology demonstrator which was test-flown between 1982 and 1985. Here at last was the aircraft that had triggered the "Shamu" reports. Developed and built by Northrop under a $165 million "black" programme which started in 1978, the single-seat Tacit Blue was developed as a potential platform for radar sensors developed under the USAF's Pave Mover and Army SOTAS ground-surveillance programmes. It may have had the secondary role of demonstrating that a stealth aircraft could be built using curved surfaces rather than faceting.

With a length of 55ft 10in (17.02m), a height of 10ft 7in (3m), and a wingspan of 48ft 2in

(14.68m), Tacit Blue weighed 30,000lb (13,600kg). It had an unswept wing, a V-tail, and a single flush inlet on the top of the fuselage to provide air to its two Garrett ATF3-6 high-bypass turbofan engines. Its novel shape required the use of a quadruplex digital fly-by-wire flight control system to stabilise the aircraft about the longitudinal and directional axes. Robert E. Wulf, the former Flight Sciences manager on stealth projects at Northrop, has described how "the only requirement was to develop the best stealth performance... It was the most unstable aircraft flown in both pitch and yaw."

Tacit Blue made its first flight on 5 February 1982, and completed 135 flights over a three year period. It often flew three to four flights a week, and on several occasions flew more than once a day. It was designed to fly at a speed of 250kt, and at an operating altitude of 25-30,000ft (7,620-9,145m). By the time it flew, the USAF had combined the SOTAS and Pave Mover projects into a single programme which eventually became Joint STARS, and in May 1984 the DoD decided that the resulting aircraft would use the Boeing 707 airframe. Tacit Blue made its last flight on 14 February 1985, and was placed in storage. After being unveiled, it was renovated and placed on display at the US Air Force Museum at Wright Patterson AFB.

JSF PROGRAMME

The next stealth fighter to begin development was not launched as a "black" programme. From the start, the STOVL Strike Fighter project was run as a normal Advanced Research Projects Agency (ARPA) programme. The original goal

was to develop a replacement for the F/A-18 Hornet and AV-8B Harrier II, but this original US Navy/US Marine Corps project was later expanded to cover the

Above: **Some stealth technology has been incorporated into the Boeing (formerly McDonnell Douglas) F/A-18E/F Super Hornet.**

US Air Force requirement for a new fighter to replace the F-16. The USAF had no need for vertical take-off, so the CALF (Common Affordable Lightweight Fighter) scheme envisaged that, on USAF examples, the vertical lift system would not be fitted, and the free space would be used to carry additional fuel to produce

longer-ranged land-based fighter. The CALF project was merged with Joint Advanced Strike Technology (JAST) programme, and in 1995 was renamed the Joint Strike Fighter (JSF).

Three teams competed for the task of developing the new aircraft. These were headed by Boeing, Lockheed Martin, and McDonnell Douglas. In

November 1996 Boeing and Lockheed Martin were selected to build concept-demonstration models of their respective aircraft. These were given the designation X-32 and X-35, respectively. Following comparative evaluation of the rival designs, a winner will be selected in late 2001. The chosen design will enter engineering

Above: It may look ugly, but Boeing's X-32 candidate for the US Joint Strike Fighter (JSF) requirement is intended to combine stealth and STOVL.

Below: The X-32 made its initial flights in conventional takeoff and landing form, proving the basic design before STOVL was attempted.

and manufacturing development (EMD), and is expected to enter service with the USAF, US Navy/Marine Corps and Britain's Royal Navy. The final JSF will not be as stealthy as the F-22 Raptor, but great emphasis is being placed on the need for its low-observable qualities to be easily maintainable.

FURTHER STEALTH

Although programmes such as the F-22 and the Joint Strike Fighter are now being conducted in the public domain, other highly classified "black" programmes are under way. Rumours abound of another US stealth aircraft about to be revealed.

The best evidence for the existence of new "black" programmes is the continued expansion of the Area 51 classified test facility at Groom Lake, a dry lake bed in central Nevada, about 75 miles (120km) north-northwest of Las Vegas. Facilities there have been used to support development of the Lockheed A-12, Have Blue tests, operations with MiGs and other potential-adversary aircraft, tests of the Tacit Blue stealth technology demonstrator, and undoubtedly other stealth programmes.

At a time when it apparently has no purpose, Groom Lake has never been busier, and never

been in such apparent need of high security. Unless some massive waste of the US taxpayers' money is taking place, one or more secret aircraft are in flight test.

PROJECT AURORA

The best candidate for keeping Groom Lake busy is the mysterious Aurora project. This first came to light in February 1985 when a Pentagon budget document accidentally disclosed that $2.3 billion, had been earmarked for a USAF project code-named Aurora. Reporting the incident, *The Washington Post* quoted unidentified Pentagon sources as saying Aurora might have something to do with the new stealth bomber or at least with stealth technology. Air Force officials declined to discuss Aurora, beyond confirming the accuracy of the numbers listed in the budget documents. "That is a classified program and we can't talk about it," said Maj. Richard Ziegler, an Air Force spokesman.

For almost three years, no more was known about this "black" programme, but in January 1988 the *New York Times* reported that the USAF was developing a replacement for the ageing SR-71 Blackbird. This was described as a long-range reconnaissance jet which used "special equipment" to

avoid radar detection. The performance claimed was a major step over the SR-71 – a cruising speed of more than 3,800mph (6,080kmh), plus a ceiling of more than 100,000ft (33,000m). This Mach 5 stealth design is widely reported to be the mysterious "Aurora".

The former Soviet Union seems to have had early knowledge of the Aurora programme. In 1984 it started development of the MiG-31M and the Vympel R-37 (AA-X-13) missile, systems designed to engage targets cruising at speeds of up to Mach 6 and altitudes of up to 130,000ft (40,000m).

Further evidence for the existence of Aurora emerged in October 1990 when *Aviation Week & Space Technology* reported sightings of what seemed to be a high-speed, high-altitude aircraft. Seen at night, it appeared as a single, bright light, sometimes pulsating.

"SKYQUAKE"

Since 1990, there have also been persistent reports of unusual aircraft noises. One of the first

was published by *Aviation Week & Space Technology* in 1990, and described how an aircraft taking off late at night from Edwards Air Force Base had made a very loud noise, which some witnesses said was a pulsing sound with a period of about one second. Since 1991, many US communities have reported sounds which appear to be supersonic booms, but of a magnitude which causes them to be confused with earthquakes. Many of these "skyquake" reports come from coastal areas. Booms heard between June 1991 and June 1992 were powerful enough to register on seismographs operated by the US Geological Service, and analysis of the times of arrival of the sound at various points showed that the culprit seemed to be aircraft smaller than the Space Shuttle, flying at speeds between Mach 3 and 4 and at altitudes of 26,000-32,000ft (8-10,00m). The estimated flight path headed

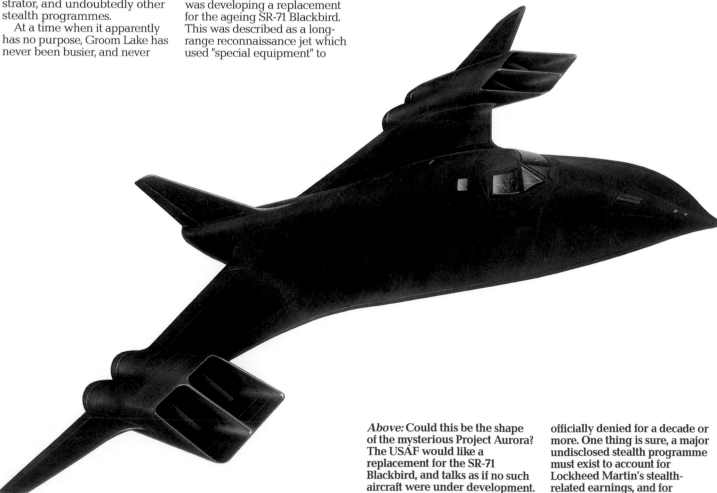

Above: Could this be the shape of the mysterious Project Aurora? The USAF would like a replacement for the SR-71 Blackbird, and talks as if no such aircraft were under development. But, as the F-117A programme has shown, the very existence of a black programme can be

officially denied for a decade or more. One thing is sure, a major undisclosed stealth programme must exist to account for Lockheed Martin's stealth-related earnings, and for unexplained "Other Production Charges" in the US defence budget.

northeast over Los Angeles and the Mojave Desert, and could have taken the aircraft to Nellis Air Force Base in Nevada or to Groom Lake.

Aviation author Bill Sweetman has nicknamed these aircraft the "phantom boomers". Writing in *Jane's International Defense Review* in January 2000, he noted that, "The phantom boomers appear to avoid densely populated areas, and the stories usually go no further than the local paper. Only a few local papers have a searchable website, so it is highly probable that only a minority of boom events are reported outside the affected area."

Frequent reports of slow-frequency (about 1Hz, and sometimes 50-60Hz) pulsing sounds, sometimes linked to the appearance of thick, segmented smoke trails or contrails, have led to suggestions that the unknown aircraft may use a pulse detonation engine. These unusual contrails – often described as "donuts-on-a-rope contrails", have been seen not only in the USA, but also in Europe, which suggests that the aircraft which is producing them is being flown on overseas sorties.

However, the evidence for a pulse-detonation powerplant has been questioned by the Federation of American Scientists, whose analysis has

suggested that "engines operating at the thrust levels associated with military aircraft would operate at between 100 and 200 Hertz (pulses per second)...While doppler shifting may reconcile this value with the reported 50-60 Hertz pulsation, it is more difficult to reconcile this with the reports of a 1 Hertz pulsation."

The FAS also notes that the apparent 100m spacing of the "donut-on-a-rope" is difficult to reconcile with a 100-200kHz pulse rate. "The association of these contrails with a pulse detonation engine would seem to be predicated on the observation that each "donut" is a product of a single pulse detonation... Assuming a detonation pulse rate of 100 Hertz, this would imply a velocity of 10 kilometers per second, or 36,000 kilometers per hour (roughly Mach 36), one-and-one-half times orbital velocity." A detonation pulse rate of 1Hz would imply a velocity of only 360kmh, which would be far too low.

MACH 8 AND ABOVE

Then there is the strange saga of the US X-30 National Aerospace Plane (NASP) programme to develop a single-stage-to-orbit launch vehicle. The project was launched in December 1985, and contracts were awarded to

Boeing, Lockheed, McDonnell Douglas, General Dynamics, and Rockwell International, but in late 1987 Lockheed and Boeing – the two contractors with the greatest experience with high-speed aircraft development – were dropped from the programme.

Following a gradual process of source selection, General Dynamics, McDonnell Douglas and Rockwell International teamed to offer a single design, a slender delta-winged lifting body with two vertical stabilisers, while Pratt & Whitney teamed with Rocketdyne on the powerplant. This was to consist of several hydrogen-powered scramjet (supersonic combustion ramjet) engines, with a single rocket engine being used for the final approach to orbit. The air-breathing units were to operate as ramjets at speeds for between Mach 2 and 6, then as scramjets from Mach 6 up to orbital velocity. (Scramjets are similar in concept to ramjets, but burn the fuel in a supersonic flow rather than subsonic as in ramjets and turbojets or turbofans, with the fuel being injected and burned near the front on the engine.)

Although the US DoD was funding 80 per cent of the work on NASP, when George Bush became US president in 1989, his newly appointed US Secretary of Defense, Dick Cheney,

cancelled the DoD's involvement in the programme, saying that there was no USAF mission for the vehicle. The entire project was wound up in 1993, having cost several billion dollars.

Given that the US claimed to have virtually no experience of air-breathing flight at speeds of beyond the Mach 3+ top speed of the SR-71, the idea of creating an aircraft able to fly at speeds of up to 18,000mph (29,000kmh) seemed technologically audacious to the point of foolhardiness – the equivalent of trying to jump from the performance of the 1918 biplane to the Mach 2 interceptor in a single design.

Much of the research conducted under the NASP programme was focused on the Mach 8+ regime, even though there seemed to be an almost equal lack of information on flight at speeds from Mach 4 to Mach 8. Curiously, although NASP was not a "black" programme, information on the low-speed portion of the propulsion system was classified. A similar pattern can be seen in more recent US high-speed flight programmes such as the USAF's HyTech project and NASA's Hyper-X. The focus is on scramjet research and speeds well above Mach 6. Four flights of the scramjet-powered Hyper-X UAV are planned –

one at Mach 5, one at Mach 7 and two at Mach 10.

It is hard to avoid the conclusion that NASP was an attempt to research flight at speeds of Mach 6 and higher without the cumbersome procedures associated with "black" programmes, and that its planners regarded flight at speeds of Mach 4 - 6 as a problem which had essentially been solved. This mysterious Mach 4 - 6 experience and the sudden removal of Lockheed and Boeing (perhaps to allow them to concentrate their expertise on a classified aircraft in this speed range) fits neatly with the dates of the first Aurora reports.

The idea that Lockheed was building a new spyplane was boosted by the obvious fact that while Lockheed Burbank had large numbers of employees, it had no apparent end product. In April 1988, High Technology Business reported that, "Aeronautical Systems Group, based in Burbank, Calif., will receive more than $1.1 billion in 1988 government funding that cannot be attributed to any known program... Also, there are more cars in the division's parking lot than can be accounted for by employees of known programs, indicating the possible existence of a new and secret project."

As experience with the B-2 had shown, the Other Production Charges line item in the USAF section of the US defence budget can be used to fund a "black" programme. In 1989, the B-2 funding emerged under its own category; the Other Production Charges fell from its 1998 peak of $2,977 million to a total of $1,075 million, and stabilised at between $460 million and $686 million in the following four years. At this reduced level, it may still have covered "black" activities.

In its analysis of these figures, the Federation of American Scientists concluded that, "The recent funding level of the Other Production Charges line item is strongly suggestive of a continuing program to procure additional stealth aircraft This connection is further strengthened by the similarity in magnitude between the funding level of Other Production Charges, and the cash flow stream and employment at Lockheed Aeronautical Systems Group."

Interviewed by *Defense News* in 1990, Ben Rich offered his explanation of what was keeping the Shunk Works busy – and that explanation was not Aurora. "I have heard and read about Aurora, and I do not know what Aurora is. And it is not

what we are doing in the Skunk Works. There are a whole bunch of programs out there, lots of them are sensor programs. And that is where we are applying our expertise."

Rich was dismissive of reports of a new Aurora spyplane. In his 1994 memoirs, he said that Aurora had been a codename for funding of the late 1970s competition between Lockheed and Northrop to win the development contract for what would become the B-2. Unfortunately for this theory, the Aurora which sparked rumours of hypersonic jets did not emerge until the mid-1980s. "Although I expect few in the media to believe me, there is no code name for the hypersonic plane," he stated, "because it simply does not exist."

It may seem like an authoritative denial, but must be considered in the light of the policy that, when questioned by an outsider, an individual cleared for access to a "black" programme is required to deny all knowledge of the programme. In the "wilderness of mirrors" created by "black" programmes, a denial may or may not be true. There is no way

of telling.

A footnote in the US Defense Airborne Reconnaissance Office (DARO) 1997 report on unmanned aerial vehicle (UAV) development referred to "the U-2 and the Air Force Special Platform". According to *Jane's International Defense Review,* DARO director, Maj. Gen. Kenneth Israel, acknowledged that this reference points to "a covert reconnaissance aircraft ... in the classified world". This led the magazine to conclude the existence of a "secret reconnaissance aircraft, probably a low-observable counterpart to the Lockheed Martin U-2".

In September 1998, Lt. Gen. George Muellner, the principal deputy, Office of the Assistant Secretary of the Air Force for Acquisition, told *Jane's Defence Weekly* that the USAF had no operational "black-world" aircraft in service, but did say that, "There may be other test programmes going on right now in demonstration and things of that nature. They are limited in number and they are not producing operational platforms. They are just designed to mature the technology."

In its article based on the

Muellner interview, *Jane's Defence Weekly* stated that it had been told by a senior source in an internationally recognised aerospace company that it has supplied major subsystems for two types of "high-flying covert US military aircraft, both of them manned", and that one of these aircraft closely matched popular descriptions of the Aurora. The magazine concluded: "If the individual's testimony is accurate, the timing would suggest that 'Aurora' is not yet in operation...but more likely to be in advanced development, possibly progressing as far as flight-test. It could also follow that sightings across the US southwest of a high-flying, very fast aircraft in the late 1980s and early 1990s were of a hypersonic demonstrator – or conceivably several demonstrators – designed to 'mature technology', as alluded to by Gen Muellner."

STEALTH TRANSPORT

Aurora is not the only pro-gramme whose existence has been deduced by a careful study of unclassified DoD documents. In 1988 the US DoD announced details of a project named

"Advanced Transport Technology Mission Analysis". Bidders were being sought for what was described as the "second iteration of pre-concept exploration studies for the next generation theater airlifter". Translated from the official "Pentagonese", this meant "a second round for studies for a new tactical military transport aircraft".

But what the DoD had in mind was not going to be an ordinary C-130-style transport aircraft. "Emphasis will be on in-depth examinations of V vs STOL, low vs conventional observables, and the employment of an advanced airlifter in-theater with the C-17, the C-130, and Army helicopters."

The appropriate part of this bid request was an eye-opener! "The bidder must be capable of conducting programs at classification levels up through top secret, special access required. This requires the bidder to have certified or certifiable secure facilities, administrative support capabilities and procedures, and personnel with access to handle, for example, low observable and other sensitive

technology and operational issues."

In plain words, any company bidding for a contract to study the new transport would have to be security cleared to handle a "black" programme.

SENIOR CITIZEN

The proposed study may be linked to a "black" project codenamed Senior Citizen (Program Element 0401316F). This is thought to be a low-observable, short take-off and landing (STOL) transport for special operations. Paul McGinnis, an individual who has been researching classified DoD programmes notes that several advanced STOL aircraft have been funded. He believes that Senior Citizen is a low-observable, V/STOL turbofan-powered troop transport, and that it is probably being manufactured by Boeing.

The USAF has studied the MC-X, a new low-observable short-takeoff and vertical-landing (STOVL) transport for special operation forces (SOF). In theory this could replace the MC-130s currently used for this role, but the anticipated quantity

of around 24 is unlikely to be sufficient to allow programme start-up.

OTHER TYPES

Several other reports of "black" aircraft programmes have been published. However, a degree of caution is required when considering these reports.

In April 2000, *Aviation Week and Space Technology* reported that unidentified US Air Force officials had told the magazine that an experimental stealth aircraft designated YF-113G had been flown more than 20 years earlier at the restricted Nevada test ranges. The magazine quoted one source as saying that the YF-113G was "an airframe that came before Have Blue and the F-117 We used it in the initial work to examine the stealth edges problem." Trials had ended by the early 1980s. In a correction published a week later, the magazine explained that the designation YF-113G applied to the MiG-23, which had been flown clandestinely in the late 1970s by two special projects units. Its source had mistakenly identified the type as a US stealth demonstrator.

Above: **Powered by a scramjet powerplant, the Hyper-X will explore speeds of more than Mach 6. Aurora may have already conquered Mach 4-5.**

The most likely of these other rumoured aircraft is a subsonic stealthy reconnaissance aircraft, which eyewitnesses suggest is around 40ft (12m) long and 60-65ft (18-20m) in wingspan. Reported as operating at low and high altitudes, and being seen flying with F-117 stealth fighters, T-38 trainers, and KC-135 tankers, its task is said to be that of collecting and transmitting near-real-time digital photo information directly to F-117As. Its range has been estimated at more than 3,125 miles (5,000km).

The designations "TR-3A" and "Black Manta" are often reported for this aircraft, but the former should be treated with caution. "TR-3A" could be a mis-hearing of "Tier 3A", the designation of a giant flying-wing reconnaissance UAV which was cancelled in the mid-1990s.

Another type of aircraft mentioned in sighting reports is described as having a planform similar to that of the XB-70

Above: The B-2 (seen here on its sixth test mission) relies on airborne refuelling to give it global range.

bomber. In 1992, *Aviation Week & Space Technology* published details of five sightings – two were near Edwards Air Force Base, and one occurred near a Lockheed-operated radar cross section test range in the Mojave Desert. Reports describe the aircraft as light-coloured with dark leading and trailing edges. It is said to have a sharp nose, a narrow fuselage with a clear-canopied cockpit, and a delta wing with upward-canted vertical fins at each outboard tip. Length is believed to be around 200ft (60m), wingspan around 150ft (45m). Some observers describe the aircraft has having a prominent canard, but others do not, causing speculation that this may be used only for take-off, landing and slow-speed flight, and may pivot or sweep for internal stowage during high-speed flight. Some observers also believe that this aircraft is a "mother ship" equipped to launch a smaller hypersonic aircraft.

One of the most reliable sightings of an unidentified aircraft was made in August

1989 by Chris Gibson, a drilling technologist for a major oil field service company. A member of Britain's Royal Observer Corps for 13 years, and a member of the ROC aircraft-recognition team for 12 years, he had produced an aircraft recognition manual for the Corps. While working on the jack-up rig "Galveston Key" in the Indefatigable oil field in the North Sea in August 1989, he observed a four-aircraft formation which consisted of a KC-135 Stratotanker, two F-111 fighter-bombers, and a triangular-shaped aircraft which he could not identify. A trained aircraft observer, he considered that it might be a third F-111 flying with its wings fully swept back, but decided that the planform of the aircraft was too long. Also he could not see any gaps between the wing and tailplane.

A triangular-shaped aircraft was reported at Beale Air Force Base in late February 1992. In this case the aircraft was flying at night, and to judge by the spacing of lights on the airframe may have been about one and a half times the length of the F-117, and about twice the wingspan.

The possible existence of a programme to develop a new stealth fighter to replace both the F-117 and the F-15E was

suggested in a chart which formed part of a paper delivered at a 1997 Air Power Conference in London, by Col. Richard Davis, commander of the USAF's Wright, Laboratory, Wright-Patterson AFB, Ohio. Intended to show the force structure of Air Combat Command over the next 25 years, this chart suggested that the new aircraft could enter service in small numbers around 2005, then in larger numbers after around 2015 when retirement of the F-15E is due to begin. In response to inquiries by *Jane's Defence Weekly*, Wright-Patterson officials said that the chart was intended to show possible future USAF systems.

NEW BOMBER

The USAF does not plan to develop a new bomber in the near future; a date of 2037 has been mentioned as the likely operational date for a follow-on to today's bomber fleet. The concept has been dubbed 'B-X', and Boeing, Lockheed, and Northrop Grumman are reported to be working on competing proposals, but have taken note of suggestions by the US Congress that a new bomber be fielded in 2015.

Northrop has the advantage in

that its B-2A is currently in service. If a 2015 IOC is needed, it proposes a new B-2 variant designed to take advantage of advanced manufacturing techniques and more maintainable stealth coatings. Further cost savings could result from simplifying the structure to create an aircraft which would operate only at medium and high altitudes. More advanced proposals for service on the later timescale are a subsonic flying wing, a supersonic design able to "supercruise" in dry thrust, and a hypersonic wave-rider concept.

According to an April 2000 report in *Aviation Week & Space Technology*, Boeing is following four lines of investigation. The simplest would be to base the new bomber on a commercial airframe. A 767 derivative with a V-tail, and powered by rear-mounted engines fed by a dorsal inlet system. Treated with RAM, this would achieve stealth performance. A second design would be based on a blended-wing body configuration which the company hopes to launch as a commercial transport by 2015. The addition of weapons bays in the aircraft's centre section and the use of low-observable materials would create a bomber variant.

If the USAF rejects the idea of

Left: **The OH-58D Kiowa Warrior scout helicopter with its all-weather, day/night, electro-optical mast-mounted sight (MMS) with visible and infra-red capability.**

obtain a signature which could identify what type of helicopter it is.

"Passive" measures able to reduce the acoustic signature of a helicopter include the use of a larger number of blades on the main rotor. This will reduce the characteristic low-frequency sound output, but the reduction in blade chord needed to maintain the same overall blade area will make the individual blades more vulnerable to hostile fire. For helicopters intended for paramilitary or police work, this may not be important, so it is possible that

some of the "silent" helicopter work in the USA. may be for the Federal Bureau of Investigation (FBI).

The tail rotor adds its own component to the sound signature. Possible noise-reduction measures include the use of offset four-blade tail-rotors rather than the traditional cruciform pattern, shrouded anti-torque rotors such as the "fenestron" on the Eurocopter Gazelle, or even the McDonnell Douglas No Tail Rotor (NOTAR) system.

Active measures could permit even greater degrees of sound suppression. An individual blade control technology (IBC) scheme devised by Eurocopter Deutschland in association with a number of other German aerospace organisations uses a

a commercial-derivative, Boeing could offer a flying-wing design powered by two engines and based on JSF manufacturing technology, or a bomber based on the configuration used by the X-45A unmanned air vehicle.

No information is available about the Lockheed proposals, but the company's experience with the SR-71 (and perhaps with Aurora) could favour a hypersonic design. Retired USAF General Chuck Horner, the air commander during the 1991 Gulf War, has predicted that work on a stealthy hypersonic aircraft could begin in the USA. within a decade. An aircraft of this type could cruise at altitudes as high as 100,000ft (30,000m).

STEALTH HELOS

Given the presence of a whirling rotor, the idea of a stealth helicopter might seem bizarre, but a degree of stealth technology has already been applied to several types of helicopter. The use of measures to reduce the IR signature of helicopters has been common since the first use of SA-7 "Grail" IR-homing man-portable SAMs during the Vietnam War, but the creation of a stealthy helicopter requires that similar attention be paid to the aircraft's radar and acoustic signatures. The main rotor generates enough radar return not only to allow the aircraft to be detected, but will also allow a Doppler radar to

Above right: **On the McDonnell Douglas/Bell LHX design, the armament is stowed out of sight of enemy radar in a combined wing/sponson.**

Right: **This Bell Helicopter artwork of a possible LHX helicopter configuration features internally-stowed missile armament.**

Above: **The futuristic, composite-constructed LO Comanche features internal weapons bays, integrated IR suppression, and a unique canted fantail anti-torque system and "T" tail.**

Above right: **The world's first truly low observable (LO) comabt scout, the Boeing Sikorsky RAH-66 Comanche was the winner of the US Army LHX competition to replace the Cobra and OH-58D.**

moving flap to introduce a very high frequency flutter in the blade at the precise moment that the advancing side would otherwise produce a loud shockwave. At present, this flap is electro-hydraulically actuated, but a piezoelectric system due to be tested around 2001 is expected to be even more effective.

In 1981 the US Army started work on a Light Helicopter Experimental (LHX) programme in which it envisaged buying 5,000 new helicopters to replace the UH-1, AH-1, OH-58 and OH-6. By the time a formal request for proposals was issued on 21 June 1988, the requirement had been scaled back to only 2,096 scout/attack helicopters. Two 23-month demonstration/validation contracts were issued to the Boeing Sikorsky First Team and Bell/McDonnell Douglas Super Team.

Artists' impressions of the rival LHX designs revealed at the 1988 Farnborough air show showed that both incorporated some signature reduction technology.

The Army specification insisted that the undercarriage be retractable, and that weapons be carried internally. The Boeing/Sikorsky design mounted ordnance on upward-swinging gull-wing doors in the fuselage sides, while the McDonnell Douglas/Bell team favoured carriage within a combined wing/sponson. The two designs also took different approaches to the tail area. Boeing/Sikorsky offer a "V" tail and a Gazelle-style fenestron rotor, while McDonnell Douglas/Bell use a NOTAR (No TAil Rotor) ducted exhaust system.

The Boeing Sikorsky design

was selected on 5 April 1991, and the team was given a contract to build four YRAH-66 demonstration/validation prototypes, plus a static test article (STA) and propulsion system testbed (PSTB). The scale of the programme continued to shrink through the 1990s. The number of prototypes was cut from four to two, and in 1999 the production quantity was reduced to only 1,096. The schedule also suffered, as the programme was delayed. A late-1990s restructuring revised and accelerated the programme, calling for the delivery of 13 preproduction aircraft from 2004. The aircraft that finally enters service will be the first combat helicopter to be given "stealth" features while still on the drawing board.

Stealth technology for helicopters is thought to have been tested in a number of classified technology demonstration programmes at Groom Lake and other locations, and there are persistent reports that the US military has developed a silent helicopter.

"PRIME CHANCE"

When Iranian surface craft began attacking commercial shipping in the Persian Gulf during the late 1980s, Bell Helicopter secretly modified a number of OH-58D Kiowa scout helicopters for armed missions. As part of an operation codenamed "Prime Chance", the aircraft were adapted to fire Hellfire air-to-surface missiles,

Right: **Taken by a US spy satellite, this photograph was "leaked in 1983 to give the world its first look at the Blackjack bomber (bottom).**

Hydra 70 unguided rockets, and Stinger air-to-air missiles. Deliveries began in December 1987, and the modified aircraft were operated by A and B Troops of 4th Squadron/17th Aviation Regiment until January 1991.

In 1999, *Jane's Defence Weekly* reported that one of the "Prime Chance" aircraft was modified locally to mount a crew seat from a Black Hawk helicopter onto the side. This crudely modified aircraft was used to attack the oil rigs used by the Iranians as bases for their fast attack-craft. Seated in the external seat, a sniper with a powerful silenced rifle could

shoot individuals on the platforms. "They never heard a thing," one source told the magazine. "It gave the Iranians a big morale problem, too, because they never knew what was hitting them."

If this report is correct, the "Prime Chance" aircraft must also have had some form of acoustic stealth measure which reduced the noise it made to the point where the aircraft could get so close to its target that a sniper on what was essentially a vibrating platform could score a useful number of hits.

Other helicopters have been retrofitted with low-observable features. By 1993 the Bell

Right: Even before the first photos of operational Blackjacks were available, US intelligence knew much about the aircraft.

OH-58Ds of 1-17th Cavalry at Fort Bragg, North Carolina, had coated rotor blades, new windscreen material and other changes intended to reduce the front-sector RCS. Bell's Stealth Kiowa Warrior $200,000 stealth kit offers a similar series of modifications, plus a reshaped nose with radar-absorbent coatings, engine and gearbox cowlings of radar-absorbent material, and radar-absorbent coatings on the windows, mast-mounted sight and landing gear. Although 18 aircraft were modified for Gulf War service, none was deployed.

The Kamov Ka-60 Kasatka variant of the Ka-62 civil helicopter is an infantry-squad transport helicopter which incorporates IR- and radar-absorbent coatings, a reduced rotor speed, and low-IR-signature exhausts. First flown on 10 December 1998, it is designed to carry up to 16 soldiers, or six stretchers and three attendants when used in the medevac role. If adopted for service, it would be fitted with a Pastel RWR and an Otklik laser warning system, while an optional transverse boom could

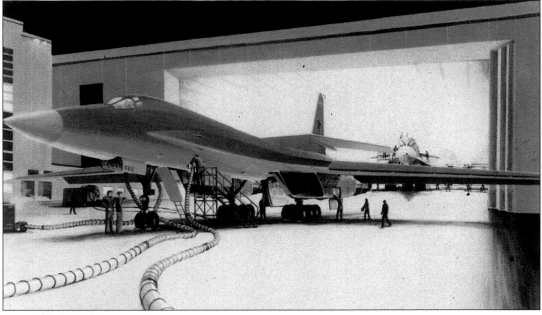

Right: Even before the first photos of operational Blackjacks were available, US intelligence knew much about the aircraft.

Above: Soviet air attache Col Vladimir Izmaylov was expelled from the USA in 1986, accused of gathering intelligence on stealth.

carry light armament such as 7.62mm or 12.7mm gun pods or B-8V-7 seven-round pods for 80mm unguided rockets. The Ka-60 has been evaluated by the Russian Army, and was displayed to potential international customers at the MAKS '99 air show in Moscow. It is reported to have attracted interest from Iran.

Little is known about a "black" helicopter programme codenamed "Grassblade". When the first edition of this book was written, Grassblade was believed to be a stealth helicopter under development for the US Army. Since then, the codename has seen virtually no further public exposure, but is still believed to be an active programme. It may be an aircraft for use by special forces, a role

which may not necessarily require low RCS.

RUSSIAN STEALTH

The greatest mystery in the world of low-observables is the status of Russian stealth technology. Having read a draft of one of the first magazine articles ever written about stealth aircraft, Nancy Biglin, then circulation manager of *Armed Forces Journal*, asked one of the magazine's editors, "Do the Russians have one of these airplanes?" Told that this was unlikely, she countered by asking, "But how would we know, if they can't be seen?" A long silence followed, as the impact of her comment sunk home.

In May 1986, *International Defense Review* quoted USAF Aeronautical Systems Division commander as saying that the US was "ten to 15 years ahead" of the Soviet Union in stealth technology, "and we may be further ahead than that". During a 1988 Aerospace Education Foundation meeting, Assistant US Air Force secretary for acquisition John J. Welch was asked if the US held a lead in stealth technology over the Soviet Union, and if so whether that lead could be maintained. He replied, "The answer has to be – yes, and hush up." His humorous response was followed by the statement that the US did have a commanding lead, and that given suitable exploitation and security "it can be an enduring one".

"When we build a technology and eventually field it, the Russians tend to do the same thing about ten years behind," said Kent Bankus, a member of the Senate Armed Services Committee. "One would hope that, given the secrecy with which we've approached this,

maybe that gap will have widened." Bankus suggested that the US had to assume "that the Russians are very actively pursuing [stealth] with all the vigor they possibly can," a view which seems to be shared by the US defence community. "Both sides are working very hard on countermeasures, reduction of radar cross section and additional stealthy components and tactics," US assistant deputy Under-Secretary of Defense James F. O'Bryon told the magazine *Aviation Week and Space Technology* in the summer of 1988.

In 1985 the US Navy predicted that Soviet aircraft and missiles incorporating stealth technology would enter service by the end of decade. The need to cope with these had been a driving force in the decision to fit the Grumman F-14D version of Tomcat with an infra-red search and track (IRST) system.

The Soviet Union must have been aware of the emergence of stealth technology by the late 1970s, by which time it was in the middle of a massive and costly programme to replace obsolescent combat aircraft with a new generation of more advanced types such as the MiG-29, Su-24, and Su-27. Like the US "teen" series of fighters, these were expected to serve well into the 1990s, so the only chance the Soviets had of exploiting the new technology would have been to embark on a project to create an equivalent to the F-117A.

Through the late 1970s and 1980s, US intelligence would have looked for signs that such a programme was under way, carefully monitoring selected areas of Soviet military research and development for indications that stealth technologies were being developed, keeping a

Above: **Mikoyan's 1.44 technology demonstrator was to languish on the ground for five years, awaiting the arrival of flight-rated engines.**

satellite watch on known Soviet aircraft plants and flight test centres, and gathering information from agents working within design laboratories and aircraft factories.

Adolf. G. Tolkachev, a Soviet national whose execution was announced by the Soviet Union in late October 1986, may have played a major role in keeping the US informed of Soviet stealth developments. Described in official announcements as "a staff worker of a Moscow research institute", he was an aviation engineer, and worked at a Moscow research institute

tasked with developing the most advanced forms of military aircraft technology. Recruited by the CIA, he was caught passing secrets "of a defense nature" to Paul M. Stambaugh, a second secretary in the US Moscow embassy.

If the Soviet Union started work on an aircraft similar to the F-117, the project must have been short-lived. No such aircraft was reported during the last decade of the Soviet Union's existence, and has not been reported since. In the early 1980s, the Russian Air Force released preliminary specifications for a next-generation proposed MFI (*mnogofunktsionalnyy frontovoy istrebitel*: multifunctional front-line fighter) and LFI (*legkiy frontovoy istrebitel*: lightweight front-line fighter). Intended to

replace the Su-27 and MiG-29, respectively, both were probably intended to make some use of stealth technology, though neither the Mikoyan 1.44 design drawn up around the MFI requirement, or the Sukhoi S-37 technology-demonstrator make extensive use of low-observable technology.

The LFI project to develop a lightweight front-line fighter able to replace the MiG-29 and act as a "low" complement to the MFI has yet to result in hardware. The MiG bureau drew up several proposals, including an F-16-style aircraft, but the requirement was suspended in 1988. In the 1990s, the designations LFS (*legkiy frontovoy samolet*: lightweight frontal aircraft), LMFI (*legkiy mnogofunktsionalnyi frontovoy*

istrebitel: lightweight multifunctional front-line fighter), and Mikoyan I-2000 have all been used to describe a concept which incorporates some low-observable features, and bears some resemblance to a scaled-down F-22. As a result of economic problems, such an aircraft is unlikely to be built in the foreseeable future. In the short term, Russia's MiG-29 follow-on will be the MiG-29SMT.

In 1995 Col. Gen. Peter S. Deinekin, who was at that time commander of the Russian Air Force, stated that, the Tupolev Tu-22 Blinder bomber and the Sukhoi Su-24 Fencer would be replaced by a new "multi-role strategic bomber". Tupolev's giant Tu-160 Blackjack has little or no stealth technology, but Russia is thought to be developing a medium-weight stealth bomber for tactical missions. The Sukhoi T-60S (sometimes called the S-60) is believed to be a variable geometry design, but a flying-wing design may also be under study.

Despite Russia's chronic shortage of defence funds, the new bomber project seems to be proceeding. In early 2000, a

Left: **Officially, the Sukhoi S-27 Berkut is a technology demonstrator, but the bureau would like to develop an operational version.**

senior Russian Air Force general confirmed that the programme was "a high priority and that research is underway".

JAPAN

Although the US is the only nation to have fielded stealth aircraft, and no other country is believed to be developing "absolute" stealth aircraft, low-observable technology is being used to some degree in a number of non-US programmes.

In its search for a suitable aircraft to replace the Mitsubishi F-1 fighter-bomber during the mid-1980s, Japan looked at several approaches. The most obvious was a new indigenously developed aircraft based on stealth technology. Some work in this area was already under way. In January 1982, the Japan Self-Defense Agency had admitted that it was carrying out research into stealth.

To draw up plans for a new stealthy fighter, an industrial team known as the FS-X (Fighter, Support, eXperimental) Joint Study Team was set up. Headed by Mitsubishi Heavy Industries, this included Kawasaki, Fuji Heavy Industries, engine maker Ishisawajima-Harima, and Mitsubishi Electric.

Working at Mitsubishi Heavy Industries' Nagoya Works under chief engineer Itsuro Masuda, a

team of 31 engineers took as their starting point a 1983 experimental conversion of a Mitsubishi T-2 trainer. The design which took shape on their drawing boards was intended to have a low-altitude combat radius of up to 450nm (833km) at Mach 0.9 while carrying a payload of four Type 80 ASM-1 anti-ship missiles.

As the new design took shape, the various companies involved began to explore some of the key technologies needed for the new aircraft. Mitsubishi joined forces with its partners to research the stealth technology needed for the FS-X. New types of RAM were developed, and tested in the anechoic chamber at Mitsubishi's Komaki South factory, while software engineers tackled the task of created computer programmes for the design of RAM and the prediction of aircraft RCS.

By 1987 the team was convinced that its FS-X would have a higher performance and lower cost than rival designs, all of which were being offered by foreign companies. Four aircraft were seen as alternatives to the indigenous design: developed versions of one of the existing Western fighters – the F-16 Fighting Falcon, F-18 Hornet, F-15 Eagle and the Panavia Tornado. Early in October 1987, Japan announced that the FS-X

would be a derivative of an existing US aircraft, the choice of the basic airframe being either the F-16 or the F-15. Defence Minister Yuko Kurihara announced that the chosen airframe would be fitted with selected items of Japanese technology such as a phased-array radar and a new fire-control system, and would also incorporate stealth technology.

By the autumn of 1987, however, discussions had focused on a design whose reported designation was SX-3 (perhaps a mis-spelling of "FX-3"). A stage beyond the "big-winged" Agile Falcon being proposed to Western Europe, SX-3 was intended to incorporate advanced technology composite materials in the forward and aft fuselage sections, and in the increased-span wings. It would also incorporate the stealth measures planned for the indigenous design.

This F-16 derivative was selected by the Japanese Self-Defense Agency, a decision which received the formal endorsement of the Japanese National Security Council in October 1987. In 1988 the two governments signed an MoU which would give Japanese industry access to many advanced US technologies. It specified that an Japanese refinements to existing

technologies must be made available to the US free of charge, while technology developed entirely by Japan had be to requested (and paid for) by the USA.

Development of the resulting aircraft was slow. The first prototype did not fly until 7 October 1995, and the first squadron to be equipped with what by now had been designated the F-2 was formed in 2000 and was expected to become operational in the following year.

The experience gained with the F-2 has given the Japanese aerospace industry the confidence to embark on an ambitious project to develop an indigenous FI-X next-generation fighter to replace the F-15J. This was expected to be around 44ft (13.4m) long and 30ft (9.1m) in wingspan, with a fuselage made from composites and incorporating radar-absorbent materials. An ambitious avionics suite was planned, including a conformal radar and an electro-optical sensor, plus digital fly-by-light and digital engine-control systems.

Below: **Outwardly, the Mitsubishi F-2 closely resembles the General Dynamics F-16 from which it was derived.**

Development of a suitable 11,240lb (5,100kg) class turbofan was started in the mid-1990s, and the first XF-7 engine was delivered for ground testing in June 1998. Construction of prototype aircraft was due to start around 2000, but the programme has been stretched in timescale. Flight tests of the XF-7 engine have been delayed until 2007, and no date has been given for prototype construction.

CHINA

China is also working on stealth technology. On 26 January 1987, Hangzhou radio reported that "practicable stealth technologies and theories" had been mastered and claimed that a "considerable quantity" of experimental data had been collected by Chinese scientists and engineers. "It will not be long before our country can make our own stealth aircraft," listeners were told.

The claim seems to have been

Above: **The dazzling flight performance of Rafale A has not blinded France to the need for RCS reduction.**

premature. No Chinese stealth fighter has appeared, but trials of low-observable technologies are known to be under way. In early 1999, trials of a Shenyang Aircraft Corporation J-8 ("Finback") with some parts of its structure covered in Xikai SF18 radar-absorbent material were reported, along with proposals to fit the same material to the Xian Aircraft Company JH-7 heavy fighter-bomber.

INDIA

India sees China as a significant potential threat, so it is hardly surprising that the use of some low-observable technologies such as radar-absorbent materials is planned for India's next-generation Medium Combat Aircraft (MCA). Intended to replace Indian Air Force Jaguars and

Mirage 2000s, the MCA is expected to be a twin-engined aircraft with a maximum take-off weight in the 40,000lb (18,000kg) class.

EUROPE

Europe has been pursuing its own stealth studies, and a significant amount of work has been done in the UK, which has been able to share stealth technology with the US. RAM-treated aircraft were tested at Farnborough in the 1950s, while a pair of Canberra light bombers belonging to 51 Sqn were treated with RAM during the late 1950s and early 1960s, and tested at Wyton, home of the Royal Air Force's small elint fleet.

In the 1990s, the UK spent around £100 million on stealth technology, building a new research and development facility, including a secure hangar, at the Warton plant of what was then BAe (now BAE Systems). In the late 1990s the company was promoting the concept of a national stealth demonstrator to be known as Experimental Aircraft Programme II. (The original Experimental Aircraft Programme had been the 1980s technology demonstrator which proved the basic concept later adopted for the Eurofighter 2000.)

Similar stealth technology demonstration efforts are probably under way at Dassault, and the UK and France have proposed the construction of a collaborative manned demonstrator. The earliest application of the results of this stealth work could be the air platform selected to meet the Royal Air Force Future Offensive Air System requirement for a system to replace the Tornado GR.4 after 2015. The latest

generation of European military aircraft – Eurofighter and Rafale – incorporate some degree of RCS reduction, but probably not enough to be militarily significant. In this respect, they are inferior to the US F-22.

Germany and Italy are known to be working on stealth technology, both individually and in collaboration. In 1986 the UK magazine *Flight International* published a drawing of the Dornier LA-2000, a proposed subsonic ground-attack aircraft. The original drawing on which the magazine's sketch was based had not been released by the company, but seems to have "leaked" from the German defence ministry. The drawing showed a small delta-winged aircraft, whose pure triangular shape was marred only by a raised section on the centreline. This incorporated a small canopy close to the apex of the delta. The aircraft's two engines were located in a propulsion bay mounted under the wing. The inlet was between a quarter and a third of the way back from the nose, and the two low-bypass-ratio turbofans – each with a thrust of 5,600lb (2,550kg) – feed a single two-dimensional vectoring nozzle at the trailing edge of the wing. Two large elevons were mounted on either side of the wing trailing edge, and would presumably share the task of controlling the aircraft. An internal weapons bay of about 200 cubic feet (6 cubic metres) capacity contains a retractable weapons platform.

This design was probably developed under the German MoD's plan to build a stealth

Below: **The curved inlets shown on the EFA mockup were a modification which reduced the aircraft's RCS.**

demonstrator. The Lampyridae (Firefly) programme was begun in 1981. Lampyridae (also known as the Medium Range Missile Fighter) was a faceted design, but used fewer facets than the F-117A. As a result, it would have been a supersonic aircraft. Although a three-quarters scale model was test-flown in a wind-tunnel, the project was cancelled in 1987, apparently due to lack of money.

In 1989 DASA and Aermacchi launched a programme to develop a light aircraft which could be used as an advanced trainer or a light combat aircraft. Aermacchi withdrew from the project in 1994, but DASA kept the programme

alive, collaborating with the South African company Denel on avionics, and Hyundai in South Korea who planned to build some non-composite elements of the structure. The design is modular, so should be easy to modify for the different roles. It incorporates a chined forward section, wing/forebody blending, and air intakes designed for minimal RCS. These measures are expected to give an RCS of around 10.76sq ft (1sq m).

Below: **The Raytheon AMRAAM medium-range missiles which arm RAF Eurofighters will eventually be replaced by ramjet-powered weapons.**

A full-scale mockup of what was now named the Mako (Shark) was displayed at the 1999 Paris Air Show, but development will begin only when DASA (now part of EADS) can find risk-sharing partners. Given a prompt go-ahead, EADS says it could fly prototypes in 2003 and deliver production aircraft towards the end of the decade.

STEALTHY RPVs

For the moment, most European stealth efforts seem to be focused in the field of unmanned air vehicles (UAVs). As already described earlier in this chapter, some the

Above: **As this British Aerospace artwork shows, the Royal Air Force's eventual Tornado replacement could be a stealthy UAV.**

pioneering US efforts in low-observables were aimed at improving the combat survivability of remotely piloted vehicles. This trend was to continue through the 1970s, 1980 and 1990s.

Soon after the combat debut of the Ryan Model 147B RPV over Vietnam in the autumn of 1964, drones were returning to base with photos of fighters flying between 5,000-10,000ft (1,500-3,000m) below them. Although SAM sites could do

nothing against these tiny targets, manned fighters were soon scoring kills. The first drone to be shot down was 147B No. B-19, which was lost over southern China on 15 November. Later reports suggest that it was attacked by 15 to 20 fighters which made a large number of passes before scoring the kill. Similar mass attack tactics were adopted by the North Vietnamese Air Force, leading to further drone losses.

The 147H model fielded in the late 1960s had a cruise altitude of 65,000-70,000ft (19,800-21,300m), and incorporated some measures intended to reduce vulnerability to interception. A RAM installation known as HIDE (High-absorbency Integrated Defense) was fitted to the inlet to reduce RCS, while the HEMP (H model Evasive Maneuver Program) system

Below: **Lockheed's YMQM-105 Aquila started life as a simple RPV which would offer many advantages over mid-1970s piston-engined designs, while having a lower RCS. As the requirement grew more ambitious, high-technology systems were added and the total cost of the system skyrocketted.**

Right: **The Northrop Grumman Pegasus UAV is intended to explore the concept of using unmanned combat air vehicles from US Navy carriers.**

used an RWR tuned to Vietnamese fighter radar frequencies to initiate programmed turns if a MiG closed in for a firing pass. A later HAT-RAC (High Altitude Threat Recognition and Countermeasures) system took the concept a stage further, responding to SAM and fighter radars by initiating flight manoeuvres.

Contrails were to remain the Firebee's weak link. The 1962 test interceptions had shown how trails could betray a drone, and work on a "no-con" system had started in that year. This involved two QC-2Cs equipped with a system which injected a chemical agent into the exhaust. It was not very successful. Some H models carried an anti-contrail system known as CRL. Developed by Cambridge Research Laboratories, it was intended to suppress the contrail at specific altitudes. A history of the drone programme describes this as "quite successful".

Successor to the 147H was the 147T. This had a more powerful

Continental J100-CA-100 engine offering 45 per cent more thrust, boosting cruise height to between 66,300 and 75,000ft (20,200-22,850m). The 147T retained the HIDE system. Other RCS-reduction measures included greater use of built-in RAM in areas such as the nose, wings, dorsal spine and tail surfaces. A wing-root fillet which blended the wing into the fuselage also helped reduce

Below: **In developing the Model 147T long-wing version of the Firebee reconnaissance drone, Teledyne engineers applied RAM to the nose, wings, dorsal spine and tail, and added a degree of wing-body blending. By 1969 it was**

RCS. Operations with the 147T started in 1969, and this basic design led to the follow-on elint model used in the early-1970s "Combat Dawn" programme, the TE and the improved TF.

The limited degree of stealth technology built into the Firebee was extended in the later Teledyne Ryan AQM-91A Model 154. Development of this large RPV was ordered in 1966, under the USAF's "Compass Arrow"

ready for service, flying into the face of Chinese and North Vietnamese air defences. Despite all the aid which the Soviet Union could give, they never fully mastered the art of downing these tricky radar targets.

Right: **The use of RAM and shaping on the Model 147T gave Teledyne the confidence to tackle the custom-designed Model 154 stealth RPV. The flat underside reduced radar reflectivity from below, while the sloped fuselage sides and tail surfaces cut RCS at higher aspect angles. The Model 154 (also known as the AQM-91A Compass Arrow) flew at high altitude3, so the dorsal engine bay screened the engine inlet and exhaust from upward-looking radars.**

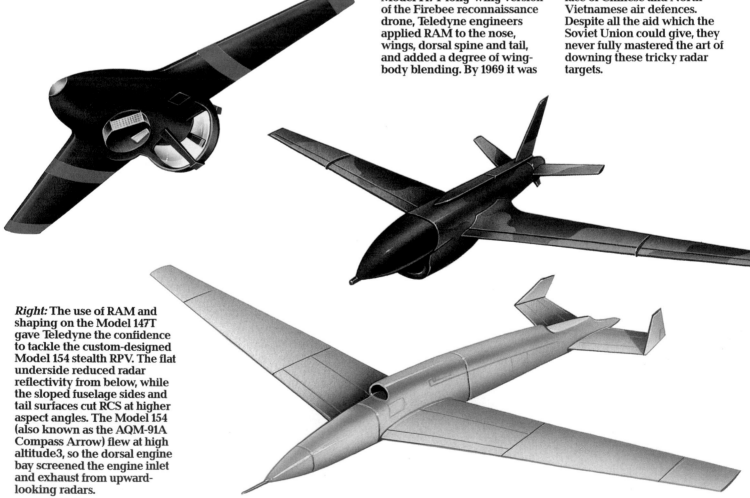

programme. In the summer of 1969, the emergency descent of one example onto a road at the Los Alamos Scientific Laboratory gave a first glimpse of the first custom-designed stealth aircraft to enter service. Almost half as long again as the Firebee, and weighing up to 5,245lb (2,379kg), the 154 had many features first proposed in the unbuilt 1960-vintage Model 136 "Red Wagon" RPV. These included a dorsal engine installation and inward canted twin fins. The 48ft (14.6m) span wing was swept, and was low-mounted on the flat-bottomed fuselage, a configuration intended to reduce RCS when seen from below.

A much lower level of technology was used in the Lockheed YMQM-105 Aquila. Intended for target acquisition, this 330lb (150kg) piston-engined flying wing first flew as a prototype air vehicle in 1975. Results seemed promising enough to allow full-scale development to be ordered in 1979. As the requirements grew more ambitious, costs soared. The programme came under repeated attack, and the Fiscal 1988 defence budget submitted to Congress in November 1987 finally killed the Aquila programme, with no funding being authorised. Aquila used much less body-wing blending than the B-2, and relied for its low RCS on a combination of small size, careful shaping, and the large-scale use of composites.

TIER II AND TIER III

Like the F-117A, the first stealth UAV may have been a Lockheed design. Designated Tier III (the alternative designation of "Q" has also been reported), this is understood to have been a 150ft (45m) span flying wing. Little is known about the UAV, which

may have been built in small numbers before the project was cancelled. The specification may have been too demanding, making the resulting design unaffordable. A unit cost of anything from $150 million to $400 million has been reported.

Two less ambitious specifications were drawn up for complementary patterns of long-endurance UAVs. To develop these Tier II Plus and Tier III Minus designs, the US DoD used the Advanced Concept Technology Demonstration (ACTD) concept. ACTDs are intended to allow a very early operational assessment of a new system concept without the need to invest the large amounts of money required by traditional development projects.

Under the first-ever ACTD, the US DoD ordered the Lockheed Martin/Boeing DarkStar (also known as Tier III Minus), a stealthy UAV designed to penetrate heavy air defences. Powered by a single 1,900lb (860kg) thrust Williams F129 turbofan engine, it was intended to operate at ranges greater than 500nm (926km), loitering for more than eight hours at altitudes greater than 45,000ft (13,700m).

The contract for a more conventional UAV to meet the Tier II Plus requirement was awarded to Teledyne/Ryan. Describing the contract award, Lieutenant Colonel Blackwelder, Lead Co-ordinator for UAV and Decoy ACTDs, stated that Teledyne-Ryan's Global Hawk was intended to be "more of a workhorse for the wide area coverage. It will be a moderately survivable system with threat warning and electronic

Right: **The Northrop Grumman Global Hawk outperformed DarkStar, but being unstealthy could prove vulnerable to attack by SAMs or fighters.**

countermeasures that will have much greater range, payload, and endurance capabilities, giving it the ability to cover 40,000 square nautical miles a day with one system. It will have the endurance to fly about 40 hours, so you can trade off that endurance for range and time over target. The objective was to produce a system that would have 3,000 nautical mile range, be able to stay there for 24 hours, and come back home again, and data link that imagery back to the warfighter so he can have it immediately."

Stealth aircraft tend to be of novel shape, and DarkStar was no exception. It had a short, disk-shaped body and long wings of 69ft (21m) span, but no vertical surfaces or tail. The wings were slightly swept forward, positioning the elevons close to the center of pressure – a configuration which gives reduced stability. With its wings detached for shipping, the vehicle could be carried by a C-130. Construction was mainly from graphite composites, but the wing has an aluminium

fuselage carry-through spar. The airframe was treated with RAM to minimise radar reflectivity. To maximise stealth, DarkStar's air intake and F-117-style exhaust were invisible from below. The design was intended to be stealthy in both the 8-12 GHz and 140-180 MHz (UHF) bands, with its radar reflections being focussed in two sideways facing "spikes".

Boeing built the wings and related subsystems, while Lockheed Martin provided the fuselage, and carried out final assembly at its Skunk Works facility. In the best Skunk Works tradition, the project moved fast, with the first example being produced just under a year from contract signature. Rolled out in June 1995, DarkStar was due to fly in October of that year, but the first flight was delayed until in March 1996, largely due to software problems. Following

the first flight, changes were made to the flight-control software and to the take-off technique. Immediately after liftoff for what would have been its second flight, DarkStar pitched up and crashed just north of the runway.

The second DarkStar made its first flight in early 1998, flying for more than two-and-a-half hours, and reaching an altitude of 25,000ft (7,600m). The flight was fully automated from take-off to landing, with the UAV navigating via differential Global Positioning System (GPS) guidance, and demonstrating its ability to update its preplanned mission during flight. The test cleared the way for further tests to evaluate its flight characteristics and system performance, and to evaluate the performance of its high-resolution synthetic aperture radar and electro-optic payloads. DarkStar was designed to carry either a Recon/Optical electro-optical camera or a Westinghouse Synthetic Aperture Radar (SAR). Both were intended to transmit real-time still images via satellite.

Early in 1999, the USAF, US DoD, and Advanced Concept Technology Demonstration officials unanimously agreed to cancel the Lockheed Martin/Boeing DarkStar in favour of the Global Hawk, which had outperformed the stealth UAV in recent flight tests. Now a Northrop programme, following that company's purchase of Teledyne Ryan, Global Hawk will be the future US long-duration UAV. Global Hawk has no low-observable features and will rely on its high operational altitude and

Below: **Boeing's X-45A is intended to test the concept of a stealthy unmanned combat air vehicle (UCAV) which could fly high-risk missions.**

Right: **This photo of the NASA/Boeing X-36 shows the general configuration of the UAV, but hides the classified thrust-vectoring system.**

defensive EW suite for survivability.

The NASA/Boeing X-36 UAV is a canard design intended to assess whether stealth and high in-flight agility could be successfully combined in a single configuration. The X-36 was developed in 28 months by a team from NASA Ames Research Center and what was then the McDonnell Douglas Phantom Works. It uses a blended wing-body design with a chined fuselage, sharp leading-edges, and no vertical tail. These give a low RCS, but poor lift and agility. Yaw control is partly via split ailerons that can be used as drag rudders, and partly via an engine thrust vectoring system. In January 2000, *Jane's International Defense Review* reported that the X-36 used "a still-classified thrust vectoring system with an externally fixed nozzle".

STEALTH UCAVs

More recently, the US has become interested in the concept of stealth UAVs able to fly combat missions and deliver weapons. Known as UCAVs (Unmanned Combat Air Vehicles), these could help reduce casualties during air strikes.

As this book was being completed, Boeing was preparing to flight test the first of two X-45A UCAVs. Being developed under a $131 million cost-share agreement with the

Below right: **An unmanned stealth aircraft, the X-45 has straight edges arranged to be parallel wherever possible.**

US Defense Advanced Research Projects Agency (DARPA), the X-45A has an aluminium sub-structure and graphite-epoxy composite skin. This choice was made to minimise cost, but any production version would have a composite sub-structure. The UCAV is powered by a single non-afterburning Honeywell F124 engine fitted with a rectangular yaw-vectoring exhaust nozzle that minimises control surface deflections.

The X-45A is around 26.5ft (8.08m) long and has a wing span of 33.8ft (10.30m). Empty weight is around 8,000lb (3,630kg), rising to the region of 15,000lb (6,800kg) at maximum takeoff gross weight. It can carry a payload of approximately 3,000lb (1,360kg) in two weapons bays, one on each side of the fuselage centreline. For trials purposes, the right-hand bay

will be used to carry avionics. The bays have been sized to carry up to six 250lb (113kg) bombs or a single 1,000lb (453kg) Joint Direct Attack Munition (JDAM) guided bomb. The maximum range is believed to be around 300-400nm, but an operational version would have the ability to loiter for up to 30 minutes over a target around 650nm from the launch point.

Tests are expected to conclude in 2002 with a mission in which the UCAV will detect and attack a simulated hostile emitter. The next stage could be the construction of a third example, which would take advantage of the experience gained with the first two, and be closer to the configuration of a prototype operational version. Engineering and manufacturing development (EMD) of an operational UCAV could begin in 2005.

EUROPE'S UAVs

Given that stealthy UAVs are less expensive than stealth aircraft, it was hardly surprising that the unmanned concept was to be explored in Europe. In 2000, three types of stealthy UAV were announced by France, Germany, and Sweden, respectively.

On 18 July 2000, Dassault Aviation began flight tests of a scale model of a low-observable UAV design. Developed under a rapid prototyping scheme, the Aéronef de Validation Expérimentale (AVE) is intended to meet a French military requirement for a low-observable target which can be used to train airborne and ground-based radar operators, but it is also intended to demonstrate to the French Ministry of Defence that the company has mastered stealth technology.

Dassault Aviation also hopes that the AVE will be the first stage in the development of a full-scale UAV demonstrator which could lead to an operational design able to carry out reconnaissance, or air-to-air and air-to-ground combat missions, perhaps under the control of a Rafale fighter. Like the X-45A, any combat version would have internal weapons bays. The version now flying is 7.87ft (2.4m) in length and wingspan. Powered by twin AMT engines, it has an empty weight of 77lb (35kg) and a maximum take-off weight of 132lb (60kg). Maximum speed is Mach 0.5, and the UAV has a maximum range of approximately 93 miles (150km).

Germany has begun the Future Airborne Weapon System (FAWS) programme to study possible replacements for the Tornado fighter-bomber. Like the UK, Germany is not sure that the solution is another manned aircraft. Cruise missiles or UAVs may be a partial solution, perhaps supplemented by a smaller number of new aircraft. In September 2000, EADS announced that it was studying a stealthy UAV configuration under the FAWS effort.

Sweden has been studying stealthy UAVs since the late 1990s. The project is being conducted under Sweden's Nationellt Flygtekniskt Forsknings-Program (National Aeronautics Research Program), and involves Saab's Avionics and Dynamics divisions, Ericsson and the Aeronautical Research

Right: **Dassault Aviation hopes that the AVE will demonstrate to the French Ministry of Defence that the company has mastered stealth technology.**

Institute of Sweden (FFA). Nine configurations were studied between April and June 1998, and a low-speed model of the resulting Swedish Highly Advanced Research Configuration (SHARC) was wind-tunnel tested starting in March 1999. The initial tests checked weapon deployment test from the UAV's internal bay, and later tests in the T1500 wind tunnel at FFA explored the vehicle's flight envelope.

SHARC is 32ft (10m) long, has a wing span of 26ft (8m), and is expected to have a take-off weight of around 11,000lb (5,000kg). It is intended to complement existing manned aircraft, providing a lower-cost method of attacking targets. However, there is currently no specific Swedish Air Force requirement for such a UAV. SHARC's low signature is intended to prevent detection and counter-attack from anti-aircraft units and fighter aircraft. Unlike non-stealthy manned aircraft, it will need no ESM sensors, or the ability to fly evasive manoeuvres with steep turns involving heavy "g" loads. This will help keep costs down. Since SHARC would be armed with existing non-stealthy weapons, it will carry these in an internal weapons bay to screen them from enemy sensors.

ISRAELI UAVs

Israel hopes to develop it own models of stealthy UAVs. These would be long-endurance designed intended to track down and destroy enemy ballistic-missile launch vehicles. In 1994, IAI, Rafael, and Wales teamed to design the HA-10 stealthy UAV, a platform intended to use two or three Moab (Python-derivative) air-to-air missiles to attack Scud-type ballistic missiles in the first 65-80 seconds of powered flight. Funded by the US Ballistic Missile Defense Office (BMDO), the study concluded that the manufacture of such a weapon system would be very expensive.

With the emerging threat of new Iraqi or Iranian long-range

ballistic missiles, the idea of a stealthy counter-weapon is again finding favour, but now the objective would be to attack enemy ballistic missile transporters, erectors and launchers (TELs) before these can launch their missiles. The proposed UAVs would have an endurance of up to 60 hours. One version would carry the sensors needed to detect TEL targets, while the other would conduct the attack.

The required airframes and propulsion systems would probably have to be imported. Although Israel has developed conventional long-endurance UAVs, Israeli stealth technology is still at an early stage can provide only reduced rather than low RCS. For example, the

Top: **Dassault Aviation's Aéronef de Validation Expérimentale (AVE) is intended to meet a French military requirement for a low-observable target drone.**

Above: **The AVE's diamond-shaped wing and V-tail combine to form a similar configuration to that devised for the Northrop YF-23.**

proposed HA-10 would have had an RCS only one order of magnitude below that of the non-stealthy Global Hawk. According to a September 2000 report in *Aviation Week & Space Technology*, Israeli researchers would have to achieve a further 10-15dB reduction in radar reflectivity to create an indigenous stealthy UAV.

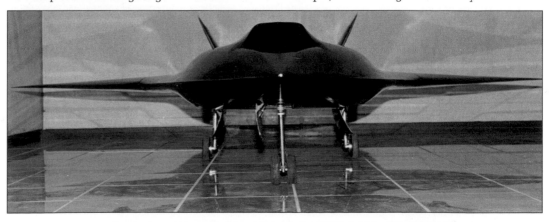

LOCKHEED U-2S

Rôle: high-altitude reconnaissance
Length: 63ft 0in (19.20m)
Height: 16ft 0in (4.88m)
Wingspan: 103ft 0in (31.39m)
Max takeoff weight: 40,000lb (18,140kg)
Max. speed: 475+ miles per hour (Mach 0.58)
Ceiling: 90,000ft (27,400m)
Range: more than 6,090nm (11,280km)
Armament: none
Power plant: one General Electric F-118-101 turbofan of 17,000lb (7,710kg) dry thrust

First flown on 1 August 1955, the U-2 was developed to meet a US requirement for a highly specialised reconnaissance aircraft able to fly over Soviet targets at altitudes of 70,000ft (21,000m) or more. The aircraft would rely primarily on height for survivability, but the need for stealth was also appreciated. Low RCS was a design goal, but in practice little could be done to reduce the radar signature. Optimised as it was for ultimate high-altitude performance, the basic design of the U-2 was so specialised that it left the design team with little leeway for large-scale modifications.

Reconnaissance operations over the Soviet Union began on 4 July 1956. When it became obvious that Soviet radars were able to track the U-2, Lockheed investigated several methods of reducing the aircraft's RCS, but most proved impractical. The only technique to be adopted was the use of a new paint scheme containing radar-absorbing "iron-ball" ferrite pigment.

Overflights of the Soviet Union continued until 1 May 1960, but fewer than 30 had been completed when a U-2 flown by Francis Gary Powers was shot down near Sverdlovsk. The "U-2 Incident" caused the collapse of the 1960 US-Soviet summit meeting between President Eisenhower and Soviet Premier Nikita Khrushchev. Eisenhower ordered an end to the overflights. They had generated about 1,200,000ft of photographic film covering more than a million square miles of Soviet territory, giving US intelligence experts an unprecedented view of Soviet aircraft, missile and nuclear deployments.

Surveillance of the Soviet Union continued, but the aircraft was now used to fly missions along the Soviet border, using sideways-looking sensors to look deep into Soviet territory. A small batch of U-2s supplied to Taiwan carried out overflights of China between 1959 and 1974. Four were shot down. In 1974, CIA involvement in the U-2 programme ended, and the 20 surviving aircraft were handed over to the USAF.

The initial production run saw around 55 aircraft built. At least seven U-2As were reworked as U-2Bs, receiving structural strengthening and the more powerful Pratt & Whitney J75-P-13 turbojet. The follow-on U-2C (a mixture of reworked and new-build aircraft) introduced a slightly extended nose, a long dorsal equipment fairing, increased fuel capacity, enlarged intakes, and the J75-P-13B engine.

The U-2D had a modified Q bay able to house specialised sensors or a second crew member, while the U-2E was a CIA version with advanced ECM systems. At least four U-2As were modified into U-2Fs by addition of a USAF-style refuelling receptacle.

The aircraft returned to production in 1968 in its U-2R form, a variant which had first flown in prototype form on 28 August 1867. Powered by the 1967? same F-75-P-13B engine as the earlier aircraft, this was intended to overcome the airframe-imposed performance limitations of the older -13B-powered aircraft, improve handling characteristics, increase the range and payload, and provide a less cramped cockpit.

The result may have resembled the earlier U-2 models, but was essentially an all-new design. Wingspan was increased by 23ft (7m), the outboard 5.9ft (1.8m) of each wing folding inwards for storage. Maximum altitude is reported to have been 75,000ft (22,860m), slightly below that of the earlier models. Most obvious new feature of the U-2R was the underwing equipment pods, which supplemented the volume of the fuselage bays. In 1978 these would be replaced by still larger underwing fairings pod known as "superpods".

A total of 25 serial numbers was assigned to the initial batch of U-2Rs but the number actually built in this initial production run was at least 14, probably 17. Aircraft were initially assigned to both the USAF and the CIA, rapidly supplanting the older models, but the surviving CIA examples were passed to the USAF in 1974.

Final version of the U-2 family was the TR-1A. Structurally identical to the U-2R, it was ordered in 1979 to act as a source of "day or night, high-altitude, all weather stand-off surveillance of a battle area in direct support of US and allied ground and air forces". The first example flew on 1 August 1981 and was delivered to the USAF in the following month. Operational TR-1As were used by the 17th Reconnaissance Wing, Royal Air Force Station Alconbury, England, starting in February 1983. The last production aircraft were

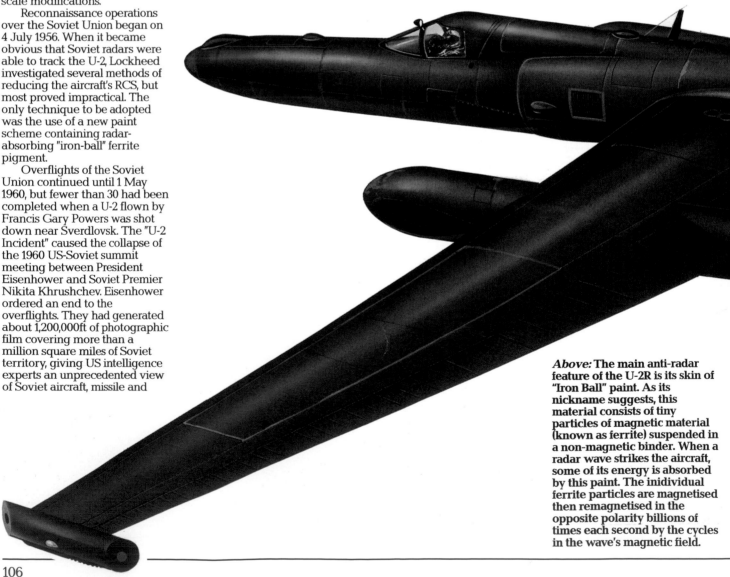

Above: **The main anti-radar feature of the U-2R is its skin of "Iron Ball" paint. As its nickname suggests, this material consists of tiny particles of magnetic material (known as ferrite) suspended in a non-magnetic binder. When a radar wave strikes the aircraft, some of its energy is absorbed by this paint. The inidividual ferrite particles are magnetised then remagnetised in the opposite polarity billions of times each second by the cycles in the wave's magnetic field.**

delivered in October 1989. In 1992 the USAF decided to drop the designation TR-1, and to classify all operational aircraft as U-2R.

In May 1988 the USAF gave Lockheed a contract to demonstrate and flight test a General Electric F118-GE-101 turbofan engine) in the U-2R. A variant of the F101-GE-F29, the new engine was lighter, produced more thrust, and burned less fuel than the older J75-P-13B turbojet. The first re-

engined aircraft flew for the first time on 23 May 1989. The upgrade proved successful, and was applied to the entire fleet. Other upgrades improved the aircraft's sensors and added a Global Positioning System (GPS) satellite-navigation system that would record geographical co-ordinates directly on the collected images. The re-engined single-seat aircraft are designed U-2S, while the trainer is the U-2ST.

The first production example

flew on 12 August 1994, and the first operational single-seaters and trainers were delivered to the 9 RW, Beale AFB, California, on 28 October 1994. The aircraft serves with four operational detachments located throughout the world, and the first operational U-2S mission was flown from Osan AB, South Korea, on 20 October 1995. It is capable of collecting multi-sensor photo, electro-optic, infrared and radar imagery, as well as performing other types

of reconnaissance, but requires a skilled pilot. An official USAF description of the U-2 notes that it "...can be a difficult aircraft to fly due to its unusual landing characteristics."

The aircraft that the Soviets once dubbed "the black lady of espionage" has outlived its supersonic SR-71 replacement. On 11 August 1994, U-2R number 0338 became the first U-2 to achieve 20,000 flying hours, and the type is expected to remain in service for many years.

Right: Originally built for the CIA as a U-2A, 66701 was later assigned to the USAF. Rebuilt as a U-2B, then as a U-2C, it was painted for the first time in 1970.

LOCKHEED SR-71 BLACKBIRD

Rôle: strategic reconnaissance
Length: 107ft 5in (32.74m)
Wingspan: 55ft 7in (16.94m)
Height: 18ft 6in (5.64m)
Max takeoff weight: 170,000lb (77,000kg)
Max speed: Mach 3+
Service ceiling: approx. 86,000 ft (26,000m)
Range: 2,600nm (4,800km)
Armament: none
Powerplant: two Pratt & Whitney J58 each of 32,500lb (14,700kg) thrust with afterburner

Despite their age, the small fleet of SR-71 Blackbird aircraft represented a unique intelligence-gathering asset right up to their moment of final retirement in 1998. More than 35 years after the type's first flight, this sinister-looking aircraft could still operate with impunity in the face of most defence systems. The Soviet Union was probably the only nation able to defend itself against Blackbirds. Others have tried – firing off SA-2 Guidelines against SR-71s has become a regular event for the North Korean air defences, but to date the exercise has proved fruitless. In 1986 Blackbirds operated in the face of the threat posed by Libyan SA-5 Gammon long-range/high-altitude missile batteries in order to record the results of US air strikes against targets in Tripoli and Benghazi.

Like the XB-70 bomber programme, the A-12 project required a long series of technological developments to make Mach 3 flight possible. Materials, lubricants, powerplants, fuels and subsystems all had to be custom-developed. When the aircraft cruised for prolonged periods at Mach 3, the external skin temperature rose to at least 450 degrees Centigrade, and to more than 1,000 degrees in areas where the thermal effects were severest. To cope with this level of thermal stress, most of the airframe was made from Beta B-120 titanium alloy.

When designing the U-2, Lockheed had been able to take only limited RCS-reduction measures, but the A-12 took the entire art a massive step forward. As North American designers working on the XB-70 bomber and F-108 Rapier fighter had discovered, creating an aircraft able to cruise at Mach 3 was difficult enough, but in creating the A-12, the Skunk Works tackled the tasks of combining this level of performance with stealth.

Comparison of the A-12 with the similar-sized F-108 is instructive. The fighter had an angular appearance which bordered on ugliness, with a slab-sided forward fuselage, box-shaped rear fuselage, and wedge inlets – features which were highly radar reflective. The

A-12 had rounded lines which made extensive use of wing/body blending, while its engines were fed by inlets whose conical centrebodies would help shield the compressor face from radar observation. The twin fins were canted inwards to reduce their radar reflectivity, while the long chines on the forward fuselage presented highly inclined surfaces to incoming radar energy.

Invisible to the untrained eye was another breakthrough in stealth technology – the use of plastic materials in areas such as the wing leading edges, chines and elevons. Developed by Lockheed, this took the form of a radar-absorbent plastic honeycomb designed to cope with temperatures of up to 600deg F (315deg C). On the A-12, it accounted for 20 per cent of the total wing area. It was not strong enough to be used structurally in a Mach 3 design, so was added to the leading and trailing edge in the form of V-shaped sections. The Skunk Works is also reported to have flown experimental components such as all-plastic vertical fins.

The dark paint finish used to help radiate heat away from the aircraft gave rise to the unofficial designation "Blackbird". It was designed with two qualities in mind. It offered high heat emissivity, so helped to radiate

friction-generated heat when the aircraft was cruising at Mach 3. It also incorporated the radar-absorbing "iron ball" pigment used on the U-2 and TR-1.

The first A-12 prototype was completed in the winter of 1961/62, and made its maiden flight (with interim J75 turbojet engines) on 26 April 1962, and deliveries to the CIA started towards the end of the year. By this time a second variant existed – the YF-12A interceptor. The first of three prototype fighters flew in August 1963 and, although extensively tested, the type was never adopted for service. Fifteen A-12s were built, all but one of which were single-seaters.

Existence of the aircraft was revealed by President Johnson on 29 February 1964, although he gave the designation incorrectly as "A-11". Four months later, he revealed that a definitive operational version was under development, but once more gave a wrong designation, referring to the new aircraft as the SR-71. It was to have been designated RS-71 (Reconnaissance-Strike) rather than SR (Strategic reconnaissance). A dedicated R-12 nuclear strike derivative of the A-12 is known to have been proposed.

The SR-71 had been ordered at the end of 1962. Like the U-2, the A-12 had been a single-seat

Left: **The SR-71 gave the world its first example of wing-body blending, a significant method of reducing RCS taken to extreme in the B-2.**

aircraft (although several two-seat trainer versions of the latter were completed). The SR-71 had a two-seat cockpit, a configuration first tested on the YF-12A. It was also slightly larger and heavier than the A-12. The chines were made from metal, and used to house the aircraft's sensors.

First flight of the SR-71 took place on 22 December 1964, the aircraft being one of an initial batch of six. Production deliveries started in January 1966 with the delivery to the USAF of the first SR-71B two-seater. The first SR-71A was delivered in May of the same year. A total of 32 SR-71s was built, all but two of which were two-seaters.

Just how well the aircraft's RCS-reduction measures worked remains debatable, but classified. Not all of the components flight-tested in plastic found their way into the production aircraft. In his book *Stealth Aircraft*, Bill Sweetman recalls with amusement how when the USAF flew an SR-71 to the 1974 Farnborough Air Show, Plessey Radar announced that its AR-5D civil air-surveillance radar had detected the plane at a range of

more than 200 miles (320km).

By the late 1980s, the USAF was operating only nine SR-71s, and decided that he cost of operating such a small fleet of special-purpose aircraft was not viable. Defense Secretary Dick Cheney retired the SR-71 fleet in 1990. Most of its aircraft were sent to or made available to museums, but at the instructions of the US Congress, five SR-71As and one trainer were set aside for possible future use.

By 1994, Congress had realized that there was a continuing shortfall in US reconnaissance capability, so ordered that three SR-71As be reactivated. The USAF reactivated two, making them fully operational, but did not use them for any significant missions.

In 1996, the SR-71 was temporarily grounded because the USAF said that funds for their operation were not authorized. Congress authorized the funds, but in October 1997, President Clinton used his line-item veto powers to delete the $39 million budgeted for the SR-71, and on 30 October 1998 the SR-71 was officially retired, after a 32-year military career.

Above: Most of the SR-71's sensor payload was packed into equipment bays within the long chines. Built from metal, these incorporated RAM and were carefully blended with the fuselage, measures aimed at reducing overall RCS.

Above: Despite being the first Western aircraft to incorporate significant RCS-reduction features, the SR-71 also offered Mach 3 performance and an undeniable beauty. This aircraft made extensive use of RAM in all the sharp horizontal edges which might be seen by an enemy radar – the chines, wing leading edges, and elevons.

Further RCS reduction was provided by the use of "Iron Ball" paint. So sophisticated was the aircraft, that it is hard to remember that the first production delivery was in 1966. Over thirty years later, the high cost of keeping the aircraft operational led to the final eight or so examples being retired.

ROCKWELL INTERNATIONAL B-1B

Rôle: strategic bomber
Length: 147ft 0in (44.81m)
Height: 34ft 0in (10.36m)
Wingspan: 78ft 2in (23.84m) swept, 136ft 8in (41.67m) unswept
Max. takeoff weight: 477,000lb (216,360kg)
Max. speed: Mach 1.25
Range: c.6,475nm (12,000km)
Armament: up to 75,000lb (34,000kg) of ordnance in three internal weapons bays
Powerplant: four General Electric F101-GE-102 turbofans of c.30,000lb (13,600kg) with afterburning

When President Reagan entered office in 1981, he was determined to improve America's defences. President Carter had ordered development of the B-2, but this was still in the earliest stages of development, and not due to fly until the late 1980s. Reagan ordered a batch of 100 improved B-1B production models, giving the USAF and Rockwell the problem of getting it into production, then into service early enough to make a useful contribution to SAC's strength before the B-2 arrived. That timescale called for a five-year programme rather than the seven to ten years normally needed to field a major weapons system.

The B-1A had already been designed to have a much lower RCS than the B-52 it would replace. By the early 1980s, Soviet development of improved defence systems intended to cope with ALCM and

Tomahawk cruise missiles – weapons such as the SA-10 and SA-N-6 – made the Rockwell bomber seem increasingly vulnerable, so steps were taken to lower its RCS. The inlets were redesigned, eliminating the variable ramps needed for Mach 2 flight. The revised design has inlet sides and splitter plates swept slightly backwards from the vertical, and incorporate curved ducts and streamwise radar-absorbent baffles. RAM was also added as a lining material.

A major move toward reducing the aircraft's RCS was the removal of the fuselage dorsal spine. This had originally been fitted to house electrical cabling associated with the aircraft's Westinghouse ALQ-153 tail-warning system. When the USAF opted to integrate the tail-warning task directly into the ALQ-161, the spine could be removed.

New absorbent seals for the B-1B wing were developed by the British company Woodville Polymers. These replaced an earlier less-absorbent design in part of an exercise which saw the entire inboard wing structure redesigned.

Among the measures taken under later 1985 contracts for RCS-reduction were a series of

modifications to the nose radome cavity and to cavities in the fuselage side fairings. A special adhesive tape was also applied to all seams in the skin once system testing had been completed, and prior to painting. This tape was probably electrically conductive, and thus linked all the skin panels together into a common conducting surface, thus eliminating surface discontinuities which would re-radiate energy.

B-1B's RCS is one hundredth that of the B-52, and a seventh that of the FB-111. In May 1986, *International Defense Review* quoted USAF Aeronautical Systems Division commander as saying that when the B-1 flew into the 1985 Paris Air show, the French were surprised by its small radar cross-section. "They didn't believe we could do it." The aircraft has also proved an elusive target for fighters during Red Flag exercises. "In order for the monitoring radar to get our position, we either have to climb or put our transponders on," the commander of SAC's 337th

Bombardment Squadron told *Aviation Week* in 1987.

In October 1986, well ahead of the Congressional 1987 deadline, the first B-1B squadron was declared operational at Dyess AFB, Texas. The base had 15 aircraft, 12 of which had enough defensive avionics to allow them to be declared operational. With delivery of the 100th and final B-1B due in April 1988, and no prospect of a follow-on order, Rockwell began to lay off staff, with more than 10,000 leaving the B-1 operation in the first half of 1987 alone. In the spring of 1988, Rockwell announced that its long-established North American Aircraft division at Columbus, Ohio, would cease operations over the next 15 months. The final example was delivered on 2 May 1988, and the type now equips three squadrons of Air Combat Command, and two of the Air National Guard. It is now supported by Boeing.

The B-1B was designed to

Left: **Careful engineering has given the B-1B a head-on RCS of around 1sq. m, making it a more difficult radar target than a small fighter.**

Below: The rounded shape of the B-1A fuselage had played a significant part in getting the RCS an order of magnitude better than that of the B-52. Reducing the B-1B RCS by as much again involved painstaking attention to detail, with RAM being applied to key areas of the fuselage and wings to damp out radar hot spots.

fly low-level, high-speed missions which impose greater strain on the airframe than the high-altitude missions of the B-52. The aircraft is expected to have a 10,000 hour service life, which should allow it to remain in service until around 2020. Like the B-2, it is expected to retire long before the much older B-52. Designed to conservative engineering standards at a time when little was known about aircraft life expectancy, the B-52 is expected to have an operating life of more than 30,000 hours, and could remain in service until around 2040.

The B-1B's ability to deliver conventional weapons is being improved under a multi-stage Conventional Mission Upgrade Program (CMUP). CMUP Block C, fielded in August 1997, gave B-1Bs the capability to drop cluster bombs, while the Block D changes due to be completed in 2003 allow the aircraft to carry up to 24 JDAM guided bombs (eight in each of its three weapon bays), fit an Integrated Defensive Electronic CounterMeasures (IDECM) towed decoy intended to enhance the survivability of the aircraft, and add a new communication/navigation system. A planned Block E modification will allow the B-1B to carry wind-compensated munitions, the Joint Standoff Weapon (JSOW), and the Joint Air To Surface Standoff Missile (JASSM), while Block F will make further improvements to the bomber's defensive system.

Other upgrades being projected for the B-1B include the addition of a satcoms terminal and a Link 16 datalink, a cockpit upgrade, and modifications to the aircraft's radar which would allow it to take synthetic aperture radar (SAR) images of the target, improving the aircraft's ability to target GPS-guided bombs. Studies have also looked at EW improvements such as an upgraded version of the AN/ALR-56M radar warning receiver, and advanced countermeasure flares.

Above: The engine nacelles (seen below in cross section) had to be redesigned on the B-1B to add anti-radar baffles and a curved duct. These moves had a drastic effect on top speed, making the aircraft subsonic under most flight conditions, but the price was worth paying. Radar signals could no longer enter the inlet and pass down to reflect from the front face of the engine. This reduces RCS, and also prevents advanced radar signal-processing algorithms being used to observe the modulation effects of the rotating fan stages, a phenomenon which can allow radars to identify the type of aircraft being tracked.

EUROFIGHTER TYPHOON

Rôle: multirole fighter
Length: 52ft 4.25in (15.96m)
Wingspan: 35ft 11in (10.95m)
Max. takeoff weight: 46,300lb (21,000kg)
Max. speed: Mach 2.0
Tactical radius: typically 750nm (1,390km)
Armament: 27mm Mauser cannon (omitted from UK aircraft) plus up to 14,330lb (6,500kg) of external stores
Powerplant: two Eurojet EJ200 turbofans each of 13,490lb (6,120kg) dry and 20,250lb (9,185kg) thrust with A/B

Under a memorandum of understanding signed in May 1988, development of this twin-engined canard-delta was begun by what were then British Aerospace (UK), MBB (Germany), Aeritalia (Italy) and CASA (Spain). Initial prototypes were powered by two Turbo-Union RB.199-122 turbofans, but later prototypes had the production engine. Known as the EJ200, this twin-shaft turbofan was developed by the Eurojet consortium, a collaborative venture set up by what were then Rolls-Royce (UK), MTU (Germany), Fiat (Italy) and Sener (Spain).

In its basic single-seat version, the aircraft is optimised for the air-to-air role, but has a secondary attack capability. A two-seater is available for training.

Much of the technology needed for Typhoon was proven using the BAe EAP (Experimental Aircraft Programme) technology demonstrator. The first prototype of what was originally known as the European Fighter Aircraft (EFA), then Eurofighter 2000, was originally expected to fly at Manching in Western Germany late in 1991. In practice, the first two aircraft (development aircraft 1 and 2) were not completed until late in 1992, but were not to fly for some 18 months, while exhaustive checks were made of the flight-control system (FCS). DA1 finally flew on 27 March 1994.

The flight-test programme remained slow, and FCS software was often a delaying factor. This led to speculation in the mid to late 1990s that the system was experiencing technical difficulties, reports which were encouraged by the development team's regular but bland pronouncements that the subject could not be discussed, but that all was well.

In practice, two factors had caused the team to be ultra-conservative when developing the FCS. One was the FCS-related accidents which had been experienced by the YF-22 (25 May 1992) and JAS 39 Gripen (2 February 1989 and 8 August 1993); the other was the fact that the Typhoon was designed to have a very high level of agility at supersonic speeds. Since stability increases at supersonic speeds, the aircraft had an even higher level of agility at subsonic speeds which posed formidable challenges to the FCS development team.

DA3, the third aircraft to fly, and the first Italian-assembled example, was the first to be powered by Eurojet EJ200 engines. The UK-assembled DA4 was the first two-seater and first with full avionics. The remainder of the development fleet consists of three more development aircraft (DA4 - 7) and five instrumented production aircraft (IPA1 -5). Drop trials of air-to-surface weapons started in 1999 using DA3, and in 1997 DA7 made the first launch on an air-to-air missile.

When the programme was set up, the UK and West Germany intended to order 250. Italy was to buy around 170, with Spain taking 100. Inevitably these figures were to decrease. By 2000 they had dropped to Germany 180, Italy 121 plus nine options, Spain 87 plus 16 options, and the UK 232 plus 65 options. Deliveries to the user air forces are due to begin in June 2002. First units to equip will be an Operational Evaluation Unit at BAE Warton, then an Operational Conversion Unit at RAF Coningsby, JG 73 at Laage, Germany, and 4 Stormo at

Below: While the aircraft is not intended to be stealthy, measures were taken to minimise its RCS. The most obvious is the "smiling" air intake. The original design featured a rectangular intake similar to that on the EAP technology demonstrator, but tests showed that a curved configuration would have a lower RCS. The aircraft will enter service with Raytheon AMRAAM missiles, but these will be replaced by the ramjet-powered Matra

BAe Dynamics Meteor. The same company's Advanced Short-Range Air-to-Air Missile (ASRAAM) will be fitted to RAF aircraft, while other users may select the internationally developed IRIS-T.

Left: Given the risks associated with test flying, building only a single EAP prototype was a gamble, but one which paid off.

Grosseto, Italy. First export customer was Greece, which in 1999 announced its intention to purchase 60 aircraft, with options for 30 more.

Flyaway unit cost was originally seen as being around £10 to 12 million ($17 to 20 million). By 1992 this had risen to an estimated £25 to 26.5 million, and by 1996 to £38 million. There was no official requirement for the Typhoon to have a high order of stealthiness. It is not a stealth aircraft, but was designed for reduced RCS, a more modest goal which does

not require the specialised and costly technology used in the F-117A and B-2. Much can be accomplished even by simple measures such as keeping size and weight to a minimum, and using rounded shapes and profiles.

Several factors help minimise RCS. It is a small aircraft, and much of its profile is rounded. The main straight areas, such as the wing and fin leading edges, are highly swept, so will reflect radar energy in main lobes well away from the frontal sector. Extensive use is also made of carbon-fibre composites. RCS is also reduced by careful attention to detail. At the 1987 Paris Air Show, a revised full-scale mock-up showed some of the

refinements made to the design in the final stages of project definition work. The most obvious was a redesigned ventral intake. On EAP and the original EFA design, this had been of rectangular shape, but the final configuration is a slightly curved "smiling" design. This has less drag, and less radar cross section. The RAF has stated that Typhoon meets the required level of low-observability. No official figure has been released, but the aircraft is understood to have an RCS of just under one square metre.

Some F-22-type capabilities might be added to Typhoon as part of its mid-life updating programme, a possibility foreseen by the RAF and

Luftwaffe before the programme was launched. These could include three-dimensional thrust-vectoring through angles of up to 10 degrees, and off-boresight weapon aiming by decoupling the fuselage by means of CCV flying surfaces and vectored thrust. Technology for such an update could be drawn from the results of flight testing of the Rockwell/MBB X-31A.

The engine manufacturing consortium has drawn up plans for uprated EJ200 variants with thrust levels of 23,155lb (10,503kg) and 26,300lb (11,930kg). A thrust-vectoring nozzle has been studied in Spain by ITP and Sener, and 20 hours of bench tests had been completed by September 1998.

DASSAULT-BREGUET RAFALE C & M

Rôle: multi-role fighter
Length: 50ft 1.25in (15.27m)
Height: 17ft 6.25in (5.34m)
Wingspan: 35ft 5.25in (10.80m)
Max. takeoff weight: 49,600lb (22,500kg)
Max. speed: Mach 1.8
Tactical radius: 570-950nm (1,055-1,760km)
Service ceiling: 55,000ft (16,760m)
Armament: up to 21,000lb (9,500kg) of ordnance, plus internal cannon
Powerplant: two SNECMA M88-2 turbofans each of 16,400lb (7,440kg) thrust with A/B

At the 1983 Paris Air Show, Dassault showed a mock-up of a technology demonstrator for a next-generation fighter. Two features of this ACX (Advanced Combat eXperimental) design proved striking – the huge vertical fin, and the novel inlets. The size of the fin had been dictated by the need for directional stability, but the

inlets, which incorporated the moveable conical centrebodies found all Mirages since the IIIC, were mounted under the leading-edge root extensions of a carefully sculpted forward fuselage.

The author assumed that this configuration had been adopted to ensure a good airflow at high angles of attack, but Northrop's Lee Begin had an alternative theory. "Take another look," he urged me, "they're shaped that way because of stealth." As the design was refined to create today's Rafale, the tail fin shrank in size, the lower fuselage assumed a V-

shaped cross-section, and the inlets were changed for a simpler pattern without centrebodies or other moving parts. There was no loss of stealth, however. The revised inlets remained tucked under the fuselage and largely screened from the attention of look-down radars.

Like the Eurofighter consortium members, France apparently concluded that the cost of developing a truly stealthy fighter was politically and economically unacceptable. Like EFA, the Dassault-Breguet Rafale is a reduced-RCS design.

In France, the task of

developing RCS-prediction software was tackled by Thomson-CSF. To allow a start to be made on the task of eliminating "hot spots" from the design, Thomson-CSF adapted existing software, and used this to study the radar cross-section of the aircraft. Three areas were quickly identified as major contributors to RCS – the radar and EW antennas, the inlets and engine, and the cockpit. A parallel effort involved developing software for the Cray XMP 18 supercomputer which will allow the design of large metallic structures of up to 10 square metres in area. This

Above: Although not a true Dassault stealth fighter, Rafale will have a lower radar cross section than today's Mirage F1 or Mirage 2000.

Below: Rafale's rounded inlets may appear very conspicuous, yet they're one of the aircraft's stealthier features. Today's air combat is at low level, and major threats include AEW radar and interceptors equipped with look-down radars. From most observation angles above the aircraft, the inlets – a prime radar target in any aircraft – are concealed by the forward fuselage. They're barely visible in the photo at the bottom of the opposite page, for example. The aircraft shown here is on an interception mission, and carries two Matra R530F radar-guided missiles, plus two wingtip-mounted Magics. If tasked with an air-superiority mission into unfriendly skies, it would probably carry the new Matra BAe Dynamics MICA.

would initially be used to carry out studies of aircraft inlets.

The Rafale A prototype flew for the first time on 4 July 1986, just ahead of the rival BAe EAP. Like the British aircraft, it was a technology demonstrator rather than a true fighter prototype. About 1,000lb (450kg) heavier than the planned Rafale D production version, it was powered by two GE F404 turbofans. First flight with a single SNECMA M88 replacing one GE F404 was on 27 February 1990.

A series of test flights were made in the winter of 1987/88 to measure the RCS and the IR signature of the Rafale A. A series of 13 missions was flown, allowing the radar signature to be assessed with different external loads and under several combat conditions. These included an air-combat sortie with the aircraft carrying two Matra Magic 2 heat-seeking missiles, and a low-level flight with two 530 gallon (2,000 litre) external tanks.

Like the UK, France had hoped that a flying demonstrator might act as the catalyst for an international programme, but the path to any agreement was made difficult by conflicting views over aircraft weight. Given the close relationship between aircraft weight and cost, and the need to attack large-scale export orders to make programmes commercially viable, Dassault has always favoured lightweight designs. French determination that the cost (and thus the weight) of a next-generation fighter had to reflect the need for maximum export potential,

and French demands to be given design leadership of any international fighter programme which might emerge from international discussions, ended any prospect of a viable programme.

The UK, West Germany, Italy and Spain chose to go their own way with the EFA, leaving France to continue with Rafale as a national venture. The programmes to develop the definitive aircraft and its M88-2 powerplant were launched in December 1992, and the first production aircraft were ordered in March 1993.

Four versions have been planned. Rafale B started out as a two-seat, dual-control version for the French Air Force, but has now evolved into an operational version suitable for single or two-seat (pilot + weapon system officer) use. The version for the French Air Force was originally to have been Rafale D, but this has now become a generic designation for French Air Force versions. Rafale C is the single-seat combat version for French Air Force, while Rafale M is the naval single-seat version for use on aircraft carriers.

The designation Rafale R has been applied to a possible reconnaissance version which would carry a pod-mounted sensor suite, and replace French Air Force F-1CR and French Navy Super Etendard reconnaissance aircraft.

The Rafale programme did

not go smoothly. When the first edition of this book was written in 1988, there were already suggestions that the project could prove an "abyss for billions". In the mid-1990s the French Government had problems with its defence budget, and demanded cost reductions for Rafale. In November 1995 the programme was suspended. Work on production aircraft was temporarily halted in April of the following year, but in January 1997 Dassault and French defence ministry agreed on a 10 per cent cost reduction and the procurement of 48 aircraft between 1997 and 2002. The arrangement had to be abandoned following a change of government, and a new deal agreed in January 1999 covered only 28 (plus 20 options) for delivery between 2002 and 2007.

The first production aircraft was a Rafale B, which made its first flight on 24 November 1998. It was followed on 7 July 1999 by the first production Rafale M. The first Rafale C is due to be delivered mid-2002.

First version into service will be the Rafale M, and the first naval squadron is due to be equipped by June 2002. Deliveries to the French Air Force should begin in late 2002, with the first squadron being equipped in 2005. The delivery rate will be slow, with the 294th and final aircraft for the French forces being delivered in 2023.

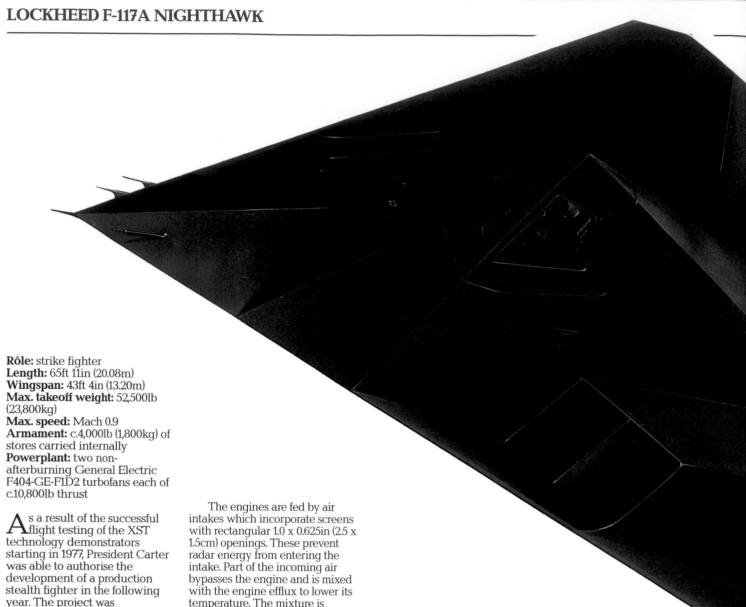

Rôle: strike fighter
Length: 65ft 11in (20.08m)
Wingspan: 43ft 4in (13.20m)
Max. takeoff weight: 52,500lb (23,800kg)
Max. speed: Mach 0.9
Armament: c.4,000lb (1,800kg) of stores carried internally
Powerplant: two non-afterburning General Electric F404-GE-F1D2 turbofans each of c.10,800lb thrust

As a result of the successful flight testing of the XST technology demonstrators starting in 1977, President Carter was able to authorise the development of a production stealth fighter in the following year. The project was codenamed "Senior Trend".

The aircraft that project head Ben Rich and his Skunk Works team created was of very different shape to the widely-projected "F-19" seen in mid-1980s books and magazines. To keep RCS to a minimum, extensive use was made of faceting. Straight lines rather than curves dominate the aircraft's configuration. Its angular lines make one half-seriously wonder whether Ben Rich had impounded every set of French curves owned by Skunk Works personnel.

The faceted panels are mounted on skeletal sub-frame, and coated with radar-absorbent materials. The wing is of two-spar construction, and has a faceted aerofoil. The original outward-canted ruddervators have been replaced by a modified design made from thermoplastic graphite composites, which give the additional strength needed to avoid flutter problems that had placed a speed restriction on the aircraft. The cockpit canopy and most access panels have sawtooth edges to suppress radar reflection.

The engines are fed by air intakes which incorporate screens with rectangular 1.0 x 0.625in (2.5 x 1.5cm) openings. These prevent radar energy from entering the intake. Part of the incoming air bypasses the engine and is mixed with the engine efflux to lower its temperature. The mixture is ejected through narrow-slot exhausts in the rear fuselage. These are 5ft 5in (1.65m) but only 4in (10cm) and have 11 vertical guide vanes.

All ordnance is carried in an internal weapon bay 15ft 3in (4.7m) long and 5ft 9in (1.75m) wide and covered by two large doors hinged on the centreline. When lowered, these greatly increase RCS, so changes have been made to minimise the length of time for which they are opened for weapon-release.

The faceted airframe plays havoc with the aircraft's inherent handling qualities. To make the aircraft flyable, it has a GEC Astronics quadruplex fly-by-wire control system. A Texas Instruments Forward-Looking Infra-Red (FLIR) sensor with dual fields of view is mounted in a cavity just below the front of the canopy, while a Downward-Looking Infra-Red (DLIR) and laser designator also made by TI is mounted in another cavity beneath the forward fuselage to starboard of the nosewheel bay. Both cavities are covered by fine mesh screen to prevent the entry of radar energy.

The designation "stealth

Below: **The side view of the F-117A reveals what must surely be the strangest shape to fly since the 1930s. The steeply-sloped fuselage sides and the highly swept wing leading and trailing edges ensure that radar energy is deflected harmlessly, rather than** being reflected back to the enemy radar. RCS is greatly reduced, but a penalty must be paid in terms of airframe drag and internal volume. Since most USAF bombs and missiles are unstealthy, they are carried in internal weapons bays.

fighter" is partly a misnomer; the aircraft is essentially a strike aircraft designed to fly close to a target at subsonic speed, launch a guided missile or "smart" bomb, then turn away. In terms of speed or agility it is no match for a traditional fighter. It would be a vulnerable target if caught by an enemy fighter. To avoid this, it normally operates at night, conditions under which it is virtually undetectable. In terms of radar penetration, the F-117A has met its specifications, but at a price of restricted speed and manoeuvrability. Its

successors such as the F-22 and Joint Strike Fighter will combine stealth with improved speed, altitude and manoeuvrability.

Although several developed versions have been proposed, none resulted in an order. F-117A+ was a development of the basic F-117A which would have taken advantage of more recent technologies to produce an aircraft with improved survivability in the face of high-threat environments, while the A/F-117X (originally known as the F-117N Seahawk) was a proposed long-range naval

strike/attack aircraft based on the F-117A. If the A/F-117X had become a firm programme, the Skunk Works planned to offer a land-based F-117B which would have used the redesigned wing and horizontal tail surfaces of the naval variant, and been fitted with GE F414 afterburning turbofan engines, and all-weather sensors.

Three upgrade schemes have kept the F-117A combat-effective. The Weapon System Computational Subsystem (WSCS) programme replaced the aircraft's Delco M362F

computers by IBM AP-102 units. The first aircraft to be modified flew in October 1986 and the entire fleet had been updated by 1 January 1992.

By this time, the Offensive Capability Improvement Program (OCIP) was already under way, with the first upgraded aircraft being delivered in November 1990. Completed in March 1995, the OCIP programme added an improved flight-management system, a digital moving map, and digital situation displays, new cockpit instrumentation with Honeywell colour multi-fuction displays, a digital auto throttle and pilot-activated recovery system.

The most recent modification scheme replaces the FLIR and DLIR sensors with a new Texas Instruments turret-mounted Infra-Red Acquisition and Designation Sensor (IRADS), while the Ring Laser Gyro Navigation Improvement Program (RNIP) adds a Honeywell ring laser gyro inertial navigation system and a Collins Global Positioning System (GPS) satellite navigation receiver.

Left: So important was faceting to the stealth qualities of the F-117A, that the USAF kept the aircraft's appearance classified until November 1988. The "butterfly tail' has not been used on a military aircraft since the days of the Fouga Magister trainer. It eliminates one of the three traditional tail surfaces and avoids a radar reflective vertical fin, but control authority is limited at high speed. A quadruplex fly-by-wire system tames the aircraft's strange aerodynamics.

NORTHROP B-2 SPIRIT

Rôle: strategic bomber
Length: 69ft (21.0m)
Height: 17ft (5.18m)
Wingspan: 172ft (52.43m)
Weights – empty: 153,700 lb (69,717kg)
    normal T-O: 336,500lb (152,600kg)
    max T-O: 376,000lb (170,550kg)
Max. speed: high subsonic (Mach 0.85?)
Ceiling: 50,000ft (15,000m)
Range (typical hi-hi-hi): 6,300nm (11,667km)
Armament: 40,000lb (18,000kg) of ordnance in internal bays
Powerplant: four General Electric F118-GE-100 turbofans each of 17,300lb (7,850kg)

Above: **The complex shape of the B-2 intakes and centre fuselage must be a manufacturing nightmare, but the shape and smoothness must be accurately controlled to minimise RCS.**

Like the Lockheed F-117A stealth fighter, the B-2 bomber has the simplest possible front profile – two straight moderately swept leading edges which meet at the nose. This layout ensures that the main RCS sidelobes in the forward sector are well away from the direction of flight. The massive sawtooth trailing edge is made up from 14 straight edges, aligned at one of two fixed angles, a layout which will direct radar energy reflected from the trailing edges into two directions well away from the immediate rear of the aircraft. Each wing side has a drag rudder and elevon on the outboard trailing edge, plus two more elevons on the next-inboard section. The central "beaver tail" forms another moving surface. The aircraft has no vertical stabiliser, a feature that helps reduce RCS. There is a quadruplex digital flight control system developed by General Electric, which incorporates fly-by-wire controls, plus a sophisticated stability-augmentation system.

Segmented inlets on the upper wing feed air to the engines buried within the fuselage. A secondary inlet mounted just ahead of the main inlet, and offset slightly outboard, also draws in air, perhaps for engine bay and efflux cooling. The inlets make a significant contribution to total RCS. A redesign was needed to get these right, and to solve manufacturing problems associated with their complex shape. The engine efflux is discharged via recessed cut-outs in the wing upper surface. Lined with heat-resistant carbon-carbon material, these open-topped ducts are probably intended to spread the exhaust laterally to reduce its IR signature. Two doors on the upper surface of each nacelle are opened when the aircraft is taxying and flying at low speed. These are auxiliary inlets used to supply extra air to the engines.

The aircraft was originally intended to be a high-altitude bomber, but in 1984 the programme was restructured to allow a redesign of the wing carry-through structure. This cost around $1,000 million, and delayed the programme by eight months, but achieved two major goals. The increased structural efficiency of the revised design gave greater strength for less weight, curing an identified weight-growth problem, and providing enough strength for terrain-following flight at low altitude. It also reduced RCS. Design goal was probably an RCS at least an order of magnitude below that of the B-1B. The latter aircraft had already taken bomber RCS to less than 1 square metre, suggesting that the likely figure for the Northrop aircraft was at least below 0.1sq m, perhaps as little as 0.05.

Since all B-2s were built on production tooling, use of the term "prototype" is almost misleading. Air Vehicle 1 (82-1066) was rolled out on 22 November 1988, and made its first flight on 17 July 1989. A total of six aircraft were assigned to development testing. The first aircraft was placed in storage in 1993 at the end of a trials programme of 81 sorties, but the others were reassigned as operational aircraft.

Although the USAF originally planned to procure 133 B-2s (the first of which would never be used as an operational aircraft), the planned force was gradually reduced, and in October 1991 was set at only 16 by the US Congress. The USAF managed to fund one more in Fiscal Year 1992 and four more in the following year. Sixteen aircraft were delivered to the Block 1 standard. Armed with B83 or Mk 84 weapons, they could operate in small numbers from Whiteman AFB.

Nos. 17 to 19 were Block 2 aircraft, and five (Nos 12-16) were retrofitted to the same standard. This equipped the aircraft with partial terrain-following capability, the GATS (GPS-Aided Targeting System), and allowed it to operate from forward bases. Block 20 aircraft could deliver 16 Joint Direct Attack Munitions (only four per target), and had a limited capability to handle the new AGM-137. Aircraft 20 and 21 were built to the Block 30 standard, to which the other 19 will be upgraded. Block 30 has full low-observability performance, full JDAM launch capability, and can carry up to 80 Mk 82, 36 M117 or 80 Mk 62 bombs.

As production ended in the mid-1990s, the tooling was placed in storage, but attempts by the US Congress to order a follow-on batch of 20 aircraft were overruled by the Clinton administration. However it was decided to remove the first aircraft from storage, and rebuild it as an operational aircraft.

The 509th Bomb Wing was formed 1 April 1993 to operate the new bomber. It was located at Whiteman AFB, Missouri, where the first operating unit – the 393rd Bomb Squadron – was formed on 27 August 1993 and received its first aircraft in December of that year. The B-2

was granted limited operational status on 1 January 1997, and Initial Operational Capability followed on 1 April 1997.

The B-2 was designed for a service life of 40,000 hours, so in theory could out-last the B-52 (with a service life of more than 30,000 hours) or the B-1B (10,000 hours). In practice, the retirement date of the B-2 will probably be determined by attrition of the small number built.

When the aircraft first entered service, caulk and pressure-sensitive tape were used to shield the gaps around panels and doors, In flight, the tape tended to peel away from the skin, allowing the exposed gaps to reflect radar energy. During regular depot maintenance, the B-2 is being given an improved anti-radar coating based on magnetic radar-absorbing materials (MagRAM), and high-access

areas of the airframe are being retrofitted with 119 easily removable panels. MagRAM is an iron-filled elastomer which stores radar energy rather than conducting it. The radar reflection from the gaps around a MagRAM-coated panel will be absorbed before it can escape, removing the need to caulk and tape the gap. These modifications will increase the aircraft's weight by 3,666lb (1,660kg), but should reduce the

time needed for low-observable maintenance from 20.8 maintenance hours per flying hour to less than ten.

The B-2 was intended to have a contrail-suppressing system. Located in two bays immediately outboard of the main wheel wells, this would have sprayed highly corrosive chemicals into the exhaust. This scheme was abandoned in favour of using a rearward-facing laser radar to detect contrails, allowing the pilot to move to an altitude where the contrails cease. The vacant spaces earmarked for the contrail-suppressing system could be used in a proposed upgrade to house small missiles with decoy or jamming payloads.

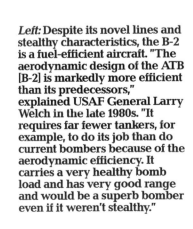

Left: **Despite its novel lines and stealthy characteristics, the B-2 is a fuel-efficient aircraft. "The aerodynamic design of the ATB [B-2] is markedly more efficient than its predecessors," explained USAF General Larry Welch in the late 1980s. "It requires far fewer tankers, for example, to do its job than do current bombers because of the aerodynamic efficiency. It carries a very healthy bomb load and has very good range and would be a superb bomber even if it weren't stealthy."**

LOCKHEED MARTIN F-22A RAPTOR

Rôle: air-superiority fighter
Length: 62ft 1in (18.92m)
Wing span: 44ft 6in (13.56m)
Weights – empty: 31,670lb
(14,365kg)
   max T-O:
c.60,000lb.(c.27,200kg)
Max. speed: Mach 2+
Ceiling: over 50,000ft (15,250m)
Range: 1,735nm (3220km)
Armament: see below
Powerplant: two Pratt &
Whitney F119-PW-100 turbofans
each of 35,000lb (15,900kg) class

The F-22 is intended to allow USAF pilots to establish absolute control of the skies through the conduct of counter-air operations, defeating threats that the F-15 will no longer be able to counter. It will use stealth and advanced sensors to give the pilot a first-look, first-shot, first-kill capability.

Lockheed Martin Aeronautical Systems is responsible for overall weapon system integration. It developed and now manufactures the forward fuselage (including the cockpit and inlets); the vertical fins and stabilators; wing and empennage leading edges; ailerons, flaperons; and landing gear.

Lockheed Martin Tactical Aircraft Systems is responsible for the mid-fuselage; armament; electronic warfare system; the integrated communications, navigation, and identification (CNI) system; stores management and inertial navigation systems; and development of the support system.

Boeing is responsible for the wings and aft fuselage, plus structures in the aircraft for installation of the engines and nozzles. Boeing also handles radar system development and testing, and operates the ground-based Avionics Integration Laboratory (AIL), and the Boeing 757 Avionics Flying Laboratory.

Although the shape of aircraft is fairly conventional, many of its features were dictated by the need to reduce RCS. The fuselage and canopy have sloping sides, the vertical tails surfaces are canted, and the leading and trailing edges of the wing and tail have identical sweep angles. Known as planform alignment, this choice of a relatively small number of angles helps direct any reflected radar energy into a small number of directions. The edges of the canopy, weapon bay doors and other opening surfaces are sawtoothed, a stealth feature first seen on the F-117A.

A serpentine inlet duct conceals the front face of the engines from radar, while the avionics antennas are mostly located in the leading- or

trailing-edges of the wings and fins, or are flush with surfaces, in order to minimise RCS. By March 1994, the companies and the USAF had identified some shortfalls in the aircraft's radar cross-section (RCS). Detected by a new computer modelling technique, these were rectified by reducing the number of drain holes on the bottom of the aircraft and combining access panels.

Final assembly of the F-22 will take place at Lockheed Martin Aeronautical Systems in Marietta, Georgia. To test the "stealthiness" of each F-22 when it comes off the assembly line, the company has built a 50,000 square foot radar cross-section (RCS) verification building. A 45-foot-diameter turntable mounted within a 150 x 210 feet test chamber will position the fighter during RCS tests. Another 60 x 210 foot chamber will be used for aircraft antenna testing. The avionics suite of the F-22 is highly integrated, allowing the pilot to concentrate on the mission, rather than on managing the sensors as in current fighters. The AN/APG-77 radar, EW suite and communications/identification are managed by single system that presents relevant data only to the pilot, and controls the level of electromagnetic emission (such as radar and radio transmissions) according to the tactical situation.

The basic concept was derived from the 1980s Pave Pillar programme in the 1980s, and locates all the signal and data processing resources in a central collection of modular processors, linked to the sensors, subsystems and pilot by high-speed data busses. The avionics suite is based on two Common Integrated Processor (CIP) units linked by a 400 Mbits/s fibre optic network, but there are space, power, and cooling provisions within the aircraft for a third CIP, when this becomes necessary. The CIP itself will be improved by a planned technology-insertion programme which will exploit new developments in computer technology. The avionics has the computing power of two Cray supercomputers, and produces a large amount of heat, so is cooled by a mixture of air and liquid cooling.

The aircraft is controlled by a triplex, digital, fly-by-wire system. Thrust vectoring via two-dimensional convergent/divergent engine exhaust nozzles (able to move 20 degrees upwards and downwards in the vertical plane) is used to augment aerodynamic pitch control, particularly at low speeds and high angles of attack.

The aircraft will carry

Below: The F-22 has a performance which eclipses that of any other fighter present or planned. Yet some critics question the need for the USA to spend large sums of money on an expensive new fighter at a time when the Russian Air Force is a mere shadow of its former self.

existing and planned medium and short range air-to-air missiles, plus a 20mm M61A2 internal cannon. AIM-9 Sidewinder missiles will be carried in bays in the sides of intake ducts, while the other weapons are carried in the ventral weapons bay. Four underwing stores stations can each carry 5,000lb (2,260kg) of additional ordnance or stores, but this will make the aircraft non-stealthy.

Internal carriage of the missiles reduces RCS, but requires weapons which occupy the minimum of space within the bay. The maximum span of the tail surfaces of the new AIM-9X short-range

Below: The aircraft's air-to-air missiles are carried in internal bays. This 1990 test firing used an AIM-9 Sidewinder.

missile is only 17.3in (44cm), less than the 25.2in (64cm) of earlier versions, while the AIM-120C5 AMRAAM medium-range missile has the clipped wings and fins needed for internal carriage requirements on the F-22 Raptor and the Joint Strike Fighter. It incorporates a rocket motor which is 5in (12.7cm) longer than the previous motor, but a shortened control section for the moving tail surfaces keeps the overall missile length unchanged in order to maintain aircraft compatibility.

The air-to-air missiles are carried on and launched from launch adapt units (LAUs). The trapeze launcher for the Sidewinder is the LAU-141/A, while the AMRAAM Vertical Eject Launcher (AVEL) is the LAU-142/A.

The aircraft has a ground attack capability, so can carry and direct precision ground attack weapons such as the GBU-32 Joint Direct Attack Munition (JDAM). This is carried and released from a BRU-47/A bomb release unit in the main weapons bay.

The USAF plans to procure 339 production F-22s, and production is scheduled to run until 2013, but this could be extended by export orders. Test and training F-22s will be assigned to the Air Force Flight Test Center at Edwards AFB, California, the Air Force Fighter Weapons School at Nellis AFB, Nevada, and the 325th Fighter Wing at Tyndall AFB, Florida, but the operational locations for the F-22 force have not yet been announced.

Boeing X-32

Length overall: 45ft (13.7m)
Wingspan (CTOL): 36ft (11.0m)
(STOVL): 30ft (9.1m)

Lockheed Martin X-35

Length overall: 50ft 9in (15.47m)
Wingspan (STOVL): 33ft 0in
(10.05m (33 ft 0 in)

The US Joint Strike Fighter (JSF) is the largest military aircraft programme ever planned in the West; it is also one of the most ambitious. Like the controversial Tactical Fighter Experimental (TF-X) programme of the early 1960s (which produced the General Dynamics F-111), it attempts to create a

high-performance design able to meet the requirements of land and naval operations but, to make life more difficult, it also plans to incorporate short-take-off/vertical landing (STOVL) capability, affordable and easy-to-maintain stealth, and an affordable price-tag.

The prize which Boeing and Lockheed Martin are competing for is a possible production run of around 3000 aircraft – around 2,000 for the US Air Force, 600 for the US Marine Corps, 300 for the US Navy, and 90 for Britain's Royal Navy. This represents a massive series of orders, but each customer has a different requirement.

While the USAF needs an attack aircraft to replace the F-16,

the USN wants a stealthy long-range strike aircraft. Both would be conventional take-off and landing (CTOL) aircraft, but the USMC and the Royal Navy are looking for a STOVL aircraft able to replace the AV-8B and Sea Harrier, respectively. Both teams competing for the job of building the JSF also envisage large export orders from nations needing to replace aircraft such as the F-16 and early-model F-18.

The JSF requirement is specifying what is essentially a CTOL strike aircraft with a tactical radius of more than 600nm, and a STOVL variant with a tactical radius of 450-500nm. Both should have a maximum speed of Mach 1.5, and a manoeuvrability comparable with that of the aircraft they will replace.

The two aircraft that Boeing manufactured were to a design which the company calls Configuration 372. This has a modified delta planform and twin fins. Both are powered by a single Pratt & Whitney JSF119-614 turbofan engine, a modified and refanned derivative of the F119 engine used in the F-22 Raptor. While these were taking shape, the company continued to refine its design, producing Configuration 373 with a smaller, swept wing, and with new horizontal tail surfaces in

Left: **Lockheed's X-32 will win no prizes for visual appearance, but the design is intended to combine stealth and affordability.**

addition to two outward-canted fins. This was further refined in Configurations 374 and 375, the first of which introduced a new backward-swept straight trailing-edge for the wing, while the second incorporated weight-saving measures needed to make sure that the STOVL variant could land while carrying a 4,000lb (1,800kg) payload.

The CTOL version of the aircraft would have a full-span wing with cambered leading edges and leading-edge flaps on the outer wing sections, but to save weight the STOVL version would have a wing of reduced span. Neither version incorporates wing folding. Production CTOL aircraft would be powered by the -614C version of the engine, while the STOVL would have the -614S version which incorporates a Rolls-Royce lift module and spool duct. There is no auxiliary lift system in the STOVL version of the aircraft; most of the engine exhaust is ducted forward to two retractable nozzles. The engine receives air via a chin inlet with a short duct. This does not provide the line-of-sight blockage needed to screen the front face of the engine from hostile radars, but the fact that photographs of the JSF radar cross-section model have been censored to obscure the inlet duct suggests that Boeing may have developed some novel method of screening the engines.

The Boeing design uses side-

Left: Full-scale mock-up of the X-35 Joint Strike Fighter proposal on the Lockheed Martin Tactical Aircraft Systems flight line.

Right: The version of the Boeing JSF designed for USAF use will not have the auxiliary lift system planned for the STOVL version.

mounted weapon bays. These will give ground crews eye-level access for maintenance and weapons loading. They will also allow the pilot to open the bay on the side of the aircraft away from enemy radar and drop a weapon without compromising the JSF's low observability. The bay design was tested in January 2001 when USAF test pilot Lt. Col. Edward Cabrera opened and cycled the X-32A's weapons bay doors as part of vibration and acoustic testing during the aircraft's 61st flight. For these tests, the aircraft carried an instrumented AIM-120 AMRAAM and a Joint Direct Attack Munition (JDAM).

Lockheed Martin's X-35 design is more conventional in appearance, and bears some resemblance to the F-22. The X-35A demonstrator was used to test Configuration 230A, which is intended to meet the USAF requirement, and was then upgraded to the X-35B standard to test Configuration 230B, the STOVL configuration being proposed for the USMC and the Royal Navy. The RN version would be similar to the USMC version, but would have folding wings. The second aircraft was built as an X-35C to test Configuration 230C for the US Navy.

All three variants use versions of the Pratt & Whitney JSF119-PW-611 derivative) turbofan. The -611C version planned for USAF and USN aircraft has an axisymmetric (thrust-vectoring) exhaust nozzle, while the STOVL variants would use the -611S version. This has a Rolls-Royce-developed three-bearing swivel-duct nozzle which can deflect the thrust downwards, while a Rolls-Royce lifting fan located behind the cockpit and driven by a shaft from the main engine increases the bypass ratio and thrust of the engine in the hover mode, balancing the aircraft via a rear vectoring nozzle. A bleed-air reaction control valve in each wingroot provides stability at low speeds.

On CTOL aircraft, extra fuel would be carried in the space taken up by the lift fan and shaft on the STOVL versions. Changes to the USN version include a wing, fin and elevator whose areas have been increased by extending the chord. The wing would fold, and have ailerons as well as flaperons, the control surfaces would be enlarged, and the landing gear strengthened. All versions would carry ordnance in internal weapons bays.

Both JSF candidates have been designed to be stealthy. The required RCS is about that of a golf-ball-sized metal sphere. While aircraft such as the F-117A and B-2 require large amounts of careful maintenance in order to maintain low RCS, the JSF is intended to be easy to maintain. This will involve the use of low-observables which are durable and easy to repair if damaged.

Given the degree to which the US tightly controls access of stealth technology, the JSF programme faces problems on the export market. One possible solution is that the selected aircraft may be built in stealthy and semi-stealthy versions, and perhaps even in a non-stealthy version.

Both designs flew for the first time during 2000. Boeing's CTOL X-32A made its first flight on 28 September, but the STOVL X-32B had yet to fly in early 2001. The Lockheed Martin X-35A flew on 24 October 2000, and was due to complete a series of flight tests before being grounded and converted to the STOVL X-35B standard. In Spring 2001 both companies were test-flying Concept Demonstration Aircraft (CDA).

The UK committed $200 million in funding to the concept demonstration phase of the JSF programme, and under the terms of a US/UK Memorandum of Understanding (MoU) signed in January 2001, the UK will participate in the formal evaluation process of the rival designs. British industry is also expected to receive about 10 per cent of the work in the EMD programme.

The winning design will not be selected until both teams have clocked up 20 flight hours on their STOVL designs, and in October 2000 Pentagon procurement chief Dr. Jacques Gansler expressed concern that the programme could be delayed if either contractor had problems with STOVL technology. In earlier comments, he had indicated that if either team failed to achieve STOVL flight, that design could "self-eliminate".

MIKOYAN 1.42 AND 1.44

Rôle: multi-role fighter (1.42);
technology demonstrator (1.44)
Length: 74ft 10.75in (22.83m)
Wingspan: 55ft 10.5in (17.03m)
Height overall: 18ft 9.25in
(5.72m)
Max. takeoff weight: 77,200lb
(35,000kg)
**Max. speed (high-altitude;
clean):** Mach 2.6
Service ceiling: 65,600ft
(20,000m)
Range: 2,429nm (4,500km)
Powerplant: Two Saturn/Lyulka
AL-41F turbofans each of
c39,350lb (17,850kg) with
afterburning

In 1983 the Russian Air Force
released its requirement for an
MFI (*mnogofunktsionalnyy
frontovoy istrebitel*:
multifunctional front-line
fighter). The USAF had issued its
own request for information on
what would become the
Advanced Tactical Fighter two
years earlier, and awarded
concept-definition study
contracts in September 1983, so
the two programmes were
started on similar timescales.

Having completed
preliminary design studies in
1985, Mikoyan were given final
performance requirements in
1988 and started work on the
1.42 in 1989. The resulting design
is a large, twin-engined, canard
delta with widely spaced
outward-canted twin tailfins.
Like other agile canard deltas,
the Russian aircraft requires a
fly-by-wire system. This is a
KSU-142 quadruplex digital
system which may be derived
from the BTsK-29 system flown
on MiG-29E testbed.

Work on a suitable
powerplant started in 1985. This
would offer performance better
than that of any fighter engine of
the time, and have the lowest-
possible number of parts to
improve reliability. The resulting
Saturn/Lyulka two-shaft
variable-bypass turbofan was
running on the bench by the
early 1990s.

To prove the basic design, a
technology-demonstrator
designated 1.44 was devised.
This would test the
aerodynamics, performance, and
integrated flight/power plant
control system of the planned
1.44 so would carry no weapons
or mission systems. The 1.44
does not have the double-delta
wing featured on MiG artist's
impressions of future fighters
and expected to be used on the
MFI. According to Russian
officials the definitive 1.42 design
would have better aerodynamic
characteristics than the
Lockheed Martin F-22, and be
able to fly faster, reaching
speeds of up to Mach 2.6, and
cruising at Mach 1.6 - 1.8 without
afterburner.

Stealth was obviously a

requirement for the new fighter.
In 1995 *Jane's International
Defense Review* quoted MiG
bureau general designer
Rostislav Belyakov as saying that
"any aircraft delivered around
the end of the century that does
not fully incorporate stealth does
not have a chance of success".
But this should not result in
performance penalties, he
insisted. A future fighter "should
not lose any of its flight
performance for the benefit of
stealth".

The structure of the 1.44
makes extensive use of radar-
absorbent coatings, and it has
been conjectured that
production examples of the
definitive 1.42 could be fitted
with the Keldysh Research
Centre's "plasma cloud" stealth
system Some observers believe
that a plasma system has been
installed on the 1.44, but the
probes which they see as being
plasma sources are more likely
to be associated with flight-test
instrumentation, or with the
aircraft's fly-by-wire flight-control
system.

Four side-by-side shallow
troughs below the fuselage of
the 1.44 are believed to be semi-
conformal missile carriage
stations, but the 1.42 is expected
to have one or more internal
weapons bays which would
allow the carriage of air-to-air
missiles.

Progress with the 1.44 was
slow. Although completed in
1991, the first prototype had to
wait for engines to become
available, and was not delivered
to the flight test facility at
Zhukovsky until mid-1994. Some
fast taxi trials were undertaken
late that year, and some reports

suggest these included an
aborted take-off. The aircraft was
then placed in storage. Various
reports attributed its fate to non-
availability of flight-rated
Saturn/Lyulka AL-41F engines,
problems with the flight control
actuators, or simple lack of
money. Work on the aircraft and
its powerplant had been
effectively halted when funding
dried up.

By this time, such a heavy
and potentially expensive
aircraft had little attraction for
the cash-strapped Russian Air
Force, which in 1996 had been
able to purchase only a single
new combat aircraft. In March
1997, the ITAR-Tass news agency
quoted unidentified Russian
government officials as saying
that cash constraints had
precluded further development
work.

The aircraft was shown to
VIPs on 24 August 1997, and in
February of the following year
Mikoyan officials claimed that
the Russian Air Force was
prepared to fund flight tests, and
that the aircraft would fly in
August. Both hopes proved vain.

In the autumn of 1998
development funding for the
AL-41F turbofan finally became
available, allowing engine
development to proceed. First
photographs of the 1.44 were
released in December 1998, and
a month later it was displayed to

the press at Zhukovsky. It finally
flew on 29 February 2000. It is
still possible that the 1.44 or the
planned 1.42 version could be
adopted by the Russian Air
Force, though the reported
price-tag of around US$70
million could limit any
production run.

At the press demonstration
in January 1999, Mikhail
Korzhuyev, general director of
what was now the Aviatsionnyi
Nauchno-Promyshlennyi
Komplex (ANPK) MiG, said that
the 1.44 was not a commercial
programme, but would form the
basis of "a new fighter that will
be smaller and cheaper, but not
worse, than the MFI".

This new design could result
from studied of the proposed
I-2000 LFS (*legkiy frontovoy
samolyot*) lightweight fighter,
which is expected to be jointly
developed by Mikoyan, Sukhoi
and Yakovlev. The LFS is

Left: **If the 1.44 is developed into
an operational fighter, its
flattened nose would be used to
house a next-generation phased
array radar.**

Below: **On paper, the 1.42/44 looks like an effective counter to the US Air Force's F-22, but the chronic shortage of defence funds in Russia makes it unlikely that such a heavy and costly fighter will be adopted for service. A new lighter-weight design will probably be flown within the next five years.**

expected to meet any of the performance goals originally set for the MFI, but with a smaller aircraft offering lower operating costs. It is expected to combine radar and infrared stealth with high manoeuvrability and short take-off and landing characteristics.

For the moment, the best fighter that Russia can offer is the MiG-29SMT-2. Flown for the first time in April 2000, this is fitted with a Phazotron Zhuk-M fire-control radar, Ramenskoye MFI-9 multifunction liquid crystal displays, and a 2,000-litre conformal fuel tank installed over the fuselage spine. New radar-dissipating coatings reduce RCS to around 1 square metre. A similar MiG-29SMT upgrade uses avionics from the Russkaya Avionika company.

SUKHOI S-37 BERKUT (GOLDEN EAGLE)

Length overall: 74ft (22.6m)
Wingspan: 55ft (16.7m)
Height 21ft (6.4m)
Max. take-off weight: 74,960lb (34,000kg)
Max. speed: Mach 2.1
Service ceiling: 59,000ft (18,000m)
Powerplant: two Aviadvigatel D-30F6 turbofans each of 20,930lb (9,490kg) dry and 34,392lb (15,600kg) with afterburning

In the late 1980s, the Sukhoi design bureau started work on a technology demonstration aircraft with a forward-swept wing (FSW). This was a private-venture project funded by payments received from export sales of the Su-27.

Russian interest in FSW technology probably started in the late 1970s. According to Valery Sukhanov, deputy head of the Russian Central Aero-Hydrodynamics Institute (TsAGI), during the 1980s work on FSW designs in the former Soviet Union and the USA had been going on "practically in parallel".

By 1982 an earlier (FSW) demonstrator is reported to have been tested at Saki test airfield, and may have been evaluated by the Russian Navy for possible carrier-borne use. It seems to have been rejected, as was a rival aircraft based on the MiG-23. The first carrier-based fighter other than the semi-experimental Yak-38 was to be the Su-33 derivative of the Su-27.

The S-37 Berkut which took shape in the mid-1990s was intended to explore post-stall manoeuvrability and "supermanoeuvrability" which could be applied to future fighters. It combines forward-swept ring wings, a short-span tailplane, and broad chord broad-chord foreplanes. The horizontal tail surfaces are of the traditional all-moving pattern, but the canard foreplanes may operate differentially or in unison. The configuration has been described as an "integrated triplane".

Wherever possible the aircraft uses major sub-assembles from the Su-27 series, such as tailfins, canopy, and landing gear. A forward-swept wing needs high stiffness, so the S-37 wing is made almost entirely from composites. The flight-control system is probably based on the quadruplex digital FBW system used on the Su-35 and Su-37.

The aircraft is powered by two Aviadvigatel D-30F6 two-shaft turbofans. This engine was originally developed in the 1970s to power the MiG-31. The version used on the S-37 is probably identical to that for the MiG interceptor, which has

completed several hundred thousand flight hours.

According to TsAGI, the combination of FSW and thrust-vectoring gives better control at high angles of attack, and super-manoeuvrability at subsonic speeds. However, the current engines do not have vectoring nozzles. At some stage in the flight-test programme the D-30F6 engines could be replaced with the Soyuz R-79M turbofans (a developed version of the R-79-300 which powered the Yak-141 supersonic V/STOL fighter), Saturn/Lyulka AL-37FU turbofans with two-dimensional vectoring nozzles (developed for the Su-35 technology demonstrator), or by the Saturn/Lyulka AL-41F AL-41F engine from the MiG 1.44/42.

The aircraft may have started life as the Su-32, but had been renumbered when the original S-37 concept was cancelled in 1994 when it failed to attract Russian or export backing. (This was to have been a stealthy long-range multirole aircraft similar in configuration to the Rafale, but single-engined.)

Although the S-37 was intended to be technology demonstrator, the designers made provision for the future installation of the mission

equipment and systems which would be needed to turn the aircraft into a prototype heavy twin-engined fighter. For example, it has forward- and aft-facing radomes, a vented gun bay with cannon port, a dummy IRST installation ahead of windscreen, and dielectric panels in the leading edges of the foreplanes, LERX, and tail surfaces which could be used to house EW antennas. The aircraft is reported to be fitted for conformal weapons carriage,

which would reduce RCS.

The design also incorporates other low-RCS features which would not be required in a pure technology demonstrator. The structure incorporates radar-absorbent materials, the twin tailfins are canted outwards to reduce front-sector RCS, the air

intakes are shaped to reduce radar reflectivity, and connect to the twin Aviadvigatel D-30F6 turbofans via S-shaped internal ducting which would screen the front faces of engine from forward-sector radar threats. Redesigned engine nozzles may be configured to help cool the engine efflux, reducing the aircraft's IR signature.

Compared with the Su-27 family of fighters, the S37 has "a lower radar signature from the front hemisphere", according to an ITAR-TASS publication

released at the 1997 Dubai air show. This also stated that the aircraft incorporated "a coating of radar absorbent materials". The first example flew for the first time at the Zhukovsky test centre on 25 September 1997, but after only eight flights was grounded in late November 1997 for modifications. The tailplane was increased in span and area, the engine installation was refined, and the avionics updated. Following these changes, flight testing was resumed, and the aircraft was

publicly displayed at the August 1999 Aviation Day at Tushino.

Although Sukhoi promoted the aircraft as an alternative to the Mikoyan 1.44/42, it seems to have attracted little interest from the Russian Air Force, though there have been suggestions that the S-37 and the 1.44 could undergo a competitive fly-off. Even if the aircraft is not adopted for service, it has tested spin-off technologies which could be used to improve or upgrade the existing Su-27 series and its derivatives.

Below: **The Sukhoi bureau makes no secret of its wish to see the S-37 Berkut adopted as an operational fighter, and the prototype has been designed for rapid conversion to a combat role. To date, the Russian Air Force has shown little enthusiasm for the concept.**

Below: **The complex planform adopted for the S-37 has led to the aircraft being described as an "integrated triplane".**

BOEING SIKORSKY RAH-66 COMANCHE

Rôle: reconnaissance/attack and air combat helicopter
Length (fuselage): 43ft 3.75in (13.20m)
Main rotor diameter: 40ft 0in (12.19m)
Empty weight: 8,951lb (4,060kg)
Take-off weight (primary mission): 11,632lb (5,276kg)
Max speed: 172kt (319km/h)
Tactical radius (internal fuel): 150nm (278km)
Armament: three Hellfire or six Stinger missiles or other weapons in each of two weapons bays; four more Hellfires or eight Stingers on optional stub-wings; General Dynamics XM-301 three-barrel 20mm cannon in an undernose turret
Powerplant: two LHTEC T800-LHT-801 turboshafts each of 1,563shp (1,165kW)

The first combat helicopter designed to incorporate stealth technology, the RAH-66 Comanche is similar in size to the AH-64 Apache which it will replace. It will handle the US Army's scout/attack mission, but will also be able to engage in air-to-air combat.

Construction of the prototype began in November 1993, with Sikorsky building the forward fuselage at Stratford, and Boeing building the aft fuselage in Philadelphia. The two sections were mated at Stratford in January 1995, allowing the completed helicopter to be rolled out on 25 May 1995. The first flight was made from Sikorsky's Development Flight Test Center in West Palm Beach, Florida, on 4 January 1996. The second prototype flew in March 1999.

The airframe has a faceted configuration, and all armament is carried internally, features intended to reduce RCS. According to official statements, the frontal RCS is 360 times smaller than that of the AH-64,

250 times smaller than that of the OH-58D, and 32 times smaller than OH-58D with mast-mounted sight. RCS of the entire helicopter is lower than that of the AGM-114 Hellfire missile it fires. If necessary, detachable stub wings can be fitted to carry additional weapons or auxiliary fuel tanks, but this will degrade RCS.

Like all modern attack helicopters, the RAH-66 has features intended to blunt the effectiveness of infrared-guided missiles. The efflux from the aircraft's twin T800 engines is ducted through long, thin slots, then ejected beneath the chine that runs either side of the tail. Total level of IR emission is around a quarter that of the AH-64D, allowing the aircraft to enter service without a built-in IR jammer. (Provision has been made for the Advanced Threat Infrared Countermeasures system to be fitted as an upgrade.)

Measures have also been taken to reduce the acoustic signature. The five-blade all-composite main rotor system has noise-reducing anhedral tips (a feature first seen on the EMD aircraft), while the eight-blade tail rotor is of shrouded "fan-in-fin" type. Head-on, Comanche is six times quieter than the Apache.

The planned level of radar, infra-red, acoustic and visual signature are intended to defeat the future threat systems postulated by the US Army. The likely level of RCS was measured during 2001 using a

full-scale model of the aircraft which incorporated all the design changes that had been added since an earlier series of model tests.

As with the earlier AH-64 Apache, great attention has been given to survivability. The cockpit is fitted with side armour, and an optional armour kit is available for the cockpit floor, while the crew seats are designed to cope with the stresses of a 38ft/sec (11.6m/sec) vertical crash landing.

The nav/attack system will consist of a nose-mounted sight with IR and TV channels, plus a laser range-finder/designator. All aircraft will be fitted out to carry a miniaturised and further-developed version of the Longbow millimetric-wave radar carried by the AH-64D Longbow Apache, but only a third of the fleet will be equipped with this sensor. Defensive aids will include radar and laser warning receivers,

plus an RF jammer.

There has been some weight growth during development; by 1992 the original target of 7,500lb (3,402kg) for empty weight had been relaxed to 7,765lb (3,522kg) to accommodate additional subsystems demanded by the customer. The new anhedral-tipped main rotor blades devised to reduce the aircraft's acoustic signature are 12in (305mm) greater in diameter than the original pattern, allowing the aircraft to maintain its specified vertical rate of climb without the need for an expensive and time-consuming weight reduction programme. The original blades had a 15in (380mm) chord, but this was increased to provide additional survivability, and to allow the use of materials for

signature control which were not practical with the narrower chord.

Tail buffeting problems uncovered during flight-tests of the first prototype were found to be a result of the airflow from the main rotor mast impinging more strongly on the vertical tail than had been expected. A redesign slightly reduced the height of the vertical tail, and added vertical endplates to the horizontal stabilizer to compensate for any reduction in directional stability. Flight-tested in the winter of 2000/01, it produced no significant weight penalty, and did not degradation the aircraft's low-observable characteristics.

The upper part of the tail folds down for air transportation. Once the main rotor has been removed, eight Comanches can be loaded into a Lockheed C-5 Galaxy. On arrival, the main rotor is re-fitted and the tail unfolded, and the helicopter can be ready for flight only 20 minutes after being unloaded.

Engineering and manufacturing development (EMD) started in 2000 and is due to end in December 2006. This phase of the programme is expected to require 13 further aircraft – five for flight-testing and eight to be used in initial operational tests and evaluations.

The US Army plans to buy 1,096 Comanches. Before production is begun, the programme will undergo several reviews to assess aircraft weight, in-flight vibration levels, and progress with integrating the aircraft's radar and other mission equipment. Initial operational capability is expected in December 2006.

Above: **This drawing shows the RAH-66 with the definitive tailplane devised to cure buffeting problems. The aircraft's sloped fuselage sides and shrouded tail rotor all help keep RCS to a tiny fraction of that of the AH-64 Apache. The built-in stealth capability is intended to defeat all known and predicted threats.**

Right: **These stealthy hunters will be formidable anti-armour weapons, but cost will limit the numbers purchased.**

AIDS TO STEALTH

"Imagine a man with a powerful flashlight trying to find another man on a dark night", says Tom Amlie, former technical director of the China Lake Naval Weapons Center. "He might find him at 100-200 feet (30-60m). The other man can see the flashlight at a range of at least one-half mile (0.8km). To pursue the analogy a bit farther, if the second man has an automatic rifle and homicidal tendencies, the fellow with the flashlight could be in deep trouble."

It is a neat little story and one which formed part of Amlie's outspoken attack on the US over-dependence on radar, a central theme of a 1987 interview with *The Washington Post*. It is also a good analogy of the problem facing operators of stealth aircraft. The use of stealth technology to reduce the detectable signature of fighters and strike aircraft does much to reduce their vulnerability but, on its own, signature-reduction is not enough. The stealth aircraft's on-board systems must also be difficult to detect.

Ideally, a stealth fighter or bomber should emit no radar, radio, IR or EO energy which might betray its position. Many of the traditional avionics systems carried aboard military aircraft, such as high-powered radars, Doppler navaids, IFF transponders and conventional communications equipment, must be eliminated as far as possible and be replaced with stealthy equivalents. In practice, this will be hard to achieve. If passive replacements cannot be devised, the traditional equipment must be redesigned to keep the amplitude of its emissions as low as possible, preferably in areas of the spectrum less intensively monitored than the radio and radar bands.

RADARS

Most obvious candidate for redesign is the aircraft's radar. Conventional systems must give way to new Low Probability of Intercept (LPI) designs. Exact details of LPI

Above: Warplanes such as the F-15 Eagle rely on their powerful radars for target detection, but such easily-detectable emissions would betray a stealth fighter.

Below & Right: A stealthy low probability of intercept (LPI) radar will use long pulses of low amplitude rather than the more detectable but traditional short high-

amplitude pulses. Its antenna will also be designed to have a narrower beam and smaller sidelobes, so will offer less stray radiation to hostile ESM receivers.

Radar Waveforms

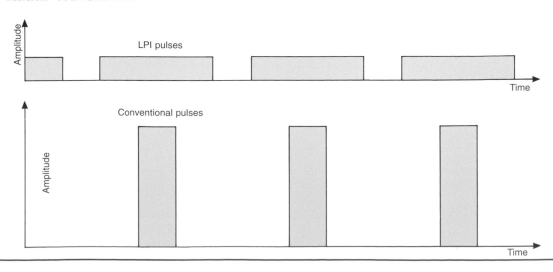

radar technology remain classified but many can be deduced.

For a start, the signal transmitted must be of a type which will be hard to detect by ESM. This involves using a wide-band waveform with a high duty cycle, ideally one which has noise-like characteristics. A conventional pulse radar has a low duty cycle and transmits powerful but narrow pulses of energy. A high duty cycle radar will transmit much longer pulses, but at a lower power level, and will spread this radiated energy over a

wide range of frequencies in the hope that it will become inconspicuous to an enemy ESM system effectively "buried" among the normal background of civil and military radar signals and communications links which clutter the microwave region.

The technique is not as simple as it sounds. One advantage of a low duty cycle is that the radar's receiver can listen for the returned echo at times when the transmitter is silent and can thus share the same antenna. The LPI radar will have to transmit and receive at the same time, so

must either use two antennas or rely on sophisticated signal processing.

To further reduce the chances of the signal being intercepted by an ESM system, it must be confined to the narrowest beam which will meet the tactical requirements for which the radar is designed. The use of a high frequency will give the narrowest possible beam from an antenna of fixed dimensions, while careful antenna design will minimise the size of the sidelobes (unwanted minor beams at different angles).

Above: **By means of the JTIDS data link, E-3 Sentry aircraft will be able to pass target information to NATO fighters, allowing the latter to avoid using radar.**

In the long run, it will be impossible to disguise a LPI radar's powerful (albeit much narrowed) main beam but denying the enemy any chance to exploit sidelobe radiation will be a major step forward. The chances of main-beam detection will be reduced largely by transmitting only in short occasional bursts, retaining the radar "snapshot" between transmissions, and updating target tracks by dead reckoning.

In an air battle involving stealth fighters, it is likely that at any one time only a few aircraft – AEW platforms and some long-range interceptors – would rely on active radar. Using LPI communications, these aircraft would pass target data to the others. It is possible to imagine tactics in which each stealth fighter in turn might use its own radar for a few seconds, then jink onto a new course while transmitting target information to the rest of the formation. Next generation radars such as those proposed for EFA and Rafale have a

Radar Beam Shapes

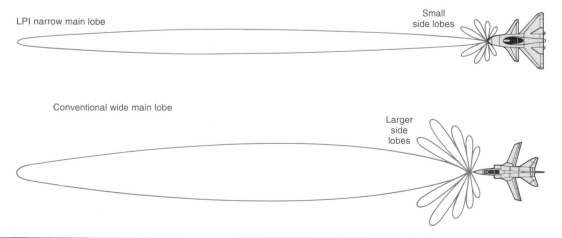

LPI narrow main lobe

Small side lobes

Conventional wide main lobe

Larger side lobes

large number of operating modes. Switching rapidly from one to another may help complicate the task faced by an enemy ESM system.

B-2 SYSTEMS

The F-117A relies entirely on electro-optics for target location and weapon-aiming, but for the B-2, Raytheon Electronic Systems developed the J-band AN/APQ-181. This low probability of intercept radar has 21 operating modes for terrain-following and terrain-avoidance; navigation system updates; target search, location, identification and acquisition; and weapon delivery.

Each B-2A carries two 2,100lb (953kg) radars, each made up of ten line-replaceable units (LRUs) including two electronically scanned antennas. The LRUs are mounted in the walls of the nose-wheel well, while the antennas are behind large radomes close to the aircraft centreline and just below the leading edge. To ensure mission reliability, all LRUs apart from the antennas are able to function as part of either or both radars.

F-22 RADAR

For the Lockheed Martin F-22, Northrop Grumman is developing the AN/APG-77 multimode radar. This uses an active electronically-scanned antenna made up of around 2,000 individual transmit/receive modules, and makes extensive use of Monolithic Microwave Integrated Circuit (MMIC) and Very High-Speed Integrated Circuit (VHSIC) technologies. Operating modes are reported to allow long-range detection of air targets (including stealth aircraft) in all weathers, target recognition, multi-missile multi-target engagement, and dogfight engagements. The radar is designed to cope with heavy clutter environments, and offers advanced air-to-surface operating modes.

With the F-22, the boundaries between radar and EW begin to blur. The AN/APG-77 is reported to have a high-gain, passive listening mode which covers a bandwidth or around 2 GHz in the forward sector. At a range of around 120 miles (190km), the AN/APG-77 is reported to have an 86 per cent probability of detecting a target with an RCS of 1sq m with only a single radar "paint" which would give the target aircraft's radar-warning receiver a minimal signal to detect. An Ultra High-Resolution (UHR) mode used for target recognition is said to have a resolution of 12in (30cm) at a range of around 100 miles

(160km), more than enough for non-co-operative target recognition.

The F-22 will not be the first fighter to offer passive identification of non co-operating targets. Under the MSIP (Multi-Staged Improvement Program) upgrades applied to the F-14 Tomcat and F-15 Eagle, both aircraft are being given a degree of passive target identification. This area is highly-classified but is largely a matter of signal processing. There is a relationship between target shape and the characteristics of the reflected wave, so inverse scattering is one of the few clues which will allow a radar to identify a beyond-visual-range target.

Aircraft approaching head-

on may be identified by analysis of the radar returns from the engine inlets, since the signal will have been modulated by the spinning blades of the first-stage of the engine fan/compressor. Such modulation effects have been known for some time. The huge contra-rotating propellers on the Kuznetsov engines fitted to the Tu-95 and -142 Bear aircraft made them easily-recognisable radar targets on analogue radar displays, while early tests of the APG-63 radar used in the F-15 Eagle showed that the modulated radar return from the engine compressors could be interpreted by the radar as a multiple target.

Above: **During this Dornier trial, an experimental laser radar produces recognisable images of a group of vehicles.**

Above right: **In-flight refuelling extends the range of the B-2, giving the numerically small force a global reach.**

Below: **The massive contra-rotating propellers on the Tupolev Bear create a distinctive and recognisable echo on western radars.**

Below right: **This Thomson-CSF photo is an example of the high-resolution imagery available from a radar which uses SAR techniques.**

LASER RADAR

Many of the problems associated with microwave radar can be eliminated by using a laser radar. The very narrow beam beam would be difficult to detect, and would have no sidelobes through which energy could leak. Performance would be dependent on weather, and laser radars would be of short range. Air-to-ground seems a more likely role than air-to-air. By scanning the terrain ahead of the aircraft, the laser radar would be able to build up an image of FLIR-like quality, also obtaining range and velocity information which could be used for targeting and terrain following.

One of the first equipments of this type was developed by Hughes in conjunction with General Dynamics. Although intended for use in cruise missile guidance systems, it clearly could be used in place of a conventional terrain-following radar. Trials have shown that a laser radar has a better resolution than that available from millimetre-wave seekers or even thermal imagers, says Hughes. Tests have shown that it can detect trees and electricity pylons.

EO SYSTEMS

In the past, some aircraft have used, infra-red or other types of electro-optical sensor for target recognition and fire-control purposes. Examples include the AAA-4 IR sensor on early-model Phantoms, the ASX-1 Tiseo ('Target Identification System Electro-Optical) in the wing leading edge of some F-4Es, and the EO systems in the nose of the MiG-29 and Su-27.

On a conventional fighter, the EO system is a secondary sensor, but the passive nature of

EO systems make them ideal for use of stealth fighters. For the F-117A, Texas Instruments developed a forward-looking infra-red (FLIR) sensor, and a downward-looking infra-red (DLIR) sensor and a laser designator. Mounted in a cavity in the upper nose, the FLIR had two fields of view, and was shielded from enemy radar by a fine mesh screen. The DLIR and laser designator were located beneath the forward fuselage to starboard of the nosewheel bay. FLIR and DLIR imagery was viewed on a large cockpit-mounted head-down display located between the aircraft's two multifunction CRT displays. Targets were initially detected by the FLIR, then at closer range were

"handed over" to the DLIR, with the laser being used for ranging and target-illumination.

In the mid-1990s, the existing TI sensors were replaced by a involved new turret-mounted Infra-Red Acquisition and Designation Sensor (IRADS).

DIGITAL MAPS

Radar is also widely used as a navaid and as a method of steering the aircraft in terrain following flight. FLIR systems are one passive alternative to radar but the pilot tasked with manually flying a long mission at very low level using only the small field of view presented by FLIR-derived HUD imagery has an

unenviable task. The development of powerful airborne computers has made possible a stealthy replacement for the conventional terrain-following radar. Known as terrain-reference navigation (TRN), this relies on careful measurement of the profile of the terrain passing beneath the aircraft and its comparison with digitally-stored geographic data.

Measurement of the terrain is done using a radar altimeter. At first sight this might seem a weak point of the system, particularly if fitted to a stealth aircraft. In practice, radar altimeters have a narrow beam-width and low power output, directing their energy downwards rather than forwards, so are thus a poor target for enemy ESM systems.

DATABASES

A conventional terrain-following radar (TFR) can only "see" the terrain ahead of the aircraft and within radar range. It has no information on terrain concealed by ridge lines. This is not shown until the aircraft has reached a position where the radar beam can illuminate the concealed terrain. Thanks to its database, a TRN system "knows" the terrain over which it is flying and can predict the profile of the ground well ahead of the aircraft's current position, even if this region is

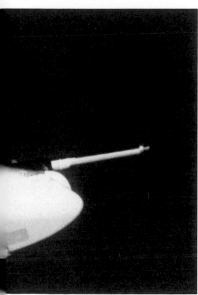

concealed by a ridge or peak. By using this information, the TRN system can initiate pull-up and descent manoeuvres at the optimum time, minimising sudden unwanted gains in height (or "ballooning") of the aircraft flight path.

TRN obviously requires terrain irregularities in order to "fingerprint" and identify its current location. Deprived of these irregularities when flying over water or flat ground, the system must rely on INS data. The use of Kalman filtering (powerful software for combining multiple inputs) allows gyro drift to be estimated, maintaining system accuracy until TRN-suitable ground is once more overflown. The accuracy of a good TRN system is a few tens of metres in the horizontal plane, and about 10 to 20ft (3 to 6m) vertically.

NAVAIDS

For routine navigation of long-range stealth aircraft such as the B-2, other passive navaids are required. Over a long mission, an inertial navigation system slowly drifts, building up and ever-increasing error. Two decades ago this could only be removed by obtaining an accurate positional fix, but modern navigation systems team INS with an integrated satellite-navigation receiver. The accuracy of the encrypted P-code signal from the US Global Positioning System (GPS) satellites is higher than that from the C/A-code signal used by civilian receivers, so aircraft fly using satnav data and rely on the INS only if the satellite signals are lost due to jamming or sharp aircraft manoeuvres.

Until the late 1980s, few individuals outside the highly classified world of "black" programmes realised that Lockheed-Sanders had become a major player in the new field of automatic mission planning. The concept had been born a year after the F-117A entered service, when a group of Lockheed engineers developed a system in only 120 days. Based on two computers loaded with geographic, intelligence, aircraft and weapon data, the system can plan sorties, routing the F-117A around the most dangerous threats, and bringing it over the target at the specified time. To maximise the effectiveness of the aircraft's low-observable features, the system generates a flight path that carefully orientates the aircraft to maximise its stealthiness in the direction of the most dangerous radar or SAM systems.

Automatic mission planning is also important for the B-2A. First introduced as part of the block 30 upgrade to the B-2A, the AFMSS provides the crew with the most effective routing that will accomplish the mission while providing the highest survivability. The system was initially unsatisfactory, but an upgrade which included a new computer with faster speeds and new software was intended to correct most of the deficiencies identified during initial operational testing. A March 1999 B-2A follow-on test and evaluation report showed that a software component known as the common low observable auto-router (CLOAR) still had deficiencies. While the upgraded AFMSS was capable

Right: **Originally used by helicopter aircrew, night vision goggles (NVG) are a stealthy alternative to terrain-warning radar.**

Above: **Hughes APG-65 radar for the F-18 uses target-recognition software whose algorithms are kept secret by the US Government.**

of planning most B-2A missions within the eight-hour operational requirement, the CLOAR shortcomings would extend the time taken to plan some missions to ten hours. Although new CLOAR software was developed for delivery to the operational B-2A wing by early 2000, the USAF accepted that even with the CLOAR improvements there would be some small percentage of missions that could take longer than 8 hours to plan because of the complexity of these missions and their plans.

Above: **Electro-optics in action: this F-4 Phantom is fitted with a wing-mounted TISEO TV sensor, and carries a GBU-15 "smart" bomb.**

ESM SYSTEMS

Since stealth aircraft operate passively for most of the time, they will make extensive use of a sophisticated ESM system to warn the crew of nearby threats. A next-generation ESM system must be able to cope with radar, millimetre-wave, IR and laser threats. It must be able to determine the location and nature of all threat systems, warning aircrew if they are being tracked, have been targeted or are being engaged.

In the long run, it should be possible for stealth aircraft such as the F-22 to detect enemy fighters via ESM, then launch fire-and-forget missiles. Not until the missiles' active seekers were energised would the enemy pilot realise that he was under attack.

ESM plays a vital role in keeping the crew of a stealth aircraft aware of the location and identity of potential threats, allowing them to make adjustments to the mission plan to ensure survivability. On the F-117A, the pilot is warned of threats to the aircraft, and according to one report the ESM system is linked to the mechanism which opens the weapon bay doors. Since opening these adds a reflective surface (the door) and a cavity (the bay) to the lower surface of the aircraft, it temporarily strips the aircraft of its stealth qualities. If a dangerous threat is illuminating the aircraft, the ESM system reportedly prevents the door from opening.

The USAF spent over $740 million to develop the defensive avionics for the B-2, only to find that this did not provide the planned capability. Developmental and initial operational testing showed the

system either incorrectly identified threats or did not provide an accurate location of threats, significantly reducing the situational awareness to the crew. The USAF concluded that these deficiencies would be too costly to correct, and decided to modify the defensive avionics system to provide a useful capability, but less capability than had originally been considered necessary. A combination of effective tactics, mission planning, and low observability features would still provide adequate survivability, it believed. The failure of the defensive avionics to provide the crew with all of the intended situational awareness information did not prevent use of the B-2A in combat operations.

ESM needs to be backed up by a reliable missile-warning system able to detect passively guided rounds, or those whose radar parameters are unknown. First attempts to develop a system of this type involved specialised radar-warning receivers designed to detect

Below: **More than 300 USN F-14A Tomcats are fitted with a Northrop Television Camera Set (TCS) target identification system.**

Above: **The spherical housing ahead of the windshield of the MiG-29 houses stabilised optics shared by an IR sensor and laster rangefinder.**

Below: **This infra-red air-to-ground image of oil tanks shows the level of liquid in each. Such information can be useful during an attack.**

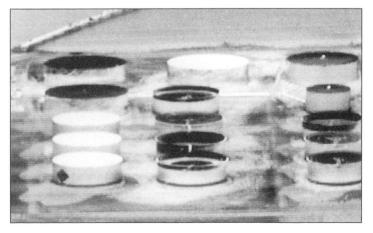

changes in radar threat signals which intelligence-gathering had identified as being indicative of SAM missile launch. Equipments of this type were designed to be effective against only one or two types of SAM. Creation of a more general-purpose missile warner initially relied on detecting the IR energy for the missile's rocket motor. Early equipments of this type were not very successful, and had a high false-alarm rate.

An obvious alternative was to use a low-powered aft-facing radar. One successful example is the Sanders ALQ-156, a tiny pulse Doppler radar which provides 360 degree coverage for US Army CH-47 Chinook helicopters. In the UK, Plessey developed the Missile Approach Warner (MAW) for use on the RAF's Harrier GR.5 (AV-8B) fighters. MAW is a low-powered pulse-Doppler radar, and has been designed to trigger the release of flares or other decoys at the optimum moment.

Active warners have two great operational advantages. They can detect unpowered projectiles such as anti-aircraft artillery rounds, and can measure range. Their Achilles heel is that they emit radar energy that might be detected by enemy ESM systems. Designers of radar warners try to keep the level of power emitted to an absolute minimum, but cannot eliminate this tell-tale energy.

In the long run, the future may belong to improved IR warners. The Honeywell Electro-Optics AAR-47 is fitted to some US P-3 Orions, helicopters and fixed-wing transports, and is also planned for the V-22 Osprey tilt-rotor. Honeywell is now working with General Dynamics to develop a version for use on the

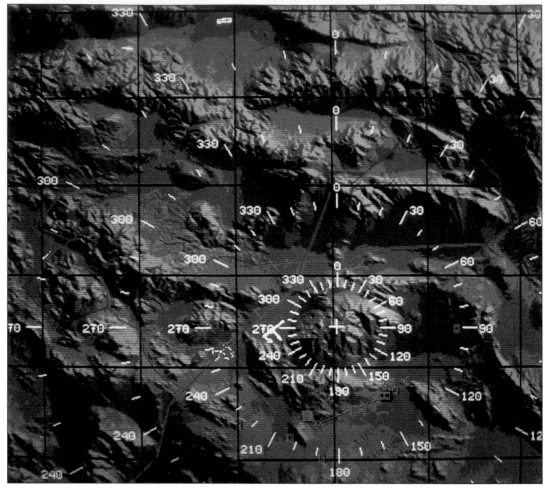

F-16 Fighting Falcon.

Data from both the ESM and missile-warner need to be integrated into a single display able to inform aircrew if they have been detected, tracked or engaged. Given a degree of artificial intelligence, such equipment might also be able to suggest the best countermeasure or mix of countermeasures.

Hughes Aircraft (now part of Raytheon) has devised a totally passive technique for locating hostile radar emitters. This is based on terrain reflections, so does not require direct line of sight to the emitter; all that is required is that there exist terrain areas that are mutually visible to both the hostile emitter and to the aircraft-mounted receiver. Tests using a brassboard system suggest that an operation version could

Above: **It's not necessary to own a spy satellite to create digital maps like these. TRN systems will work with Landsat or Spot data.**

locate non-co-operating emitters to within a CEP of less than 1,640ft (500m) independent of range and azimuth. Since no line of sight is required, the sensor would allow the pilot to locate radar

Terrain Following System

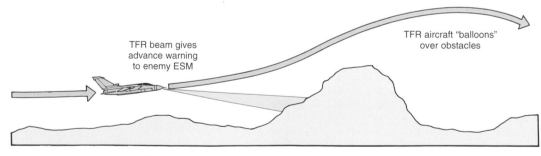

TFR beam gives advance warning to enemy ESM

TFR aircraft "balloons" over obstacles

Left and below: **A terrain-referenced navigation (TRN) system compares radar altimeter readings with pre-stored geographic data, so can pinpoint its location. An aircraft relying on terrain following radar will tend to gain height by "ballooning" over obstacles (top left), but the TRN-equipped aircraft (bottom left) can predict the terrain ahead, so can fly closer to the ground.**

Terrain Reference System

TRN signals give no advance warning

TRN aircraft anticipates future terrain contours

TRN Grid

TRN compares ground with stored database

AIDS TO STEALTH

Burn-Through Range

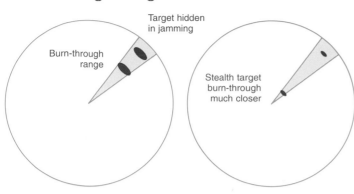

Above: Even when hidden by a jamming strobe, a target will eventually become visible once its echo is strong enough to burn through the jamming (left). Reduce target RCS and you reduce the echo strength. The target must come much closer (right) before the new burn-through range is reached.

threats before being exposed to them, giving him the chance to use terrain masking and avoid detection. Such a capability would reduce the tactical advantages normally obtained by deploying mobile air-defence systems whose position cannot be predicted by the attacker.

Reducing aircraft RCS provides advantages when designing self-protection jammers. Since most EW techniques rely on swamping the echo from the target with noise, or seducing the hostile radar away from the true target by providing it with an acceptable but false substitute, any reduction in the size of the genuine echo must be of benefit.

EW engineers use the term "J.S. ratio" to describe the ratio between the strength of the normal radar return from an aircraft and the signal which the hostile radar receives from the jammer. As the distance between the radar and the target is reduced, this ratio degrades, with the true echo becoming stronger and stronger until it is detectable through the jamming.

JAMMING

The term "burn-through range" is used by engineers to describe this vital distance at which the EW system gives no further protection. Its value depends on the power of the radar transmitter, the sensitivity of the receiver, the power of the jammer and the RCS of the target. The need to keep burn-through range as large as possible led Soviet designers to install a massive

Right: The Visually Coupled Airborne System Simulate programme was expected to provide technology for the cockpit of the YF-22/23 ATF.

600kW transmitter in the Fox Fire radar carried by the MiG-25 Foxbat.

If the RCS of an aircraft is reduced, the amount of jamming power needed to achieve the same burn-through range falls by the same amount. Since high levels of jamming power involve large, bulky and power-hungry transmitters, stealth is obviously good news for the designer of EW systems. If the aircraft plans to rely on the use of chaff rather than jamming, the reductions in the amount of chaff needed are similar to those for jamming power.

Over the life of the B-52, some $2,600 million has been spent on EW upgrades. The current system weighs about 5,500lb (2,500kg) and consists of 238 LRUs (line-replaceable units). Given that the B-1B has a radar echo only 1 per cent of that of the older bomber, it would at first sight seem reasonable to assume that the lower levels of jamming power needed would result in a lighter EW suite. In practice, the Rockwell aircraft carries about 5,000lb (2,250kg) of EW equipment, virtually no weight saving.

The likely reasons are not hard to guess. If RCS is reduced by a factor of four while keeping the amount of jamming power constant, the burn-through range will be halved. Reduce it by a factor of ten and the burn-through range will fall to less than a third; while an RCS of one

Right: On the B-52, high levels of jamming power were required to swamp the bomber's huge radar echo. Less power is needed to mask the B-1B's reflection, so the designers of this EW suite were able to allocate more weight to sophisticated signal processing.

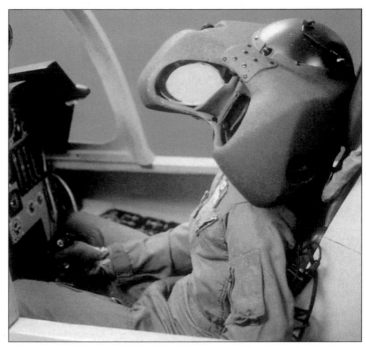

B-1B Defensive Avionics

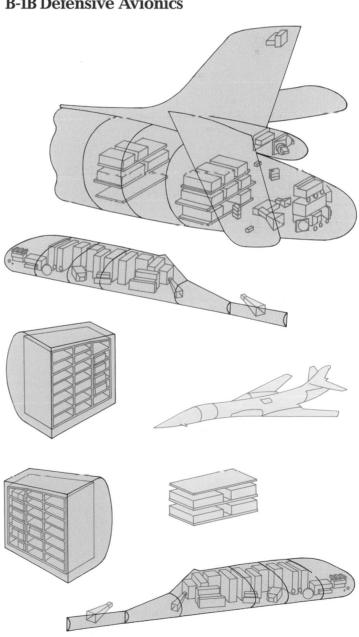

137

Above: Every four-vehicle battery of these SA-6 SAMs relies on a single Straight Flush radar, so is vulnerable to stealth.

Right: Flares remain an effective counter to IR-guided missiles, and are cheaper to develop and deploy than IR jammers.

hundredth of the original value will reduce burn-through range to a tenth of its original value.

Rather than accept all of the potential weight saving which a lower level of transmitter power would allow, the USAF will have opted to have extra power in hand in order to increase burn-through range well beyond that available to the B-52. The ALQ-161 system on the B-1B is also likely to devote more of its weight to signal-processing circuitry, allowing the use of the most advanced decption jamming techniques.

EW SYSTEMS

EW systems must be updated to adapt to the latest threat technologies. Even today no single EW technique can cope

with all types of radar-guided weapon. Next-generation ECM suites will have to incorporate the normal radar bands, plus millimetre waves and IR wavelengths. They will also be tightly co-ordinated both with the aircraft's ESM and missile-warning system and with the systems which release towed or expendable decoys.

Some indication of future trends in EW was provided in the spring of 1988 when French electronics giant Thomson-CSF revealed the direction which its own electronic-warfare efforts were taking. Stealth technology and low-level operations may reduce the vulnerability of future combat aircraft, explained Thomson-CSF Technical Director Pierre Baratault, but the importance

of electronic countermeasures is undiminished.

Low-peak radars, such as pulse Doppler radars and missiles fitted with solid-state active seekers, force an increase in EW receiver sensitivity, while new jamming techniques designed to counter techniques such as monopulse radars demand higher levels of transmitter power. "Detailed analysis of potential threats indicates that all of the most significant technical characteristics (of EW systems) will have to be increased by one or two orders of magnitude." To complicate the problem, these future high-power transmitters and sensitive receivers will be required to operate simultaneously.

Radar, IR and laser warning systems, jammers and decoys must be integrated into a coherent defensive system, which in turn must be fully integrated into the aircraft which carries it.

TOWED DECOYS

One relatively new type of EW system is the towed decoy. Widely used by warships since the early 1940s as a method of countering acoustic homing torpedoes, towed decoys were not seriously promoted for aircraft use until the late 1980s. These devices take the form of a small radar jammer towed behind the aircraft it is protecting. Being vulnerable to destruction or accidental loss, this is kept as simple as possible, with most of the signal processing being carried out by avionics mounted within the aircraft and linked to the decoy via the towing cable.

The current US towed decoy is the E-Systems ALE-50, which was selected for use on the FA-18E/F, B-1B, and F-16. The aircraft-mounted hardware includes the onboard techniques generator, a sub-system that combines a receiver and a

Left: This *Luftwaffe* Tornado has a BOZ chaff pod and Cerberus jammer. Stealth aircraft will also require EW systems.

Right: Matra developed the Sycomor chaff-dispensing pod for use on fighters such as the Mirage F1, but it could also be used to protect Rafale.

processor. The jamming modulations devised by the techniques generator are converted from electrical signals into pulses of light, which pass down a fibre optic towing cable, and control a travelling-wave-tube (TWT) transmitter in the decoy. The fuselage-mounted receiver will monitor the signals from the threat being jammed, and can use the resulting information to refine the jamming signals being sent to be decoy.

Similar decoys are being developed in Europe. GEC Marconi (now part of BAE Systems) started development work on towed decoys in the mid-1980s and the resulting Ariel decoy entered service on the British Aerospace Nimrod in 1990. The company has already tested towed decoys at supersonic speeds using Tornado trials aircraft, and is responsible for the wingtip-mounted towed decoy which forms part of the defensive aids sub-system (DASS) of the Eurofighter 2000.

The Swedish company CelsiusTech has developed the BO2D towed decoy to provide protection against radar-guided missiles which use Doppler signal-processing. After release, it acts as a wide-band repeater jammer which can be turned on or off and switched from one mode to another by signals sent down the tow line by the aircraft. BO2D operates in H, I and J bands, and can counter several Doppler-based threats simultaneously.

Although Daimler-Benz Aerospace is developing a towed decoy, this does not form part of the current Kampfwertanpassung/Kampfw erterhaltung (KWA/KWE) mid-life improvement programme for Luftwaffe Tornado IDS, but is likely to be fitted as a future upgrade. Suitable for use on fighters or transports, and for installation in existing EW pods, it uses a monopulse angle jamming technique.

For a long time the primary threat to aircraft was seen as being radar-guided weapons, so the bulk of Western EW funding was applied to the creation of RWRs and radar jammers. This was the result of the large-scale use of SA-2, SA-3 and SA-6 missiles in the conflicts of the 1960s and 1970s. A recent US Department of Defense study of combat losses in the decade from 1975 to 1985 revealed that 90 per cent of the tactical aircraft downed fell to IR-guided air-to-air missiles or IR-guided SAMs.

CHAFF AND FLARES

In the past, such IR threats were detected visually and countered by manoeuvring and/or the release of flares. This worked well against threats such as the AA-2 Atoll or SA-7 Grail. These older missiles were essentially "tail-chase" threats but the latest models of missile have better seekers, offering all-aspect attack capability and good resistance to countermeasures.

Flares will have some effect against such weapons, particularly the newer types being developed in the late 1980s. Current dispensers are used to release chaff, IR cartridges or expendable

Above: Even zero RCS would do nothing to protect an aircraft from this Stinger SAM. IR signature must also be kept to a minimum.

Below: ALQ-159 IR jammer on the tail of a Chinook. Many current units of this type were developed for helicopter applications.

Above: The hunter and the hunted – the F-117 can deliver laser-guided ordnance on high-priority targets such as this hardened shelter.

active decoys. Future trends are likely to be the use of "smart" dispensers, able to release decoy payloads only in the direction of the threat, and also by the development of multi-spectral expendable cartridges.

IR JAMMERS

Countering the more sophisticated IR threats will require the use of IR jammers but to date such systems have only been installed aboard helicopters and transports. The technology needed to create IR jammers for fighter use was not available; the existing models of IR jammers were large, power-hungry and unable to mimic the high nozzle and efflux temperatures of after-burning engines. In the case of a stealth aircraft, the low IR signature would in theory make current IRCM technology usable but, in practice, new types of IR jammer will probably be created for deployment on stealthy and non-stealthy fighters alike.

The earliest IR jammers used electrically-powered or fuel-heated hot elements as their source of IR energy, but by the early 1980s, IR tubes were being used. All these patterns of IR jammer radiate their limited jamming energy over a wide volume so may be too weak to jam advanced seekers.

For a fighter-based IR jammer,

Above: Most RWR systems incorporate a small CRT screen which shows the bearing and nature of detected threats.

Left: Five antennas, two electronics units, a control unit and a display are all that is needed to locate radar threats to a helicopter.

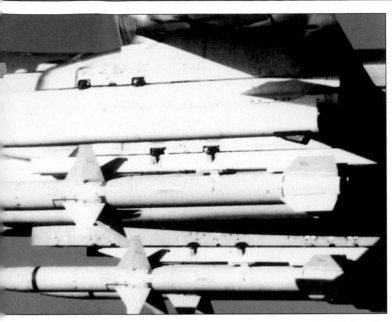

Above: AGM-88 HARM, seen here on a German Tornado, is the most effective anti-radiation missile. The EW pod is Germany's Cerberus.

Below left: The EF-111 Raven was an effective jamming aircraft, but the decision to phase out the F-111 doomed it to early retirement.

Below: AGM-88 HARM anti-radiation missiles, (wings and fins not yet installed), are wheeled toward a FLIR-equipped A-7 Corsair.

a more likely power source would be an IR laser, whose narrow beam would generate the high levels of power needed to defeat the latest types of imaging IR seeker. The only practical solution is a directional jammer that uses some form of sensor to track the incoming missile, then aims a highly directional beam of modulated IR energy at it. Since the jamming energy is concentrated in the direction of the threat, the jammer-to-signal ratio seen by the seeker is maximised.

The two main directional IR systems currently under development are the Northrop Grumman Nemesis Directional Infra-Red Countermeasures (DIRCM) system and the Sanders ALQ-212 Advanced Threat Infra-Red Countermeasures (ATIRCM). Nemesis uses a modified version of the Westinghouse AAR-54 (V) ultra-violet missile warning receiver to detect and track targets and to steer its jammer, while ATIRCM relies on the AAR-57 Common Missile Warning System. At present both systems use an arc lamp as a source of jamming energy. In the longer term Nemesis could be fitted with a laser to supplement the arc lamp, while

the ALQ-212 will switch to a multi-band laser. Both are intended for use on transports and helicopters, but work is under way to miniaturise this technology to the point where it can be used on fast jets.

EW FOR FIGHTERS

Integrated EW installations are planned for all next-generation fighters. The Sanders AN/ALR-94 electronic warfare EW system for the F-22 is part of a highly integrated avionics suite which effectively combines the radar, ESM, communications and identification functions into a single system while presenting the pilot with the relevant data, and controlling the level of emissions from the aircraft to match the tactical situation. It is made up of apertures, electronics, and processors that detect and locate threat signals and control the release of expendable countermeasures such as chaff and flares via AN/ALE-52 dispensers. It also provides a missile launch detection capability.

Similar systems are being developed in Western Europe. The BAE Systems towed decoy mentioned earlier as part of the DASS on Eurofighter 2000 forms part of an integrated suite which also includes an RWR, LWR, MAW, and chaff/flare dispensers.

In 1989 Dassault Electronique teamed with Thomson-CSF to work on the electro-magnetic detection and jamming system for Rafale. It is responsible for the warning and ESM parts of the resulting Spectra system, plus the jamming techniques generators, while Thomson-CSF has teamed with Elettronica to produce the system's solid-state jamming transmitters. Full-scale

development of Spectra began in 1990, and eight prototypes have been built. These have been tested on a Mystere 20 and on a Mirage 2000 prototype devoted to Spectra development and integration.

JAMMERS

Just like conventional fighters and bombers, stealth aircraft need the support of stand-off jamming aircraft. In the late 1980s, the USAF relied on the EF-111A Raven stand-off jamming aircraft, F-111A fighter-bombers which had be rebuilt in the early 1980s as EW assets. These had been expected to remain in service until around 2010, but when the collapse of the Soviet Union and the Warsaw Pact allowed the USAF to retire its F-111 fleet, the economics of retaining the EF-111A proved unviable, so the EW variant was retired in the summer of 1998, leaving the USAF dependent on the US Navy's force of EA-6B Prowler jamming aircraft.

This in turn required the USN to increase the number of Prowler squadrons from 14 to 20, expanding the 80-strong force to more than 100 by returning stored aircraft to operational service. The limitations of such a small force were demonstrated in 1999 when the US found itself involved in two simultaneous air campaigns in the skies over Iraq and Yugoslavia.

Before the start of Operation Allied Force against Yugoslavian forces operating in Kosovo, the DoD had to dispatch an additional eight EA-6B to the region, where the Yugoslavian air defences were assessed as being far more dangerous than those in Iraq. Most combat missions flown over Yugoslavia

during Allied Force were supported by EA-6Bs.

During that conflict, the USAF studied the possibility of modifying a B-52H bomber for the EW mission. The resulting EB-52 would have carried ALQ-99 jamming pods under its wings. Although not put into practice, it generated longer-term interest in the possibility of creating a dedicated EW variant of the B-52, B-1B or even the B-2. If the plan goes ahead, the end result could be an EB-52 fitted with the Improved Capability-3 (ICAP-3) jamming system being developed for the EA-6B. The aircraft would be able to stay on station about 12 hours, standing off at ranges of more than 150 miles (240km). A similar upgrade of the B-1B could create an EB-1 able to escort strike forces into enemy airspace. Operating much closer to the radars it is jamming, an EB-1 would need a much lower level of jamming power than an EB-52.

SUPPORT AIRCRAFT

Stand-off jammers mounted in aircraft such as the EA-6B and EF-111 are best used against early warning and GC1 radars, where their high power can prevent the enemy predicting the direction from which strike aircraft or fighters may be coming. Deprived of this tactical information, target acquisition and tracking radars must carry out their own search for the incoming formations.

Since the high-powered jammers on an EA-6B would be a good target for a SAM launched in home-on-jam mode, a group of several jamming aircraft can protect themselves by sharing target data via a data link, and taking turns to be the jammer. Faced with a target that seems to be jumping around the sky, the missile will expend its propulsive power in a vain attempt to chase the source of jamming energy.

The EA-6B is currently expected to serve until around 2015, and various potential replacements are under study. These include a "Command & Control Warfare" (C2W) variant of the two-seat F/A-18F (a design tentatively designated F/A-18G Growler), a SEAD version of the Joint Strike Fighter, a jammer-equipped version of the F-22, and a jammer-equipped UAV. One feature of stealth aircraft which makes them attractive as jamming platforms is that they carry their armament in weapons bays, internal spaces which could easily be adapted to house EW hardware.

There have also been reports that the USAF is developing – presumably as a "black"

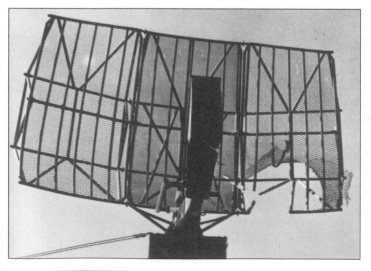

Top: **The F-4G Wild Weasel has been retired; advances in digital electronics allowed the anti-radar mission to be assigned to HARM-equipped F-16 aircraft.**

Above: **HARM ignites its rocket motor after a trials release from a German Tornado. Further export orders for this defence suppression missile are anticipated.**

Left: **During a 1980 flight test at China Lake in the USA, an unarmed HARM round gouged this hole through the target antenna.**

deleted to make room for the internally mounted EW avionics.

A developing trend is the installation of ARMs on many types of strike aircraft. HARM may be carried on any aircraft which has digital avionics and sufficient computer capacity. The US Navy was ahead of the USAF in this respect, since its main HARM carriers became standard F/A-18 Hornets and A-7 Corsair IIs, the types which gave the weapon its combat debut during operations against Libya in April 1986.

MISSILE GUIDANCE

In parallel with this work to install HARM on a wider range of platforms, improvements are being made the to missile's guidance system. A new reprogrammable memory allowed the seeker to be modified in the field in order to match new threats or changes in tactics by means of software changes. One effect of these is to give the missile a degree of awareness of its geographical position by using information from its mechanical gyroscopes to create a crude form of inertial navigation. This limited capability can probably be used to restrict the weapon's attack capability to an area of terrain when enemy emitters can be expected.

Under a more advanced International Harm Upgrade Program (IHUP) being conducted by the US, Germany and Italy, the missile will be given an inertial measurement unit and a GPS receiver. These will provide a precision navigation capability, and may allow the missile to attack radars which have shut down following the HARM launch.

Technology for a longer-term HARM replacement is being explored by the Advanced Anti-Radiation Guided Missile (AARGM) programme. Being developed by Science Applied Technology, the proposed missile would have a dual-mode seeker which combines passive antiradiation homing with active

programme – a stand-off jamming pod which could be carried by a fighter such as the F-15.

There is a limit to what even the best EW techniques can do. Defence suppression is also needed to ensure that an aircraft will survive in hostile airspace. This is largely a job for anti-radiation missiles (ARMs). Weapons of this type first saw service during the Vietnam War on dedicated anti-radar aircraft known as "Wild Weasels". A more general term would be SEAD aircraft.

Although the USAF pioneered the "Wild Weasel" concept, and used the F-4G to good effect during the 1991 Gulf War, the aircraft has since been retired. The USAF no longer operates dedicated anti-radar aircraft, but relies on Block 50/52 F-16CJ aircraft fitted with HARM ARMs and the HARM Targeting System (HTS) pod. Developed under a "black" programme, the HTS detects and identifies radar threats, and provides target location information to the pilot.

US air operations over Iraq

Right: **Decked out in a high-visibility paint scheme, Northrop's Tacit Rainbow anti-radar drone flies over a US test range.**

following the 1998 Desert Fox air strikes has built up useful operating experience for the F-16CJ/HARM combination. In 1999 the journal *Electronic Defense* reported that pilots had discovered "both some limitations and some capabilities" of the system. In August 1986 the US Navy began to fit HARM to its EA-6B Prowler EW aircraft. The EA-6B has proved an effective HARM carrier. The effectiveness of any add-on ARM installation can be enhanced by linking the missile seeker to the aircraft's ESM system, so that high-priority threats which it detects may be automatically assigned to the ARMs. Prowler's on-board ESM system is well-suited to this task.

The unique mixture of hard and soft-kill capability offered by the aircraft was summed up by one pilot following the April 1986 US attack on targets in Libya. "As soon as they come on, you squirt 'em, with electrons or with missiles," he told a US reporter.

Outside of the USA, Germany is the only NATO ally to have ordered SEAD (Suppression of Enemy Air Defences) aircraft – the Tornado ECR. Based on the standard Tornado IDS, the ECR carries two AGM-88A HARM missiles, two AIM-9L Sidewinders for self-defence, a jamming pod, a chaff/flare dispenser pod, plus two external fuel tanks. It lacks the twin 27mm Mauser cannon of the strike version. These were

Left: The small size and non-metallic structure of RPVs such as the Israel Aircraft Industries Scout keep RCS to a minimum.

Right: The weapons bay of an FB-111 bomber opens to reveal the ultimate defence-suppression weapon – the nuclear-tipped SRAM.

Below: Britain's Royal Air Force adopted the lightweight Alarm anti-radar missile, but the only other user is Saudi Arabia.

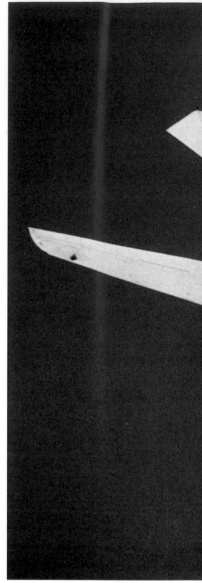

millimetre-wave terminal guidance. AARGM will normally rely on passive guidance, but if the threat radar shuts down, it will switch to active millimetre-wave guidance and continue to home. AARGM is an advanced technology demonstration programme, and is expected to conclude with several guided launches late in 2001.

At least two other projects to develop dual-mode ARMs are under way. Under a private venture, Raytheon is investigating dual-mode seekers which would combine passive anti-radiation homing with imaging infrared seekers, laser-radar or millimetre-wave guidance, while the German company BGT is studying the Armiger, a high-speed ARM which would use a combination of passive RF and imaging infra-red guidance. Armiger would be ramjet powered, and a similar powerplant is being considered for AARGM. Both missiles would probably have a top speed of around Mach 3.

Below: Like a hungry mosquito in a darkened bedroom, an anti-radar drone can loiter waiting for an opportunity to attack. If no emitters are present, or if the intended victim shuts down, the drone climbs back to cruise height to await a fresh signal on which it may home. An endurance measured in hours keeps radars silent.

Lightweight self-protection ARMs are a relatively recent development. Weapons of this type can be carried in addition to a strike aircraft's normal armament. The only example to have entered service is the British Aerospace ALARM, a weapon whose parachute-borne target search and near-vertical attack profile remain unique. Problems with the original design of the rocket motor delayed flight trials to the end of 1986. A new powerplant was developed by the German company Bayern Chemie, and the missile was rushed into service to arm UK Tornado strike aircraft during Operation Desert Storm in 1991.

DECOY RPVs

Despite years of stop-go development work, progress with anti-radiation and decoy RPVs has been slow. Israel used decoy RPVs to good effect during its battles against Syrian-manned air defences in the Bekaa valley during the 1982 invasion of Lebanon, and has since fielded Harpy, a piston-engined drone which carried a passive anti-radiation seeker and a small warhead. Harpy can loiter over the battlefield, then dive onto any hostile emitter which it detects. Cheap enough to be launched in significant numbers, this type of anti-radar UAV can force the enemy to keep his radars off for long periods of time.

The US used ground-launched

drones as decoys to confuse the Iraqi air defences during the opening stages of Desert Storm. In the mid-1990s Teledyne Ryan was asked to develop a miniature air-launched decoy (MALD) which would be powered by a 50lb (22.7kg) thrust Sundstrand TJ-50 turbojet, and carry an EW repeater payload able to mimic the VHF, UHF and microwave radar returns from a full-sized combat aircraft. MALD was tested from the F-16 during the late 1990s, but the B-52H was seen as a likely first operational application. Mimicking a B-52 would involve increasing the strength of the apparent radar return (probably by an amount which varies with frequency band), and a similar but smaller increase would be needed to mimic a conventional fighter.

If the energy emitted by the

repeater payload were to be only slightly boosted, and perhaps made erratic by turning the repeater on and off at frequent but ransom intervals, MALD or a similar type of free-flying decoy might be able to imitate the tiny and fleeting radar returns from a stealth aircraft. Enemy pilots and SAM operators would have no way of telling whether the target they were struggling to locate was a $60 million stealth aircraft or a $30,000 decoy.

Anti-Radar Drone

Target identified

Transit to loiter area

Loiters over enemy territory

Terminal dive

Launch vehicle

Northrop Grumman and TRW's Avionics Systems Division, the new antenna was embedded in a specially built tip mounted onto the aircraft's right vertical stabiliser. Connected to the airframe electrically as well as physically, it made both its own structure and the aircraft skin operate as an antenna.

Addressing an Air Force Association symposium in June 1986, Brigadier General Eric B. Nelson, AFSC deputy chief of staff for plans and programmess, revealed another potential application of smart skins. Future US warplanes might try to match their apparent radar signature with that of ground clutter. An antenna array on the underside of a low-flying aircraft could be used to sample the ground clutter from the terrain being overflown. "If you can make the topside of the aircraft look like the clutter in a frequency and power sense, then you have done something nearly ideal – you have made an [electronic] chameleon out of your airplane."

A February 1996 report by the magazine *Aviation Week & Space Technology* suggests even more bizarre qualities for future aircraft skins. According to the magazine, the skin coating on a new classified stealth aircraft being tested at Groom Lake uses a 24V electrical charge to trigger an active method of reducing radar cross section. It also claimed that the colour of the skin could be changed to blend the aircraft into the sky background if viewed from below, or the terrain if seen from above.

It may read like science fiction, but science fiction has a habit of becoming science fact. It is possible that smart skins may help tomorrow's stealth aircraft vanish amidst the ground clutter.

ACTIVE SKINS

As counters to stealth technology become available, stealth designers will be able to look toward the avionics industry for new aids to stealth. In its futuristic forward-looking study "Forecast 2", the USAF predicted that one of the key technologies for tomorrow's aircraft and avionics would be the use of "outer skins containing embedded phased arrays to permit aircraft to sense and communicate in optical and other frequency bands, and in any direction from any aircraft attitude". The concept was rapidly dubbed "smart skin". These phased arrays would consist of arrays of microscopically tiny active transmitting elements buried within the aircraft skin. Given suitable signal processing, these would work together like the active elements of a phased array antenna.

The most obvious use of smart skins will be for communications. Radar applications would be expected to follow, but these require increasing levels of power. In March 1997 the F/A-18 Systems Research Aircraft (SRA) based at the Dryden Flight Research Center was used to test an experimental Smart Skin Antenna. Developed jointly by

Below: **Long obsolete, the tiny Quail decoy equipped SAC's B-52 fleet in the 1960s and 1970s. Able to fly as fast as a bomber, this jet-powered drone carried equipment which boosted its RCS to B-52 proportions, allowing it to mimic the bomber which had released it.**

STEALTH IN ACTION

The F-117A Nighthawk had been developed as a "magic bullet" which could help even the odds between the US and the former Soviet Union in the event of a conflict between the two superpowers. However, once the aircraft was in service, the US Government began to consider it a possible tool for use in military strikes against other nations when such operations were required by US policy. The question that had to be answered at the highest political and DoD levels was – what sort of crisis would warrant using the Nighthawk in combat, stripping away part of the veil of secrecy that protected the aircraft?

By 1983 three squadrons of F-117A were operational at Tonopah, and in October of that year two operations were apparently contemplated. The first would have involved the aircraft in Operation Urgent Fury, the October 1983 US invasion of Grenada, while a second would have targeted Palestine Liberation Army (PLO) sites in the Lebanon. Support for the Grenada operation could have been given by F-117As based on US territory, but the Lebanese strike would have

involved deploying a small number of aircraft to a European base, reportedly Rota in Spain.

In April 1986, preparations were made to use the F-177A in Operation El Dorado Canyon, the planned air strike against the Tripoli-based headquarters of Libyan leader Muammar Gaddafi. A batch of between 8 and 12 aircraft would deploy from their Tonopah base to an airfield on the US east coast. From there, they would fly across the Atlantic and into the Mediterranean, supported by refuelling aircraft. After attacking their targets at around 3am in the morning, they would return to the USA.

Hours before the planned departure from Tonopah on 15 April, the plan was scrubbed. The attack on Gaddafi would be mounted by carrier-based US Navy aircraft instead, supported by UK-based F-111s, allowing the F-117A to remain secret.

The crisis that would see the first operational use of the F-117A developed much closer to the USA. In 1988 two US Federal grand juries in Florida indicted General Manuel Antonio Noriega, the leader of Panama's military forces on

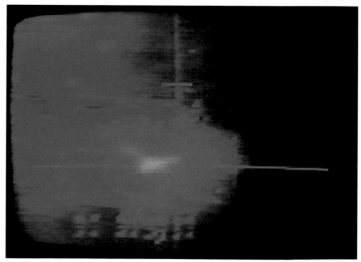

charges of drug smuggling and racketeering in the USA. When Panamanian President Eric Arturo Delvalle dismissed Noriega from his command, he suffered in indignity of being forced out of office by Noriega's supporters, and seeing the general become Panama's new leader. A furious US Government imposed economic sanctions against Panama.

In the following year

Guilleremo Endara opposed Noriega in a presidential election, and apparently won, only to have the Noriega government declare the election invalid. When the US provided some assistance to an attempt by a group within the Panamanian military who attempted unsuccessfully to topple Noriega, the stage was set for a confrontation between the US and Panama. The sight of General Noriega declaring

Left: The F-117A's combat debut came in 1988, in support of US ground forces in Operation Just Cause, Panama.

Below left: As captured on FLIR tape, an AC-130 pounds the Panama Defense Forces Comandancia headquarters with 105mm cannon rounds.

Above: When US Rangers captured Torrijos Airport it had the support of USAF special operations aircraft as well as F-117 fighter-bombers.

war on the United States seemed closer to farce than international politics, but the killing of a US Marine provided the impetus for the US Government to act. President George Bush ordered US forces to invade Panama and bring Noriega to the USA to stand trial.

Just before 1am on the night of 20 December 1989, a massive blast shook the Panamanian Defense Forces base at Rio Hato, 80 miles (130km) southwest of Panama City. The strike, delivered by an unseen F-117A, was part of a co-ordinated US attack. The base was about to be attacked by the US Army's 82nd Airborne Division, and a pair of F-117As dropped two 2,000lb (900kg) high-explosive bombs close to a barracks that housed some of Noriega's best soldiers. The two stealth fighters flew the

mission directly from the USA, refuelling in flight four or five times.

This combat debut for the F-117A was soon to be the subject of controversy. The US DoD claimed that the Panamanian forces defending the compound at Rio Hato were quickly subdued, thanks to the distraction caused by the stealth fighters, but US paratroopers who captured the base were reported as saying that they landed into an intense firefight. Several days later, US newspaper reports quoted unidentified government sources as claiming that some F-117As had been tasked with attacking Noriega. On 26 December the US DoD confirmed that US military commanders had considered but rejected other missions for the aircraft during the attack. Pentagon spokesman Pete Williams refused to say how many aircraft took part, what type of ordnance had been dropped or what other missions had been considered for the aircraft.

He repeated earlier DoD claims that the objective of the F-117A strike had been "not to hit the barracks, but rather, in fact, the mission was to miss the barracks and hit the field – and by nature of the explosion, disorient and stun and confuse and frighten" the Panamanian defenders. "The mission was

successful," he said.

Williams explained how Defense Secretary Richard B. Cheney had been told several days earlier that the bombs from the F-117As had "precisely hit their targets . . . I'm told that the F-117 hit it very precisely and that it was the precision of the F-117's bombing capability that was the reason it was used." He also conformed that the attack on Rio Hato had been the sole mission assigned to the stealth fighters. "Others were considered but they were discarded."

Given that Panama had no effective air force or air defences, the use of the F-117A seemed strange but, following a factfinding trip to Panama in early January, Senate Armed

Services Committee Chairman Sam Nunn stated that Army Lt. Gen. Carl W. Stiner, commanding general of the Joint Task Force South that implemented the invasion plan, had asked for the F-117A not because of its radar-evading capability, but to exploit its advanced nav/attack systems. "They hit exactly where they were meant to," he told reporters, adding that the strike was intended not to kill large numbers of Noriega's troops, but to stun them by dropping bombs

Below: Following the US invasion of Panama, US agents arrest General Noriega and prepare to return him to the USA to stand trial.

outside their barracks.

The entire affair of the bombs that missed came to a head in April, when the *New York Times* and the industry newsletter *Aerospace Daily* revealed that one of the F-117As had missed its intended target by more than 300 yards (275m). A few days later a spokesman for Cheney explained to news reporters that the USAF had not told his boss that the two F-117As had dropped a bomb "way off target", until a few days before. As a result, Cheney had for months been praising the aircraft's accurate weapon delivery, unaware of the facts. "The pilots were told to drop their bombs no closer than 50 meters" from two separate PDF barracks buildings, explained Pete Williams. Due to a last-minute misunderstanding between the pilots, the second F-117A dropped its bomb on a hillside some distance away, Williams said. "The first bomb hit 55 meters from one of the barracks, but the second bomb was way off target."

In July 1990, Lockheed delivered the 59th and final F-117A stealth fighter to the US Air Force. The aircraft was delivered under budget and two months ahead of the schedule first drawn up in 1978. A month later, the Lockheed fighter was

Below: **A line-up of F-117A stealth fighters before deployment to the Gulf. Beneath the open weapons bays are cargo pods for spares.**

on its way to a war that would more than vindicate its reputation.

THE GULF WAR

At 2am on 2 August, units of the Iraqi Army rolled over the border with Kuwait, rapidly overwhelming the Kuwaiti armed forces and occupying the country. Ostensibly this action had been taken at the request of a newly established revolutionary government that had toppled the government of the Emir of Kuwait, Sheikh Jaber Ahmed al-Sabah. In practice it was Iraq's response to a breakdown in talks between the two countries held in Jeddah the day before.

With an army of around 100,000 men poised on the frontier, Iraq had demanded that Kuwait pay reparations for the oil Kuwait had "stolen" from Iraq via the border oilfields, write off loans made to Iraq during the Iraq/Iran war in the 1980s, and accept Iraq's territorial claims to Bubiyan and Warba, Kuwaiti islands that controlled the waters through which Iraq maintained in access to the Gulf. Kuwait rejected these demands, and walked out of the talks. With Kuwait firmly occupied, the pretence of a "revolutionary government" was soon abandoned. On 8 August Iraq formally annexed Kuwait as its "19th province".

On 6 August, a UN resolution called for mandatory sanctions

against Iraq. With Iraqi troops now along the border between Kuwait and Saudi Arabia, the latter nation feared for its own security, and requested that US troops be sent.

On 7 August, US President George Bush ordered the start of Operation Desert Shield, which would protect Saudi Arabia and other Gulf States from the threat posed by Iraq. The first US units sent to the area were an initial force of fighter aircraft plus 4,000 troops. Responding to further UN resolutions, other Arab and

Above: **General Norman H. Schwarzkopf ("Stormin' Norman"), Commander of US and Allied forces in the Gulf, in a typically forceful pose at a press conference.**

Western nations joined the rapidly growing Allied Coalition, while the UN passed further resolutions calling for a naval blockade, then for UN members to use "all necessary means" to restore international peace and security in the area.

The Coalition was directed by

Headquarters US Central Command, under the command of US Army Gen. H. Norman Schwarzkopf. USAF Lt. Gen. Charles A. Horner was made the Coalition's supreme air commander, and within days had established the Headquarters Central Command Air Forces (Forward) in Saudi Arabia. From this headquarters, he would command the subsequent air campaign.

Within five days, five fighter squadrons, a contingent of AWACS, and part of the 82nd Airborne Division had moved into the area. A total of 25 USAF fighter squadrons flew non-stop to the theatre, and within 35 days the USAF fighter force in the region matched the numbers of Iraq's fighter strength. Soon after the buildup of military strength had started in August, it became clear that the US was dispatching forces which would give the Allies an offensive capability. Besides Marine amphibious forces, units sent to the Gulf included a squadron of F-117As, triggering press speculation that they might be used to attack Iraqi supply depots or oil installations.

Col. Anthony Tolin, until recently commander of the 37th Tactical Fighter Wing at Nellis, and by now assistant deputy chief of staff of the Tactical Air Command at Langley, was blunt about the aircraft's capability. "I

guess it would be tough to classify the F-117A as a purely defensive weapon. Its defensive nature is its ability to penetrate enemy radar without detection," he told reporters who visited the base on 19 August to see the squadron's arrival en route to Saudi Arabia. "They give us an ability, should we need it, to get in with the least amount of casualties and attack those important targets if necessary."

A total of 22 F-117As 415th TFS "Nightstalkers" had arrived at Langley, but only 20 set off across the Atlantic on the following day. The two other aircraft had been spares, brought to Langley to make sure that 20 could be despatched overseas. Flight time to Saudi Arabia was approximately 15 hours, the aircraft refuelling in flight from KC-10 Extenders. Like most fly-by-wire aircraft, the F-117A is more stable during the refuelling operation than older types, but its faceted upper fuselage and flat-plate canopy limited upward visibility as its pilot approached the refuelling boom. The pilot of one of the KC-135Q tankers used to fuel the F-117As during the flight from Tonopah to Langley told an *Aviation Week & Space Technology* reporter that he was aware of this poor visibility, and was ready to rapidly break away if the boom operator thought the situation was becoming dangerous. In all other respects,

refuelling is normal, with the boom mating with a receptacle just aft of the "peak" on top of the F-117A fuselage.

The F-117s were deployed to King Khalid Air Base near Khamis Mushait in the southwestern corner of Saudi Arabia. This was more than 1,000 miles (1,600km) from Baghdad, which meant a round-trip operational mission would average more than five hours and require multiple refuellings. It is likely that the air base at Khamis Mushayt was one of the few in the area with sufficient hangars to house the F-117 force and protect its sensitive radar-absorptive coating from the elements. It was out of range of Iraqi Scud missiles and, given that the F-117 was designed for night attacks, the aircraft was not able to exploit a more forward base in the way that aircraft flying several sorties by day could.

On arrival at King Khalid Air Base, the pilots of the 20 F-117As started a programme of training. Initial sorties intended to familiarise them with the local terrain were carried out by day, but the emphasis was soon switched to night flying. The local area was similar in environment and altitude to Tonopah. An exotic aircraft built in small numbers might be expected to have reliability problems. In practice, serviceability of the F-117As sent

Above: **An F-117A refuels from a USAF tanker during the long flight from the USA to a new operation location in Saudi Arabia.**

to Saudi Arabia remained high, with mission readiness rates equalling those of conventional fighters.

Soon after arriving in Saudi Arabia, the F-117A was again attracting publicity. On 13 September, the French magazine *L'Express* claimed that a Thomson-CSF military radar in service with the Saudi Army had on several occasions successfully detected F-117As at a range of up to 10.5 miles (17km). The story, which was based on sources "close to the Saudi Army", claimed that, following the incidents, US commanders had moved the Lockheed aircraft away from the front lines, relocating them at a base in southwest Saudi Arabia, close to the Yemen. In another incident, Saudi troops are reported to have been puzzled by the failure of a US-built radar to detect the angular-looking black jets flying from a nearby airfield.

In November, Defense Secretary Cheney announced that a second squadron of F-117As was being sent to Saudi Arabia. This was the 416th TFS "Ghostriders". By the time that hostilities broke out early in the following year, they had been joined by the 417th TFS "Bandits". More than 40 of the 56 available aircraft were to take part in Desert Shield.

COALITION BUILD-UP

By mid-January 1991, a massive military force from 30 nations was in place ready to enforce the UN resolutions. In particular, the scale of the US air deployment was huge. Within two months of Desert Shield beginning, it had reached the equivalent of five tactical fighter wings, and included – besides the F-117As – F-15C/Es, F-16Cs, F-4Gs, RF-4Cs and A-10As drawn from more than 20 different US and Europe-based wings. F-111 strike aircraft and B-52 bombers had been redeployed to Turkey and the Indian Ocean, respectively. Carrier-based air units had added at least 100 more combat aircraft, with the USMC providing another 150 aircraft.

By the time the Coalition's land, sea and air build-up was complete, Saddam Hussein was thought to have stationed 590,000 troops and 4,200 tanks in Kuwait and southeastern Iraq. Total air strength of the Iraqi air force was around 500 aircraft and 250 combat helicopters.

The F-117A was the only stealth aircraft taking part in the war, but several of the conventional aircraft were modified to make them less easy

to detect. Royal Air Force Tornado F.3 fighters – the interceptor version of the aircraft used for strike missions – had been fitted with a spray-on RAM along the leading edges of the wing, tailplane, and vertical fin, plus the nose and leading edges of its underwing stores such as the Phimat chaff/flare pods. RAM tiles were also added to the inlets to dampen their radar response. This feature initially gave trouble, with several tiles coming loose in flight and being ingested by the engine. The RB.199s kept running in every case, but were changed as a precaution after the aircraft had landed. Better adhesive had cured the problem by December 1990. The effectiveness of this improvised signature-reduction programme was never tested in action. No Iraqi warplane would ever challenge a Tornado interceptor.

A few weeks before the invasion of Kuwait, the US Navy had installed NVG systems, blue-green NVG-compatible cockpit lighting, and windscreens with better IR transparency on some of its A-6E Intruders. These gave visibility out to around seven miles (11km) under good conditions, which allowed the crew turn off the aircraft's radar, denying Iraqi elint units any signal that might warn of an incoming attack. As a bonus, it also overcame some of the radar's limitations. Crews

could now fly as low as 200ft (60m) on a clear night rather than the 500-600ft (150-180m) allowed by radar, banking the aircraft more aggressively to make best use of terrain features. (The radar allowed bank angles of no more than 45 degrees.) Radar was better than NVGs during the actual attack, so was turned at the last moment.

US Army AH-64 Apaches also went stealthy, but only on the ground. Brunswick-developed desert-camouflage netting delivered in November 1990 was designed to absorb radar frequencies from 6-140GHz. Five hundred two-piece 78 x 100ft (23.75 x 30.5m) covers were ordered to protect parked aircraft.

SIGINT

During the Vietnam War, the USAF and US Navy had each run its own air campaign, an arrangement which fostered inter-service rivalry, and which made co-ordination difficult. The air campaign against Iraq would be fought to a single integrated plan devised by two men. Lieutenant-General Charles

Right: **Armed with Skyflash and Sidewinder air-to-air missiles and carrying long-range fuel tanks, this RAF "Desert Eagle" Tornado F.3 flies a combat air patrol (CAP) along the Saudi/Iraq border.**

Horner was General Schwarzkopf's air commander, while Brigadier-General Buster C. Glosson, commander of 14th Air Division became US Central Command's principal USAF target planner. Under their command, intelligence officers drew information from USAF target files, supplemented by the

Below: **Part of the array of Russian-built air defence systems the Coalition forces faced in the Gulf War. Below left, the SA-13 SAM system, which has four missile launchers, although only one can be fired at a time.**

Below: **The SA-6 is more compact than the SA-4 (below right). It proved effective in the 1973 Middle East Conflict, but the US and its allies had devised suitable countermeasures long before the 1991 Gulf War.**

Below: **The SA-8 Gecko replaced the 57mm towed anti-aircraft gun and is in service in two versions, the SA-8a shown here, with missiles on open launchers, and the SA-8b, which has the missiles in long boxes for both transport and launch. Iraq uses both SA-8a and SA-8b.**

SA-13   SA-6   SA-4   SA-8

results of a massive intelligence-gathering effort. As US reconnaissance satellites photographed Iraqi military positions, Lockheed TR-1s equipped with the Advanced Synthetic Aperture Radar System (ASARS) gathered detailed sideways-looking radar imagery of terrain up to 35 miles (56km) to one side of its flight path.

Sigint aircraft such as the RC-135 sampled Iraqi communications signals, identifying the location of the transmitters, and listened to Iraqi radar signals as Allied fighters made high-speed dashes towards Iraq to test the defences. To counter such elint probing, the Iraqis began to shut down parts of their early-warning radar network for extended periods of time. It was a habit that would help the Allies when they finally attacked.

It is possible that some F-117As slipped across the border at night to take FLIR imagery of high-value targets such as chemical-weapons sites and nuclear installations, but any operations of this type would have been kept highly classified.

As the months wore on, the strategic plan for the air war was expanded to include about 300 targets. US and Allied intelligence officers drew up not just lists of targets to be attacked, but also the floor plans of facilities such as hardened concrete command centres which in some cases had been designed or even built by Western companies. As plans to use the unique capabilities of the F-117A were drawn up, the

USAF faced the prospect that one of these highly classified aircraft might be shot down over Iraqi territory. If this happened, strike aircraft would have to be assigned the task of systematically and intensively bombing the wreckage, to ensure that no useful information reached Iraqi (or Russian) hands.

The Iraqi air defences facing the Coalition looked formidable on paper. SAM systems were mostly Soviet-supplied, and included the S-75 (SA-2 "Guideline"), S-125 (SA-3 "Goa"), Kub (SA-6 "Gainful"), 9K33 Osa (SA-8 "Gecko"), 9K31 Strela 1 (SA-9 "Gaskin"), S-10M Strela (SA-13 "Gopher"), and the man-portable Strela (SA-7 "Grail"), Strela 3 (SA-14 "Gremlin"), plus Franco-German Roland 2s and Chinese HN-5A. To some US planners it must have seemed more than a little reminiscent of the North Vietnamese defences that the US had faced around quarter of a century earlier.

Iraq had purchased what was widely described as a state-of-the-art integrated air defence system (IADS) from France. Codenamed Kari (Iraq spelled backward in French), it was a computerised and highly-centralised network which linked the national air-defence operations center (ADOC) in Baghdad to four sector operations centres (SOC), one for each of the four sectors into which the country was divided. These SOC were linked to a total of 17 intercept operations centres (IOC) which were connected to observer and early-warning reporting posts. Around 500 radars were located at approximately 100 sites. The IOCs controlled air bases with interceptor aircraft, more than 50 surface-to-air missile sites, plus widely-deployed antiaircraft artillery sites. The system was equipped with multiple and redundant communication modes, so in theory could rapidly detect attacking aircraft, and direct fighter, missile, or antiaircraft artillery fire against

them.

The Iraqi Air Force had 24 main operating bases and 30 dispersal fields, many equipped with the latest types of hardened aircraft shelter. Most potent fighter in the 750-strong force of combat aircraft was the MiG-29, but Iraq also had the MiG-25, the older MiG-23 and -21, plus Mirage F1s.

The most heavily defended areas of Iraq were Baghdad, Basrah, Tallil/Jalibah, H-2 and H-3 airfields, and Mosul/Kirkuk. These were protected by five types of SAM system. The S-75, S-125, Kub, and 9K33 Osa had been supplied by the Soviet Union, while France and Germany had supplied the short-range Euromissile Roland.

More radar-guided SAM systems were deployed to the Baghdad area than any other part of Iraq, and were dispensed throughout the Baghdad area (as were the targets they were protecting). The greatest concentrations of radar-guided SAMs were not in the centre of

Number and location of Iraqi SAM batteries

Location	SA-2	SA-3	SA-6	SA-8	Roland	Total in area
Baghdad	10	16	8	15	9	58
Mosul/Kirkuk	1	12	0	1	2	16
Basrah	2	0	8	0	5	15
H-2 & H-3 airfields	1	0	6	0	6	13
Talil/Jalibah	1	0	0	0	2	3
Total number operational	15	28	22	16	24	

the city but in its outlying regions. The lethal range of these defences extended over the general Baghdad area, covering up to 60 miles (100km) outside the city.

The maximum engagement ranges of the systems varied from 3.5 miles (5.6km) for the Roland to 27 miles (43km) for the SA-2, so their firepower did not converge over the downtown area. Indeed only the elderly SA-2 had sufficient range for the firepower of individual batteries to converge over the centre of the city. As a result of this dispersed deployment pattern, the densest concentrations of overlapping radar SAM defences were outside downtown Baghdad, and the latter had no greater protection than the overall metropolitan area.

A critical weakness in Iraq's SAM defences was that the SA-2 and SA-3 had been first deployed around 30 years earlier, so were at the end of their operational lifespan. As the result of combat experience in Vietnam and the Middle East, their characteristics and operational limitations were well known, and the USAF and other Coalition air forces had long-established countermeasures to these systems.

The short-range Strela-2M and Strela-3 shoulder-fired SAMs were used by field units of the Iraqi Army. Most of these infra-red guided weapons were deployed in the area of Kuwait. None was used around Baghdad.

A total of around 4,000 anti-aircraft guns (mostly 23mm ZSU-23 towed guns and ZSU-23-4 Shilka self-propelled guns were in Iraqi service. There were more anti-aircraft artillery (AAA) sites in the Baghdad area than elsewhere in Iraq. Like the SAM systems, they were positioned throughout the greater metropolitan Baghdad area, not just downtown. Although linked to the IADS, few of the AAA guns were radar-guided. Most relied on barrage-style firing, and posed a threat which would require attacking aircraft to fly at altitudes of more than 12,000ft (3,660m) for most of the war.

The entire system had been designed to counter threats from Israel or Iran, so was deployed to cope with attacks coming from the east or west. The air forces now poised to strike Iraq would be attacking from the south and north, and on a much larger scale than the defences had been designed to cope with. The defences could track only a limited number of threats, and had very limited capabilities against stealth aircraft.

The Coalition had six months to gather intelligence on targets, develop its war plans, deploy the necessary assets to the theatre, allow aircrew to become familiar with the operating environment, and practise strikes and deception measures. Since France was a member of the Coalition preparing to liberate Kuwait, it was able to provide Allied planners with full details of the Kari computer system., allowing them to identify the key IADS nodes whose early destruction would inflict the quickest and heaviest degradation of the Iraqi air defences. Before attacks began, the US Navy's Strike Projection Evaluation and Anti-Air Research (SPEAR) department concluded that "the command elements of the Iraqi air defense organization are unlikely to function well under the stress of a concerted air campaign."

In early January, the UK magazine *Flight International* described the Iraqi air force as "no match for the forces arraigned against it – not at any level, not in any role. It is hard to see how the IrAF can retain any resemblance of cohesion after the first three allied sorties."

Before that issue had a chance to reach IrAF crew rooms, the validity of these comments would have been cruelly established.

DESERT STORM

In late November, the UN had given Iraq until 15 January to withdraw from Kuwait, but by early January it was becoming obvious that this would not happen. Even before the UN deadline ran out, President Bush consulted with Coalition allies, obtained formal permission from King Fahd of Saudi Arabia to begin hostilities from Saudi territory, then signed the executive order which would begin Desert Storm.

The night of 16 January was clear, with a new moon giving near-total darkness – near-perfect conditions for the FLIR systems of the F-117A and other Allied fighter-bombers. The months of pre-war intelligence gathering had paid off. At pre-flight briefings, pilots were in some cases assigned targets that were not just the building itself, but the key area within these buildings that was to be destroyed.

First off the ground, at 12.50am local time, were the USAF F-15E Eagles from Tabuk, the most distant of the Allies' forward bases. Stripped of their long-range fuel tanks to increase their weapon load, they refuelled in the air en route to Iraq. Starting at 1.30am, Tornado GR.1s of the Royal Air Force and Royal Saudi Air Force took off from Muharraq in Bahrain and from bases in Saudi Arabia. Other strike aircraft followed from bases in the Gulf states and the flight decks of US carriers.

At 2.38am on 17 January 1991, AGM-114 Hellfire missiles fired by AH-64 Apache helicopters slammed into two Iraqi early-warning radar sites in Western Iraq. These were the first shots of

Desert Storm. Having fired 27 missiles, 100 70mm unguided rockets, and 4,000 rounds of 30mm cannon ammunition, the two four-helo formations headed back to base. Within minutes, more than 100 Allied aircraft had slipped through the gap blown in the Iraqi radar network. The most intense air bombardment since the 1972 Linebacker II B-52 raids on North Vietnam was about to begin.

Ahead of this armada of warplanes flew around 30 F-117A fighters of the "Nightstalkers" and "Ghostriders". The first aircraft to cross into Iraqi airspace, they had been assigned the task of knocking out key enemy communications facilities, and were about to bring war to the capital of Iraq.

On the ground far below, Iraqi radars scanned the skies, but saw nothing of the US aircraft. The powerful radar pulses that should have reflected back from the US fighters to indicate the presence of a target were instead being largely absorbed by the black coating on the F-117As, while the remainder were deflected at bizarre angles which matched those of the oddly-shaped aircraft. Invisible to the defenders, the F-117s could fly at will over the city at medium altitudes that would have been suicidal in any other warplane, giving pilots plenty of time to identify their targets.

Carefully, the pilot of the first aircraft aligned the crosshairs of the night-vision system mounted under the belly of his aircraft with a carefully selected building close to the Tigris river. Satisfied that all was correct, he pressed a switch to activate a laser built into the same turret as the FLIR. The bomb doors under the centre fuselage opened, and a 2,000lb (900kg) laser-guided bomb (LGB) fell away into the darkness, its seeker following a patch of laser light reflected from the building far below. Crashing into the roof of the Iraq's most important communications centre, the weapon plunged through several floors, exploding deep within the structure, throwing debris from the windows, and smashing the central telephone system of the city. Within minutes, LGBs began falling on other command and control facilities such as microwave repeater stations, early-warning radars, and underground command bunkers.

As the main Coalition force swept in to begin striking their own targets, the Iraqi air defence system was already near-impotent. Anti-aircraft guns and surface-to-air missile (SAM) sites fired into the sky above Baghdad, vainly trying to find the attackers.

In the opening hours of Desert Storm, the F-117s attacked 80 targets, including the Iraqi Air Force headquarters in Baghdad, and an air-defence headquarters near the city. Videotapes taken by the attackers showed a direct hit on the multi-storey IrAF headquarters, with the LGB landing almost dead-centre on the roof. The attack on the air-defence HQ was even more impressive, with the bomb entering one of the bunker's three rooftop ventilation shafts, then demolishing the interior of the structure, the blast blowing out the NBC-protected building's airlock door. Some of the best-protected targets were buried under so much concrete that several bombs had to be dropped in order to break through the thick roof.

Their job done, the F-117As left the skies over Baghdad. As they did so, the first wave of Tomahawk cruise missiles launched from US warships struck heavily defended targets such as Saddam Hussein's palace, the Ba'ath Party headquarters, and the Iraqi Ministry of Defence. The only support needed by the departing F-117As had been flight refuelling, but almost 30 minutes ahead of the lead attack aircraft of the massive strike formations that now approached their targets were dedicated support aircraft such as the USAF EF-111A Raven and US Navy EA-6 Prowler electronic-warfare platforms. These had the task of confusing Iraqi early-warning, surface-to-air missile and ground-control intercept radars until the arrival of the F-4G Wild Weasel anti-radar fighter armed with AGM-88 HARM anti-radiation missiles, and Tornadoes equipped with the lighter-weight Alarm anti-radar missile.

Almost half the sorties flown were support missions by tankers, fighter escorts, jamming aircraft, and defence-suppression planes. The speeds and timings of the attacks mounted by aircraft such as F-15Es, Tornadoes, F/A-18 Hornets and A-6E Intruders had been arranged so that several incoming waves should share the services of the support aircraft. Some Iraqi MiG-29 and MiG-25 fighters were airborne that night, but failed to intercept the EW aircraft, or the strike formations that followed.

The Allied attack achieved total tactical surprise, and all the aircraft taking part in that first

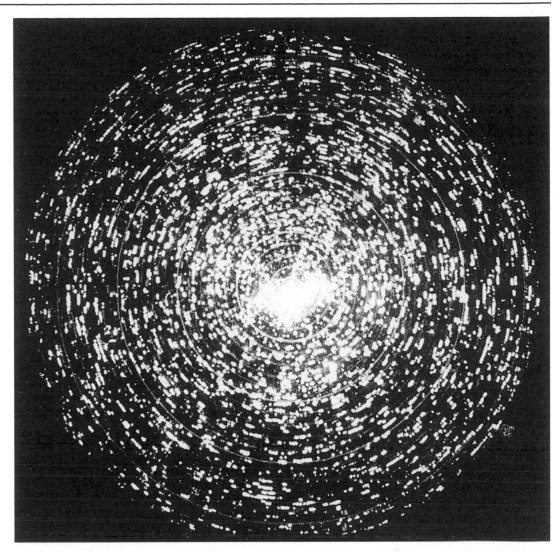

Above: **False target generation is a technique which reduces a plan position indicator (PPI) display to an unusable mess. All but one of these blips could be a** false target, and somewhere among them is the true target. This declassified photo shows only a fraction of the technique's capability.

Below: **The Gulf War was the swan-song for the EF-111 Raven. The USAF now relies on US Navy Prowlers for stand-off jamming coverage.**

wave of air strikes returned safely to base. USAF officials were quick to credit the success to the effects of the initial F-117A strike. By the time that the F-117As had attacked all 80 targets, Iraq's air defence system was near helpless. Radar sites, command centres, air and missile control facilities all lay in ruins, along with the communications needed to allow these to function. Long before dawn, the Royal Air Force and Royal Saudi Air Force Tornadoes had completed their initial series of dangerous low-level sorties against Iraq's major air bases. The sun rose on an Iraqi Air Force that had been virtually decapitated. It would never recover.

Describing the F-117A attack as a brilliant success, 37th TFW commander Col. Alton C. Whitley told reporters that this had been the result of stealth having allowed the aircraft to reach their targets undetected, plus the split-second timing with which the strike had been executed.

Through the day of 17 January, the 37th TFW pilots slept, in the vampire-like lifestyle to which they were accustomed, while the rest of the Coalition air force flew by day to pound more targets in Iraq and occupied Kuwait. Rising between 3 and 4pm, pilots were briefed on the next night's targets and routes in and out of Iraq, spending several

hours studying the information. Once darkness had fallen, they were airborne once again, along with the British and Saudi Tornado crews, flying sorties until just before dawn.

Target list for the 37th TFW that second night of the war included one of Iraq's nuclear reactors, but this was initially kept secret. NBC reporter Rick Davis, part of the press pool at the F-117A base in Saudi Arabia, found himself with a story he couldn't file. The returning pilots wouldn't divulge where the reactor was located, Davis later reported. "They didn't say . . . just that it was a nuclear reactor." In an interview with CBS on 20 January, Gen. Schwarzkopf stated that four nuclear facilities in Iraq had been destroyed.

Each day and night the process would be repeated, the F-117As taking to the air each night, while by night and day the rest of the Coalition air force flew to a daily battle plan whose complexity and detail required up to 700 pages of daily tasking orders. Within a few days, Iraqi radar activity had declined to around a quarter of the peak level that had been attained when war broke out. A week into the war, it had declined by 95 per cent. By night, the defences could do little more than to fire AA shells, SAMs, and even 7.62mm AK-47 assault rifles blindly into the darkness in the hope of hitting an attacker.

Despite the threat posed by these massive barrages, the F-117As were able to loiter over the target area, sometimes for several minutes, in order to positively identify difficult targets such as underground bunkers.

The stealth fighters were given standoff jamming support, but experience soon showed that this was best kept for the post-strike portion of the mission, when the defenders would fire for up to five minutes in an attempt to hit the attackers. Jamming support prior to

Above: **The view over Baghdad on the morning of 17 January, 1991. Tracer fire shoots upwards at unseen aircraft as Allied bombs hit key strategic targets.**

Above right: **From the TV targeting display of an Allied aircraft, this remarkable image shows an Iraqi target seconds before destruction by an LGB.**

Below: **Within a month of the 59th and last F-117A to be delivered by Lockheed to the US Air Force, the type was performing well in the Gulf War.**

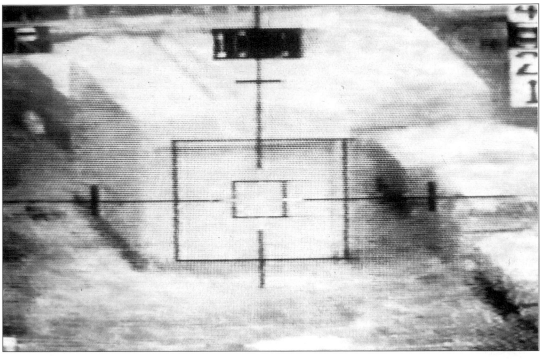

weapon release did help protect the F-117As, but also warned the Iraqis that an attack was imminent.

The initial goal of the plan devised by Lt. Gen. Horner and Brig. Gen. Glosson was the destruction of Iraq's command and control system, nuclear, chemical and biological facilities, its main military installations, and the supporting military-industrial infrastructure. Almost as important were the attacks on enemy airfields and air-defence sites. The mounting toll of destruction inflicted on these allowed US and Coalition aircraft to operate freely over ever-growing areas of Iraqi territory, beginning the task of severing the lines of supply to the Iraqi Army in Kuwait and southern Iraq, and attacking front-line units such as the Republican Guard divisions located between the Rumaila oilfields and the city of Basra.

DIVERSE TARGETS

As the war progressed, the targets attacked by the F-117s became more diverse. According to an F-117 after-action report, the doctrinal target list for the F-117 "went out the window". Although the F-117s were used against at least one example of each of the 12 target categories devised by the planners, they concentrated on a narrow range of target types within each category. These were typically fixed, small, and deeply buried or protected by concrete, and were at known locations. F-117s conducted relatively few strikes against area or mobile targets.

Within 10 days of offensive operations, 10,000 combat sorties had been flown. By the time that Gen. Schwarzkopf gave the world's press an hour-long summary of the first 14 days of combat, the air war had achieved much. Iraq's air defences had been shattered to the point where the only IrAF

aircraft taking off were those attempting to flee to sanctuary in Iran, while the Army's communications was so degraded that corps commanders sometimes could not speak directly to their divisional subordinates.

One reason for the IrAF's exodus to Iran was the nightly attacks by F-117As on Iraqi airfields. With the IrAF aircraft largely unwilling (and often unable) to come up and fight in air-to-air combat, on 25 January the Allies had started the systematic destruction of the hardened shelters in which these were hiding. Much stronger and thicker-roofed than NATO shelters, many of these had been designed by British companies, who passed the plans to the USAF. The strongest, built by Yugoslavian contractors, had roofs between 10-12ft (3.0-3.65m) thick. Study of the plans had shown that the best way of knocking out these

super-hardened shelters would be to attack them with LGBs. A special shelter needed a special bomb, and the USAF had the ideal shelter-busting weapon at hand in the form of the I-2000 warhead.

A conventional LGB uses add-on guidance and fin sections plus a standard high-explosive bomb. Bomb casings are normally cast, but the engineers at Eglin AFB who designed the I-2000 created a 1in (2.5cm) thick bomb case which was forged from a single piece of high-grade steel. It is an expensive way to make a bomb, but when assembled into a GBU-24 LGB, this hard shell gave the 2,000lb (900kg) weapon the ability to penetrate several feet of concrete before detonating. Alternate patterns of TV, IR or laser guidance allowed this 8ft (2.4m) long bomb to be configured for day or night use from high or low altitude.

The task of delivering the

I-2000 was passed to the 37th TFW. Within 24 hours of the first anti-shelter missions, Iraqi aircraft began fleeing to Iran, another major victory for the F-117A and its pilots. Detonated within a bunker or shelter, the I-2000 warhead "does a good job of destroying almost anything that's in it," an Eglin official boasted. If aircraft were in the bunker, the resulting secondary explosion of fuel and ordnance added to the destructive effects, as could be seen in videotapes of anti-shelter attacks released by the USAF in late January.

F-111F, B-52G and Mirage F1s also flew anti-shelter missions, attacking with the GBU-27s (another LGB fitted with a steel-cased penetration warhead), GBU-15 smart bombs, Paveway II and III LGBs, and AS.30L laser-guided missiles. By day 14 of the war, 100 of the 300 shelters had been destroyed, around 70 by the 37th TFW. By the end of hostilities, 375 of Iraq's 594 hardened aircraft shelters had been damaged or destroyed by Coalition bombing, and an estimated 141 aircraft within these shelters had been destroyed, while 122 had flown to Iran.

Describing the F-117A's record several days later, Secretary of Defense Richard Cheney said that "we found it comes and goes pretty much as it pleases, and in all of the missions that have been flown to date, it's been virtually invisible to enemy radar."

The only airborne radar in

Left: **As darkness falls, the F-117As head for the runway to begin their mission. The night and their stealth capability will allow them to penetrate defences.**

Iraqi service that seemed to have any chance of glimpsing an F-117A was the huge Fox Fire set carried by the MiG-25. This has a maximum power output of 600kW, a level intended to burn through massive amounts of jamming. At close range, it might have obtained a faint but usable echo from a stealth fighter, but the IrAF command and control system had no way of vectoring one of these steel-built Mach 3 jets close enough to its target. At least one of Iraq's 20 Foxbats was shot down in air-to-air combat, while five more are thought to have fled to Iran.

One Iraqi Cyrano-radar equipped F.1E did manage to detect an F-117A, but it was not able to track the stealthy intruder. The F-117A pilot who reported encountering what he described as a Mirage F.1 equipped with a searchlight may have been the intended victim. The light in question was probably the retractable landing light mounted beneath the nose of the Mirage F.1E, and the Iraqi pilot seems to have been attempting to catch the Lockheed aircraft in the beam. The F-117A pilot changed course by a few degrees, giving the

Mirage the slip.

Baghdad remained a major target throughout the war. By early February, Iraq was installing increasing numbers of anti-aircraft batteries on civilian rooftops in Baghdad and Kuwait City. Given the Allies' tactic of trying to avoid unnecessary civilian casualties, this protected the guns from attack, but this could do nothing to halt the onslaught. Around 80 per cent of the air strikes against the capital were being made at night by the two F-117A squadrons.

In February, the USAF attacked a hardened bunker in the suburbs of Baghdad. To avoid the risk to civilians using a mosque and a school in the next block, US planners opted to attack the bunker at night, when neither would be in use. The job was assigned to the 37th TFW. Two LGBs were delivered in the sort of attack pattern found best against such heavily armoured targets – one weapon to break open the roof, a second to plunge deep inside to destroy the interior. The bombs hit at around 4.30am on Wednesday 13 February, at a time when the bunker was being used as a civil air raid shelter. More than 300

people sheltering inside were killed. However, US officials claimed it had another use as a shelter for military personnel and command/communications equipment actively engaged in the defence of Iraq.

A senior Pentagon official claimed that another Iraqi command centre was operating from the basement of the Al Rashid Hotel in Baghdad, the building in which Western reporters and other foreigners were staying. The presence of the latter had prevented it being targeted, he said. Journalists invited to tour the basement found only one room equipped with relatively simple equipment consoles and manned by two operators. It was, they were told, the hotel's telephone exchange. If Iraq were indeed reduced to depending on such simple communications hardware to maintain links to its armed forces, the idea of a dual-use bunker becomes more feasible.

GROUND FORCES ATTACK

After 38 days and nights of bombing, it was the turn of the ground forces. At 8pm on

Sunday 24 February, Allied units rolled over the border into Iraq and Kuwait. The land attack was nine days behind the schedule originally planned. The weather in the early stages of the air war had been the worst ever recorded in the Gulf, and had slowed the campaign, while the diversion of aircraft to hunt down and destroy mobile Scud launchers had contributed further delays.

Instead of the "Mother of All Battles" promised by Saddam Hussein, the land war against a demoralised Iraqi Army rapidly deteriorated into a rout. After less than 100 hours of ground combat, Allied forces were on the Euphrates river, and Iraq's elite Republican Guard formations south of Basra had been reduced to a single retreating division, plus the battered remains of several others. President Bush appeared on US television to announce that "Kuwait is liberated, Iraq's army is defeated. I am pleased to announce that at midnight tonight, exactly 100 hours since ground operations commenced, and six weeks since the start of Operation Desert Storm, all United States and Coalition

BAGHDAD BKS BDE AND DEP ABU GHURAYB, IRAQ

PRE-STRIKE
AREA 1
AREA 1

POST-STRIKE
AREA 1

AREA 2

AREA 2

Above: Pre-flight checks are carried out on an F-117A Nighthawk at Langley Air Base, prior to the 15-hour flight to the Gulf.

Left: Many US air strikes against Iraqi targets displayed high precision. These facilities at Abu Ghurayb show no signs of collateral damage

forces will suspend offensive combat operations."

Iraq's collapse after 43 days of war was due in large part to what had been the most intense aerial bombardment ever mounted. The F-117A had made up less than 3 per cent of the Allied aircraft numbers, but was tasked with attacking more than 40 per cent of the targets. The stealth fighter force had flown some 1,270 sorties, with each aircraft flying around 30 missions. In more than 6,900 flying hours, the force had dropped more than 2,000 tons of bombs. LGBs accounted for only 6,520 of 88,500 tons of bombs dropped on Iraq and occupied Kuwait by US aircraft during 43 days of air attacks. This was around 7 per cent of the total, and one and a half times the number used during the eight-year-long Vietnam War. Success rate was around 90 per cent, compared with around 30 per cent for the 81,980 tons of

unguided bombs used in action in Southeast Asia. Circular Error Probability (CEP) of ordnance delivered by aircraft such as the F-15E, F-16 and F/A-18 was around 30-40ft (9-12m) – a fifth of that achieved during the Vietnam War. CEP of LGB and IR-guided bombs was in the order of a few feet (less than 1 metre).

In the weeks that followed the ceasefire, the Iraqi Army was again in action, this time engaged in suppressing revolts by Iraq's Shi'ite and Kurdish population. The Coalition forces took no action to prevent this, beyond downing several Iraqi fixed-wing aircraft that broke the ceasefire conditions by attempting to fly. For most of the Allied air force, and for the F-117As, the war was over. On 1 April, eight of the first 14 stealth fighters to leave the Gulf landed back at Nellis, the others flying to Tonopah.

THE F-117A LEGEND

By the mid-1990s, the exploits of the F-117 force during the Gulf War had been boosted into what could be called "The F-117 Legend", earning the aircraft a reputation which its manufacturer and user did much to encourage. Newspaper stories, magazine articles and books recounted how the F-117A

had been the only aircraft to attack central Baghdad, and the aircraft that smashed the Iraqi aid-defence system in a single night, opening up holes that non-stealthy aircraft then used to successfully attack other targets. It was the aircraft that shattered Iraq's nuclear reactors in a single strike after massive attacks by conventional aircraft had failed. It managed all this without the intensive support formations needed by conventional aircraft, delivering its weapons with pin-point accuracy.

Like most legends, the one surrounding the F-117 did not stand up to detailed scrutiny. When the General Accounting Office (GAO), the investigative arm of the US Congress, prepared a report on "Operation Desert Storm: Evaluation of the Air Campaign" this originally appeared in classified form, but in response to GAO concerns the DoD unclassified approximately 85 per cent of the originally classified material in the in the report. When the resulting declassified report was published in June 1997, it provided an unprecedented glimpse of the achievements and limitations of the F-117A.

The aircraft casualty rate during Desert Storm was very low compared to historic experience from earlier wars,

and the planners' expectations. It was only 0.17 per cent – 1.7 aircraft per 1,000 strikes. The GAO believed that this low casualty rate was due to three factors:
· the ban on low-altitude tactics after day two,
· the degradation of radar SAMs and the IADS in the early days of the war,
· a high proportion of strikes were flown at night.

The F-117 was the only aircraft to sustain no losses or even combat damage. "However, these aircraft recorded fewer sorties than any other air-to-ground platforms and flew exclusively at night and at medium altitudes – an operating environment in which the fewest casualties occurred among all types of aircraft," said the GAO. "Moreover, given the overall casualty rate of 1.7 per 1,000 strikes, the most probable number of losses for any aircraft, stealthy or conventional, flying the same number of missions as the F-117 would have been zero."

According to the USAF Desert Storm white paper, "the F-117 was the only airplane that the planners dared risk over downtown Baghdad", and the Air Force has also stated that "so dangerous was downtown Baghdad that the air campaign planners excluded all other attackers, except F-117s and

cruise missiles, from striking it."

In joint testimony to the US Congress on stealth and Desert Storm, Generals Horner and Glosson stated, "F-117s were the only aircraft that attacked downtown Baghdad targets – by most accounts more heavily defended than any Eastern Europe target at the height of the Cold War." The GAO disagreed, saying, "we found that five other types of aircraft made repeated strikes in the Baghdad region – F-16s, F/A-18s, F-111Fs, F-15Es, and B-52s. Large packages of F-16s were explicitly tasked to "downtown" targets in the first week of the air campaign, but these taskings were stopped after two F-16s were lost to radar SAMs over the Baghdad area during daytime." It stated that "after the third day, planners concluded that for the types of targets and defenses found in Baghdad, the F-117 was more effective."

Although US Congressional researchers tasked with compiling the official US Government "after-action" report on the Gulf War were given the widespread access to classified information that their task required, one highly classified report stayed firmly closed to

them – the study of all Iraqi attempts to engage stealth fighters. The GAO was also unable to obtain this information, so the topic of stealth aircraft vulnerability was to remain a closed book for almost a decade.

IRAQ DEFIANT

Iraq was to remain a thorn in the side of the United Nations. Although required to admit UN inspectors whose task it was to locate and destroy all Iraqi long-range missiles, chemical and biological weapons, and the facilities used to develop and manufacture these, Iraq persistently harassed these teams, and launched a major programme of concealment, moving and hiding equipment and records. In August 1996 Saddam Hussein sent forces into northern Iraq and captured the city of Irbil, a key city inside the Kurdish haven established above the 36th parallel in 1991. In September, US ships and aircraft attacked military targets in Iraq in response to this military operation.

In October 1997, Iraq accused US members of the UN inspection teams operating

inside Iraq as being spies, and expelled them. In November it expelled the remaining six US inspectors and the United Nations withdrew the rest of the team. This was to be start of a protracted confrontation with Saddam Hussein. UN inspectors were re-admitted to Iraq after the US and UK began a military build-up in the Gulf, but Iraq announced that it would not allow them to visit sites designated as "palaces and official residences." Such sites were suspected of being used to conceal possible weapons.

Angered that the UN seemed to be making no moves to end its economic sanctions, in August 1998 Iraq ended its co-operation with the inspectors, and on 31 October stopped their operations. The US and UK warned of possible military strikes, and started a new military build-up in the region.

B-1B IN ACTION

The B-1B had not been used against Iraq during the 1991 Gulf War. There were not enough crews qualified to deliver conventional weapons, and B-1B operations had been suspended following the loss of an aircraft

on 19 December 1990 due to an in-flight engine fire. Modifications had been deemed necessary to improve engine fan blade containment, and the fleet had been grounded until 6 February 1991.

In November 1998, two B-1Bs from Ellsworth AFB and two from Dyess AFB were deployed to a their forward operating base in Oman for possible military action against Iraq. On 11 November the UN withdrew most of its staff from Iraq. By the time on the 14th that Saddam Hussein agreed to re-admit inspectors, B-52s were in the air and within about 20 minutes' flying time of their targets. They were recalled, while two more B-1Bs already en-route to the Gulf were diverted to Pease AFB, New Hampshire.

The respite was short-lived. On 8 December the chief UN weapons inspector Richard Butler reported that Iraq was still preventing effective inspections, and the UN teams once more withdrew. On 15 December a formal UN report accused Iraq of not allowing access to records and inspections sites, and of moving equipment records and equipment from one to site another. A day later, the US and

Above: A UK-based B-1B is prepared for a strike mission against Yugoslavia. In 74 missions, the aircraft delivered more than 1,100 tonnes of bombs.

Left: Three days into Desert Storm, planners decided that the F-117A was the most effective strike aircraft for Baghdad operations.

Below: A 500lb conventional bomb about to be loaded into a B-1B during Operation Desert Fox, which saw the bomber's operational debut.

UK began Operation Desert Fox, an air campaign against military targets in Iraq.

During the course of the four-day campaign, US and British combat aircraft flew more than 650 strike and strike support sorties. USAF B-52s launched more than 90 cruise missiles, while naval vessels launched more than 325 Tomahawk cruise missiles. On the first night, around 50 targets were attacked by US and British air and naval forces and, by the end of the four

nights of strikes, had attacked about 100 targets.

The strike forces were following a plan that had been developed and refined over the previous year. The main targets were:
· Iraq's air defense system
· The military command and control system
· The security forces and facilities involved in concealment operations
· The industrial base for Iraq's WMD (Weapons of Mass

Destruction) and missile programmes
· The military infrastructure, including the elite Republican Guard forces
· A refinery used to produce oil products to be smuggled out of Iraq in violation of economic sanctions.

On 18 December, the B-1B had its combat debut when two aircraft from Dyess Air Force Base, Texas, and Ellsworth Air Force Base, South Dakota, took part in air raids over Iraq. 86-0135 Watchdog was from the 9th BS at Dyess, while 86-0096 Wolf Pack was from the 37th BS at Ellsworth. The target for this first B-1 strike included a Republican Guard barracks in the Al Kut area. This was attacked not with PGMs, but with conventional Mk 82 500lb (225kg) "iron" bombs, said Rear Admiral Thomas R. Wilson, USN. "This pilot walked a stick of bombs across this barracks facility." On the following night 86-0135 flew a second mission, accompanied by 86-0102 Black Hills Sentinel from the 37th BS. Although a fourth aircraft (85-0067 from the 7th BW) had been deployed to the region, it was unserviceable, so flew no combat missions.

On both nights, the aircraft flew at an altitude of around 21,000ft (6,400m), and reported "heavy" AAA fire. Iraq made little use of its surface-to-air missile systems. "These systems are important to suppress, degrade, or in some cases destroy to support the strike... These are mobile targets," Admiral Wilson told reporters on 19 December. "They get up and move sometimes every 12-24 hours... But the main thing about the SAMs and integrated air defense system is that to date, we have been able to fly in the system and not been successfully engaged by any of the Iraq air defense systems."

On 18 December each base

despatched a single B-1B to the region, raising the total number of B-1Bs available to Desert Fox planners to three from each base. They arrived too late to see any action.

CRISIS IN THE BALKANS

The next crisis that would see US stealth aircraft in action occurred in Europe. The Balkans is a region that has been a battleground for millennia, a crossroads between cultures and religions and an area which formed the frontier for at least four empires. Following World War II, during which the country was occupied by Germany, the Yugoslav monarchy was abolished and the Socialist Federal Republic of Yugoslavia was set up. When this disintegrated in 1992, wars broke out in the former republics of Slovenia, Croatia, and Bosnia-Herzegovina. In the latter two, Serbs seized control of significant parts of the country, and in a process dubbed "ethnic cleansing" tried to expel the non-Serb portion of the populace.

This process of conflict drew attention away from a mounting crisis in Kosovo, a province within Serbia. In 1974 the Constitution had been amended to grant greater autonomy to Kosovo, giving the ethnic Albanian majority who lived there bilingual public education, bilingual public signs, and an alternate judicial system. In 1989 the Serbian Parliament voted to alter the constitution to reduce Kosovo's autonomy to the federal standards that had existed prior to 1974. Coming as it did on the 600th anniversary of the loss of Kosovo to the Ottoman Empire, this decision created anger among the Albanian Kosovars. In response to rising separatism in the Albanian Kosovar community, in 1991 Serbia

dissolved the Kosovo Assembly and all Albanian-run schools. In the following year, separatists proclaimed the Republic of Kosovo, but this was recognised only by Albania. When the Communist regime in Albania collapsed in 1996, Albanian Kosovar separatists found it easier to obtain weapons, a process which speeded the rise of an armed group calling itself the Kosovo Liberation Army (KLA). As the process of violence spiralled, Kosovo and a new campaign of "ethnic cleansing" formed an ever-growing part of news reports, and a source of international concern.

Fighting between Albanian separatists and Yugoslav forces escalated in March 1998, creating new waves of refugees. By September 350,000 people were estimated to have become internally displaced or fled abroad. In May 1998, NATO

Below: **A B-1B takes off from RAF Fairford to begin a combat mission against Yugoslavian targets. The base also housed ALCM-armed B-52s.**

planners started to study a wide range of military options for intervening in the growing crisis, including the use of both air and ground forces. As the situation in Kosovo deteriorated, these plans gradually evolved.

On 23 September 1998 the UN Security Council approved Resolution 1199, demanding a cessation of hostilities in Kosovo and warning that, "should the measures demanded in this resolution ... not be taken ... additional measures to maintain or restore peace and stability in the region" would be considered. Next day, NATO threatened military intervention in Kosovo, and approved two contingency operation plans, one for monitoring and maintaining any cease-fire agreement which might emerge, and a second involving air strikes against Yugoslavian forces operating within Kosovo.

On 6 February 1999, peace talks intended to halt ethnic violence in Kosovo opened in Rambouillet, France. As these continued, NATO was assembling the air forces

needed to conduct an air campaign against Yugoslavia. These would eventually include aircraft from the USAF, USN, Royal Air Force, and French Air Force, and for the first time since World War II would involve Luftwaffe aircraft in a combat role.

Most of the strike aircraft were tactical fighters or fighter-bombers, but a key ingredient of any large-scale bombing campaign would be the veteran B-52 bomber and the F-117A Nighthawk. On 17 February, six B-52s from Barksdale AFB, Louisiana, were redeployed to Royal Air Force Fairford, England, and four days later the first F-117As began arriving at Aviano Air Base in Italy. During the flight of almost 14 hours from Holloman AFB to Italy, each Nighthawk had been refuelled 18 times by three different groups of tankers during the journey – KC-135 Stratotankers from Grand Forks AFB, North Dakota; KC-10 Extenders from McGuire AFB, New Jersey; and forward-deployed KC-135s from Fairchild AFB, Washington.

Around 250 maintainers and support personnel were already in position at Aviano, having been flown there aboard C-17 transports.

The F-117s found themselves at a crowded base which was already playing host to F-16s from Spangdahlem Air Base, Germany; F-15Es from RAF Lakenheath, England; EA-6Bs from Marine Corps Air Station Cherry Point, North Carolina; EC-130s from Davis-Monthan AFB, Arizona; A-10s from Spangdahlem; KC-135s from the Mississippi Air National Guard; Portuguese F-16s; Spanish EF-18s; and Canadian CF-18s.

By late February, the USAF had committed two air wings to the growing forces. The 16th Air & Space Expeditionary Task Force included the 16th and 31st Air Expeditionary Wings (AEW). The 16th AEW included B-52s, U-2s, F-15C/E, and KC-135s, while the 31st operated F-16CJ/CG fighters, O/A-10 ground attack aircraft, and the growing F-117 force, plus EC-130E airborne battlefield command and control centres,

EC-130H electronic warfare aircraft, and KC-135 and KC-10 tankers. By the end of the month, a third wing was assigned to the region. The 100th AEW included RC-135 reconnaissance aircraft and KC-135s.

The Rambouillet talks were finally abandoned in failure on 19 March. By this time, around 40,000 Yugoslav army (VJ) and special police (MUP) troops, and around 300 tanks had been deployed in and around Kosovo. On 20 March, these units launched an offensive in Kosovo, driving thousands of ethnic Albanians out of their homes and villages, summarily executing some, displacing many others, and setting fire to many houses.

AIR DEFENCE

NATO faced a two-level integrated air-defence system. The Yugoslav Air and Protective Defence force (JRV i PVO) – a largely volunteer force – was responsible for the early-warning radar network, the fighter force, and most of the heavy and medium SAMs, as well as the command, control, and communications network which controlled them. The fixed SAM sites included eight battalions of Russian-built S-75M Volkov (SA-2F) with 60 launchers, and 15 battalions of S-125 Pechora M (SA-3B), again with 60 (mostly quad) launchers. Locally produced electronic

decoys were available to protect some of the early-warning radars and SAM sites from attack by ARMs.

An unknown portion of the "Low-Blow" target-engagement radars associated with the S-125 system were fitted with a 15-mile (25km) range TV camera which could act as a fair-weather substitute for the radar. This add-on TV system was probably devised by Nis Electronic Industry and the Military Technical Institute in Belgrade. At least some of the S-125 systems were thought to have been upgraded. Yugoimport-SDPR was known to have developed an upgrade and overhaul package incorporating digital sub-systems including digital MTI, and other retrofit schemes were being marketed by Russia, China, Poland and Ukraine.

The Army (VJ) controlled some mobile medium SAMs, plus organic air-defence assets including most short-range and man-portable missile systems, and self-propelled AAA. Missile systems in VJ service included a small number of 9M33M Osa-AK (SA-8b), 130 9K31 Strela 1 (SA-9), plus a large number of the local S-10M2J version of the 9K35 Strela 10M (SA-13). Man-portable SAMs included around 300 9K310 Igla-1 (SA-16) and Strela 3 (Sa-14) and over 500 variants of the SA-7, including the locally produced Yugoimport-SDPR Strela 2M/A.

To prepare the way for the air

campaign, NATO mounted a major electronic intelligence-gathering operation using USAF RC-135U Combat Sent and RC-135S Rivet Joint aircraft, the US Navy's little-known EP-3 Reef Point Orions and the Royal Air Force Nimrod R.1.

During the final 72 hours before hostilities, the JRV i PVO and VJ displayed a high standard of electronic silence and emission control. The resulting lack of transmissions from air-defence radars made it difficult to locate Yugoslavia's mobile SAM systems.

With a total of 214 US and 130 allied aircraft ready for action, late in the evening of 23 March, NATO Secretary General Javier Solana gave NATO's Supreme Allied Commander Europe, US Army General Wesley Clark, authority to launch Operation Allied Force. Its goals were to demonstrate NATO's resolve to end the crisis, and to degrade Yugoslavia's military

Above: **In March 1999, B-2s from Whiteman Air Force Base, Minnesota, began bombing raids on hardened targets in Yugoslavia.**

capabilities to carry out future attacks against Albanians in Kosovo.

B-2s IN ACTION

Attacks began with on the night of Wednesday 24 March with the firing of RGM/UGM-109C and D Block 3 109 Tomahawk Land Attack Missiles (TLAM) from US Navy ships, and the launching of 27 AGM-86C Block 1 Improved CALCMs from B-52H aircraft operating from RAF Fairford. In the early morning hours of 24 March, two

Below: **From the United States to the Balkans was a 31-hour round-trip mission, including over-target loiter, involving air refuelling.**

Block 30 B-2s of the USAF's 509 Bomb Wing left Whiteman Air Force Base, Minnesota, to take part in operation Noble Anvil. Each was armed with 16 2,000lb (900kg) Mk84 or BLU-109 warhead variant Boeing Joint Direct Attack Munitions (JDAM). Following several midair refuellings, the two bombers spent several hours loitering in Yugoslavian airspace and successfully attacked multiple hardened targets, including command bunkers and air-defence systems. The two aircraft landed safely back at Whiteman AFB after 31 hours aloft. A similar mission was flown the following night, setting a pattern for nightly raids. Often, the aircraft were back in the air to begin another mission as soon as they had been refuelled and given a new load of bombs.

Using rotary launchers in their internal weapons bays, each B-2 was able to carry and deliver up to 16 JDAMs. A selectable fuse on each JDAM was set before the munition was loaded, and allowed for a variety of time delays – before or after impact – for the weapon's explosion. It took 30 minutes to convert each "dumb" bomb into a smart bomb. Ten technicians had to work for four hours to build a full load of 16 JDAMs for an awaiting B-2. Since JDAM can be dropped from up to 15 miles (24km) from the target, its use reduced the risk to the B-2. Immediately after releasing weapons, the aircraft could retreat, leaving the self-contained guidance system within each bomb to guide the round to its specific target. An inertial navigational system, updated by GPS, steered the bomb by way of movable tail fins.

Four phases of military operations were originally planned. Phase 1 was intended to establish air superiority over Kosovo, and to degrade command and control and the integrated air-defence system over the whole of the Federal Republic of Yugoslavia. Phase 2 would attack military targets in Kosovo and Yugoslav forces that were providing reinforcement to Serbian forces in Kosovo. Phase 3 would expand air operations against a wide range of high-value military and security force targets throughout the Federal Republic of Yugoslavia. Phase 4 would redeploy the available

Left: **The General Atomics Predator UAV was used to monitor Yugoslavian force movements. Several were shot down.**

After landing in a freshly ploughed field approximately 50 yards (45m) from a road and rail track intersection, he buried the life raft and other items of survival equipment which had automatically deployed during the ejection sequence. The pilot spent the next six hours hunkered down in a "hold-up site" in a shallow culvert 200 yards (180m) away from where he had landed, and waited in hope of rescue. More than six hours after the bale-out a US special operations unit reached the area. After a careful and discreet authentication of his identity, search and rescue specialists trained to recover combat air crews rescued him.

F-117A WRECKAGE

In downing the F-117A, the Yugoslavians scored a propaganda boost. Serbian television showed video of the burning wreckage, and in other news footage Yugoslavian civilians danced triumphantly on the aircraft's wing. For the first time, the legendary stealth fighter had proved vulnerable.

"We are fairly confident we know what happened that caused the loss of this airplane," Maj. Gen. Bruce Carlson, USAF Director of Operational Requirements, told journalists shortly after the incident. "But because of the fact that this is an ongoing operation – I'm concerned about the safety of the air crews – I'm not prepared to divulge it... Any further comments of the cause of the F-117 loss are unlikely to be made until the current combat and high-threat operations have ended," he added. "And then if we think that there's an operational advantage to not telling you, we probably won't tell you." This tight-lipped approach was echoed at a 26 April press conference, when NATO spokeman Major General Wald bluntly said, "We're not going to tell you what happened."

The damage visible on the F-117 wreckage included what press reports have described as "bullet holes", plus a pitting visible in areas such as the wing surface. "Both are classic examples of the type of damage which would result from a near-miss detonation of a blast/fragmentation warhead of the type frequently employed on early Soviet heavy/medium SAM systems," reported *Jane's Missiles & Rockets*. At first sight, the distribution and condition of

the wreckage seemed incompatible with a direct or proximity-fused hit at typical F-117 operating altitudes. However, the crash of an F-117A at a US air show in Maryland in September 1997 showed that the aircraft behaves oddly when out of control, descending in a fluttering flight path similar to that of a sycamore seed.

Press reports have suggested that the stealth fighter was downed by a lucky shot from an S-125 battery which had obtained some idea of the aircraft's position from short-lived temporary tracks that had been established by widely distributed radars or had detected the aircraft by using its back-up electro-optical tracking channel. In practice, the aircraft's route may have taken it over a Yugoslavian test site used for radar or missile trials, giving experienced crews equipped with upgraded systems the chance to obtain a useful radar return.

Whenever stealth fighters had crashed in the USA, the crash site had been sealed off and all fragments of the aircraft gathered up, but here was a wreck in distinctly unfriendly hands. Asked if he was concerned that parts of the wreckage of the F-117 might have been shipped to Russia for analysis, USAF Director of Operational Requirements Maj. Gen. Bruce Carlson said, "If they shipped the parts to Russia, would that concern us? Sure, it concerns us. We don't like to give anything away." However, he added, the F-117A is " what we called second generation stealth. And we've put a lot of distance between second generation and the airplanes that we're building now. We think that the result of that material, should it have gone to Russian hands ... we think that the loss is minimal." He defended the decision not to bomb the wreckage. "The airplane was lost and crashed in a rather remote location. It takes time to find those things. And I'm not sure that the commander in the field felt it was worth the risk to go in there and try to bomb it."

At least one piece of F-117A wreckage is still in Yugoslavia. The canopy of AF 82 806 is on display in a new section of the Yugoslav Aeronautical Museum. Inaugurated by Gen. Spasoje Smiljani, commander-in-chief of the Yugoslav Air Force, the exhibition features NATO aircraft and weaponry shot down during Operation Allied Force. Other exhibits include parts of an F-16CG lost on 2 May 1999, an RQ-1a Predator unmanned air vehicle (UAV) rebuilt from parts recovered

forces as required.

The air-defence system did its best to resist the effects of the NATO attacks, and to avoid being engaged. JRV i PVO fire and signature-control discipline is reported to have remained good. Following early strikes against the IADS, NATO spokesman Air Cdre David Wilby, RAF, stated that "..we have degraded it hard, there's no doubt in our minds that it is shaky. I'm not saying it's down, I'm not saying it's a totally neutralised threat, there will always be a threat from that air defence."

F-117A DOWNED

At about 8:45pm on 27 March, the IADS was to demonstrate that is was still functioning by downing an F-117A. Aircraft AF 82 806 had attacked a target near Belgrade and was heading back to base, when it was struck by a missile. As the aircraft entered an uncontrolled dive, the pilot struggled against strong negative g-forces. "The one fragment of this whole event I can't remember is pulling the handles. God took my hands and pulled," he said.

from two of the downed UAVs, the wreckage of a Luftwaffe CL289 UAV, and a near-intact example of the Raytheon AGM-145 JSOW.

On the day that the US announced the rescue of the F-117 pilot, NATO Secretary General Javier Solana stated that NATO was moving into phase two of the air campaign. Air strikes would be focus more on the Yugoslav Army and special police forces operating in Kosovo. There the campaign against the Albanian population was growing in intensity, and would continue to do so. In early April, 13 more F-117As deployed from Holloman AFB to take part in Operation Allied Force. One would replace the Nighthawk lost on 27 March, and the others would increase the number of F-117As available in the treatre.

B-1Bs DEPLOY

By this time, the USAF's third model of heavy bomber was in action. On 29 March, B-1B bombers were ordered to deploy to Europe in support of NATO operations over Yugoslavia. Before the aircraft could be despatched to Europe, they

required a block-cycle software update to their defensive avionics system. Carried out in less than 100 hours with the assistance of the 53rd Wing at Eglin AFB, this would allow the aircraft to accurately identify and jam Yugoslavian radars

Five B-1Bs from the 28th BW at Ellsworth arrived at RAF Fairford, England, on 1 April. Four were from the 77th Bomb Squadron, and one from the 37th BS. That night, two flew their first combat mission, dropping munitions over Yugoslav military targets in Kosovo. The targets for this first B-1B mission were a series of staging areas that the Yugoslav Army had set up to bring together fuel, repair and provisioning trucks in order to re-supply tank, armoured personnel carrier, and artillery units. "These staging areas are not constant places, explained a Pentagon spokesman. "They move around. They're in different places every day, and obviously we look hard for these staging areas. The B-1 is well equipped to deal with those types of wide-area targets."

Speaking at a Pentagon press conference on 14 May, Gen John Jumper, Commanding General of US Air Forces in Europe, revealed that on that first night, the B-1 bomber "was shot at and targeted very precisely by SA-6s. The defensive systems on the

airplane worked exactly as advertised." Later reports credited the aircraft's Raytheon AN/ALE-50 towed decoy as having successfully lured away missiles that had been fired at the aircraft. By the end of the campaign, the AN/ALE-50 was reported to have lured around 10 missiles away from B-1 bombers.

B-2 missions were still continuing, and by 5 April a total of 384 JDAMs had been dropped by B-2s against Serbian targets. This total suggests that two aircraft had flown sorties on 12 consecutive nights. The composite skin of the aircraft was "holding up very well", 509th Logistics Group commander Col. Bill Hood said on 5 April. "This should lay to rest concerns people may have about the aircraft's stealthiness."

The degradation of the Yugoslav defences was now severe. As early as the first week in April, the Yugoslav air defences were firing SAMs in ballistic rather than radar-guided mode in order to avoid being counterattacked by a HARM. Speaking in Washington on 22 April, US Joint Staff Director of Intelligence Adm. Wilson announced the results of the bombing on the Yugoslav forces operating in Kosovo. All four of the main lines of communication into Kosovo had been inter-dicted, reducing movements into

that region by around 50 per cent. Damage to ammunition production facilities had resulted in Yugoslav attempts to import more and different kinds of ammunition, said Wilson. "They're not having any success in that regard." The end result of the NATO air campaign was to leave Yugoslavia with "...a force which has been in the field for six weeks, seven weeks, eight weeks conducting operations, low on fuel, low on ammunition, low on food."

NATO Supreme Commander Europe (SACEUR), General Wesley Clark, reported that around 4,400 strike sorties had been flown. Although the weather was average for the time of the year, it was creating problems. "On about two-thirds of the days we have had more than half of the strike sorties cancelled," said Gen. Clark. Nevertheless, attacks on military industries, and in particular ammunition production were said to have been effective. "We have had some very good success against ammunition stocks and we have done very serious damage to his ability to

SAM SITE IVO SABAC, SERBIA
POST STRIKE

repair and maintain his aircraft, military vehicles, armaments and munitions."

The F-117 may have been hard at work, but the headlines in the field of stealth were going to the B-2. By early May, the B-2 force had dropped more than 1 million pounds (450,000kg) of ordnance on Yugoslav targets. This warload had included more than 500 JDAMs. Since each B-2 can carry up to 32,000lb (14,500kg) of ordnance (16 JDAMs), this means that at least 32 missions had been flown. "The jet's performance really has exceeded all of our expectations," Brig. Gen. Leroy Barnidge Jr., 509th Bomb Wing commander, told the press on 5 May. On a typical sortie, each bomber carried up to 16 2,000lb (900kg) JDAMs instead of the two carried by the Nighthawk. As a result, "A B-2 is equivalent to eight F-117s. We can take this thing thousands of miles; we can go into very lethal environments, and we can put the bombs exactly where we want them. Then we bring the guys home, turn the jets and do it again." The combination of the B-2 and JDAM was highly accurate. "I've seen zero collateral damage from our strikes," Barnidge said, "and that's a pretty good record."

It was inevitable that this high operational tempo would highlight problems with what was still a relatively new aircraft. Because of an airflow-cooling problem, the actuator remote terminal (ART) which works the various control surfaces was one of the high-failure items, but this was repaired on the spot.

By mid-May, NATO had flown around 20,000 sorties against targets in Yugoslavia, and estimated that the defences had fired more than 600 SAMs. Although Yugoslavia claimed the destruction of more than 80 NATO fixed-wing aircraft, helicopters, and UAVs, in fact the total NATO losses of manned aircraft had been only two – the F-117A, plus an F-16CJ shot down on 2 May. A small number of NATO aircraft – estimated by a NATO

Top left: The GBU-30 JDAM is the weapon of choice for the B-2A, and about 500 were dropped on Yugoslavia in the spring of 1999, using the CPS targeting system. This amounted to over 450 tons of munitions.

Far left: In USAF post-strike imagery, Craters mark the position of what had been a Yugoslavian SAM site at Ivo Sabac.

Left: In the hours of darkness, a B-2 is prepared for the long flight to attack targets in Yugoslavia.

spokesman as "about five to ten" – had received some combat damage, but the US DoD would not comment on a report that an F-117 had sustained damage following a near-miss from an SA-3 round. Spokesman Major General Chuck Wald would only say, "We have no indication whatsoever that they can track [F-]117s."

In previous wars, air defences equipped with missiles such as the S-75 (SA-2) and S-125 (SA-3) had achieved hit rates of only a few per cent. Before the conflict, Yugoslavia is reported to have been confident that it would be able to inflict attrition rates of about six per cent on NATO strike aircraft. In practice, they had managed a SAM kill rate of 0.3 per cent (two aircraft for 600 missiles launched), and an overall attrition rate of around 0.01 per cent (two aircraft downed from more than 20,000 hostile sorties). These figures made Yugoslavia's air defences the least successful of any major missile-equipped force used in recent wars.

The first week of June saw the effective collapse of the Yugoslavian air-defence system as a result of sustained NATO attacks, and on 9 June Yugoslavia finally agreed to accept the NATO demand to withdraw its forces from Kosovo.

By the end of the campaign, NATO had mounted 38,004 strikes in 10,484 sorties. The Fairford-based B-1Bs had flown 81 combat mission. On the 74 missions in which weapons were released, the force dropped more than 1,100 tonnes of bombs, mostly Mk 82 bombs and CBU-87 cluster bombs.

The B-2 force had set its own record, with 51 of the 53 pilots of the 509th having flown combat missions. Eight B-2s were used, flying a total of more than 45 missions with only one turn-back. Although the stealth bomber flew only 1 per cent of the total number of Allied missions flown, it delivered 8 per cent of the bombs dropped.

During a 21 October hearing of the Senate Armed Services Committee hearing, Gen. Wesley Clark stated that Allied crews delivered more than 23,000 bombs and other munitions with less than 20 incidents of collateral damage. "That's an incident rate of less than one-tenth of 1 percent," Clark said. "There's never been anything like it in the history of a military campaign, and I think it's a real tribute to the skill and proficiency of the men and women who flew and executed this campaign, to achieve that kind of precision."

COUNTERS TO STEALTH

Having created the first stealth aircraft, it is hardly surprising that the US DoD has funded the development of counter-stealth technologies. This has required a dual approach. An effective anti-stealth defence will require sensors able to detect low-RCS targets, along with weapons able to attack these elusive opponents.

The primary sensor is still radar, which can be inproved in three ways – increasing power output to obtain stronger radar returns form stealthy targets, using improved digital processing techniques to detect faint returns in the presence of background clutter and hostile jamming, and moving to lower frequencies where today's stealth technology is less effective.

Claims by radar manufacturers that their equipment have detected US stealth aircraft must be treated with scepticism. When not in combat, the F-117 is fitted with radar reflectors so that it shows up on air traffic control radars, and the same probably applies to the B-2.

To strip away the protection offered by a low RCS involves placing more energy on target, and having a more sensitive receiver to detect this energy. Both measures create their own problems. Greater power can be delivered on target by using a larger radar antenna and a more powerful transmitter, but these increase the size, weight and

cost of the radar, and reduce its mobility. Increasing the sensitivity of a radar receiver brings its own problems, since the output can contain enough clutter and other false targets to place a massive load on the processing hardware.

Rather than pursue such "brute force" solutions to the problem of detecting low-RCS targets, radar designers are trying new operating modes. For example, the fast scanning speeds possible with an electronically scanned array

Below: **Early test flights confirmed the flying characteristics of the B-2, but testing of its stealth capabilities was to be prolonged.**

Right: The E-3A was designed before the era of stealthy targets but a planned upgrade programme will improve its effectiveness.

Below: The Boeing E-3 Sentry is operated by the USA, UK, France, and collaboratively by other members of the NATO alliance.

Left: A variant of Marconi's Martello radar was a candidate in the mid-1980s competition to select a radar for a joint military/civil US radar network.

Below: The MiG-25 Foxbat was designed to intercept high-flying bombers, but by 1977 missile firing trials against simulated cruise missiles had begun.

make it possible for the radar to take note of suspect signals whose value lies below the threshold set for a true target, then re-examine them once the rest of the scan has been completed.

This is the approach which Ericsson Microwave Systems has adopted with its Giraffe and Sea Giraffe Agile Multi-Beam (AMB) 3-D radars. Intended for use with the RBS 23 Bamse SAM system, Giraffe uses a "priority tracking"

scheme against difficult targets, and can detect a 1.08sq ft (0.1sq m) target at around a third of the radar's normal range. Sea Giraffe uses a single "omnibus" transmitter beam, plus a series of receive beams which give around four times the time budget possible with a single beam. This allows the radar to spend more time observing targets of interest.

Several years ago researchers at the Mitre Corporation revealed a

novel operating mode which shows how computing-intensive algorithms may help with the detection of stealthy targets. "Track-before-detect" was proposed as an aid to air-to-air radars, but could be applied to ground-based sets. Instead of measuring suspected signals against a pre-defined threshold to determine whether they represented a target, a "track-before-detect" radar treats all

signals as potentially genuine and attempts to build these into tentative tracks. A true target will gradually result in a "sensible" track, while false tracks can soon be eliminated due to their unreasonable and unrealistic behaviour.

One way of degrading the effects of stealth technology is to use radars which operate at VHF and UHF frequencies, rather than in the microwave band. Most Western long-range surveillance radars operate in D-band (1-2GHz), E-band (2-3Ghz) or F-band (3-4Ghz), but Russia has long preferred to use C-band (0.5-1GHz), B-band (250-500MHz) or even A-band (100-250MHz). Similar low frequencies are also used in some Chinese surveillance radars. In the past, these equipments have often been dismissed as examples of Soviet technological backwardness. VHF and UHF radars are relatively easy to design and manufacture, the reason why all the early Second World War radars were of this type.

The need for smaller size, better low-altitude coverage and improved target discrimination soon led to most radars being built to operate at microwave frequencies but, even today, UHF and VHF frequencies still have some military advantages. For one thing, their antennas tend to be bulky. This is a problem for the user but it does give virtual immunity from attack by anti-radar missiles – it is just not possible to cram a VHF homing antenna into a missile seeker. They also offer good long-range performance. To see the reason for this requires a detour into basic radio theory.

High frequency microwave radio signals require a direct line of sight between the transmitter and receiver. Thus transmitted signals can be obscured by terrain features and maximum range is constrained by the curvature of the Earth. Operating at such frequencies makes long range communications difficult, and the first radio stations used the much lower LF or MF bands. At these frequencies the "surface wave" effect becomes apparent. The signal emanating from the antenna tends to hug the Earth's surface, travelling well beyond the horizon.

At the still higher VHF and UHF bands, the skywave is not refracted back to the ground and is lost. There is still a useful degree of ground-hugging surface wave, however, which allows radio reception some way over the horizon. The previously

Above: **The envelope of a non-rigid airship makes a near-perfect radome for a surveillance radar, and the helium atmosphere will not affect performance.**

Below: **The model shows the gondola of one proposed USN solution to the problem of detecting low-RCS targets – the Airship Industries/ Westinghouse YEZ-2A.**

Top right: **Developed by Russia's Nizhny Novgorod Radio Technical Institute, the 1L13 is a mobile two-dimensional radar operating in the VHF band.**

Right: **The massive antennas of the Cape Dyer station of the DEW line look impressive, but this network of North-facing radar stations is obsolescent.**

mentioned "obsolete" UHF and VHF radars also make use of this effect, giving much longer ranges than direct line-of-sight microwave systems.

VHF PROBLEMS

In designing a stealth aircraft, RCS engineers work to defeat the 1 - 20GHz microwave frequencies used by most radars. Equipments operating at lower frequencies will be less affected by RAM and other RCS-reduction measures, giving them some ability to detect and track stealth aircraft.

Luckily for the operators of stealth aircraft, UHF and VHF radars are no panacea, so they

Nizhny Novgorod Radio Technical Institute are confident that they have cracked the problem of tracking stealth aircraft. Nitel's 55G6 family of VHF-band radars are physically large, but can track low-RCS targets such as cruise missiles and stealth aircraft, says the company. According to Nitel, the basic advantages of VHF-band radars are low cost, good all-weather performance, and resistance to jamming. Since a directional antenna at such long wavelengths must be very large in order to achieve a narrow beamwidth, it cannot be fitted to an anti-radiation missile, so the radar is invulnerable to ARM attacks. Nitel claims that VHF radars were the only Iraqi air-defence sensors to survive the 1991 Gulf War, but says it does not know what success (if any) the Iraqis had in detecting or tracking USAF F-117 stealth fighters. Given the scale of the Russian post-conflict analysis of earlier military campaigns in which its equipment was used, this professed ignorance seems strange, unless Iraq is refusing to provide feedback.

In the past, Western analysts have often dismissed Russian VHF radars as primitive, but in a 1997 discussion with the Nizhny Novgorod Radio Technical Institute's Dr Alexandr Zatchchepitsky (General Designer) and Valery Marskin (Deputy Director of Research, and Chief Engineer) the author learned that a surprising degree of sophistication is built into these huge radars. In early VHF-band radars, the signal detected by each antenna element was carried at radio frequency down to a central receiver, but the 55G6-U has analogue to digital converters built into each of the individual elements which make up the vertical and horizontal array. Although the huge inverted-T-shaped antenna of this radar has vertical and horizontal legs 100ft (30m) long, and an azimuth beamwidth of three degrees, the Russians claim a performance similar to that of the US AN/TPS-70 E/F-band radar, with an accuracy of 33ft (100m) in range, 0.2 deg in azimuth, and 1,970ft (600m) in altitude. Keeping the signal to noise ratio of the radar as low as possible was the key to achieving angular accuracies of around 1/15 of the beam width in azimuth, and between 1/15 and 1/25 of the beam width in elevation.

France's Parasol alerting radar operates at even lower frequencies in the HF band (3 to 30MHz). Built under a contract from the French ministry of defence, Parasol was developed

still make up a small portion of the total number of threats. Long wavelengths create their own tactical and engineering problems.

For instance, such radars tend to be physically big, since large antennas are needed in order to obtain adaquately-narrow beam-widths and high antenna gains. A side effect of the relatively wide beam created by even a large VHF antenna is that the radar's resolution in azimuth is poor.

When the designer sets out to combine VHF operating frequencies with mobile operation, the resulting systems are often reminiscent of the Second World War German Freya and are cumbersome to deploy.

Russian electronics company Nitel and research organisation.

OTH Radar System

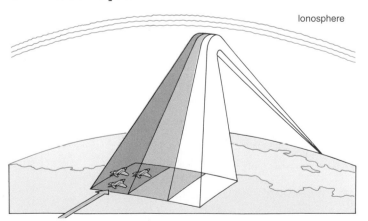

Ionosphere

Above: **General Electric's FPS-118 over-the-horizon radar bounces HF signals off the ionosphere in order to track aircraft flying far out over the Atlantic. The beam can be** **electronically steered in azimuth, while range is adjusted by varying the frequency (and ionospheric bounce behaviour) of the transmitted signal.**

by Thomson-CSF to detect stealthy threats and anti-radiation missiles. It was tested in the mid-1990s.

Under contract from the German Federal Office for Defence Technology and Procurement, Alcatel Defense Systems is developing a demonstration UHF cueing radar for missile-defence applications. The primary role of this radar is the detection of tactical ballistic missile (TBM) threats, and at UHF frequencies the radar cross-section of these is typically 10 to 100 times greater than that at microwave frequencies, while atmospheric loss and clutter are considerably lower. However, Alcatel SEL has commented that at UHF frequencies the use of stealth technology (what Alcatel SEL terms "radar camouflage" of missile targets) is practically impossible.

Surface-to-air missile systems use radars which scan large areas of sky and carry out several air-defence tasks simultaneously. The cueing radar is able to handle the task of searching for incoming threats, then hand over newly

detected targets to the weapon system radar. By concentrating its radar energy into the 5deg x 5deg cueing window defined by the cueing radar, the weapon-system radar will be able to acquire the target at the earliest possible time.

The USAF insists that the stealth features designed into the F-117 and B-2 cannot be circumvented by long-wavelength radar, but during the 1991 Gulf War a Royal Navy warship is reported to have picked up radar echoes form F-117 stealth fighters. If true, this may be due to the relatively long wavelengths used by older British naval surveillance radars. The now-obsolete Marconi Type 965 operated at metric wavelengths, presumably A or B band.

OTH RADARS

One of the most promising methods of detecting a stealth aircraft is by means of over-the-horizon (OTH) radars. In the United States, research on equipment of this type has been under way for about 25 years, with the aim of developing better defences against conventional bomber

US Defensive Radar Coverage

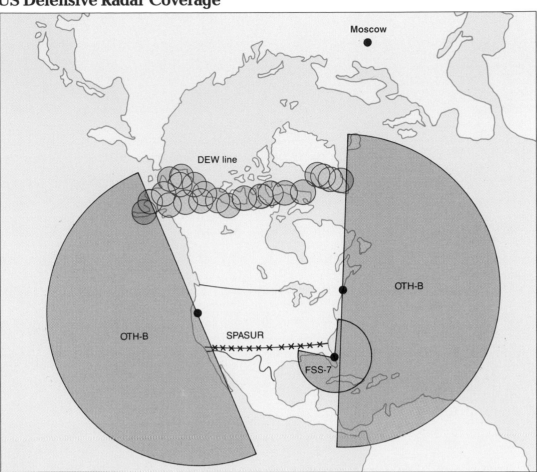

Above: The Pave Paws phased-array radar on the US East and West coasts are anti-SLBM systems, intended to detect sneak attacks by missile firing submarines.

Above right: By the 1970s, the US radar early-warning radar network had shrunk to this emasculated form. Although the development by the then Soviet Union of the Tu-26 "Backfire" and Tu-160 "Blackjack" bombers provided the impetus for improvements, the collapse of the Soviet Union ended most of these.

Left: Based at Shemya in the Aleutian Islands, the Cobra Dane radar covers the Eastern tip of the USSR, including the strategic Kamchatka Peninsula.

threats. The aim was to create long-range radars able to track aircraft which are masked from the view of conventional ground-based radars by the curvature of the earth's surface.

Radars of this type direct a powerful sky wave towards the earth's ionosphere. This is refracted and returned towards the earth's surface,

illuminating a distant patch of terrain or sea. Any targets present in this area create radar echoes which follow the reverse route back up to the ionosphere and thus back to the receiver of the OTH radar.

One problem in such dependence on sky waves is that the signal is redirected not by reflection but by refraction, so propagation conditions cannot be calculated by simple geometry. The amount of refraction experienced depends on the frequency of the signal and the density of the ionosphere. The latter varies with time, as does the height of the ionosphere. Variations occur on both daily and annual cycles and cannot be predicted accurately. As the amount of refraction being experienced alters, so also does the distance between the transmitter and the location where the sky wave returns to the earth's surface a distance know to radio operators as the "skip distance".

Studies of a possible US OTH system began in the early 1970s and system definition work was completed by November 1973. The contract to develop a prototype of what was then called the over-the-horizon backscatter (OTH-B) radar was

awarded in March 1975 but the programme soon ran into difficulties with both cost and timescale. A restructuring began in December 1976 which put the effort on a more realistic basis, allowing technical feasibility tests four years later.

The initial goal of the programme was to develop and test a limited coverage prototype radar. Based in Maine, this was used to assess the level of technical performance required by an operational system. At the same time, further work was carried out on basic OTH radar technology in order to increase the effectiveness of the final system. Areas explored by this research effort included ionospheric modelling and prediction, adaptive beam-forming, low-sidelobe antennas and computer algorithms for signal processing and radar control.

The prototype system was handed over to the USAF in May 1980, allowing the start of nine months of system performance tests. These gave the confidence needed to make the decision in October 1981 to proceed with the development and deployment of an operational system, a contract for which was

awarded to General Electric in June 1982. This called for the upgrading of the experimental system in Maine to a fully operational 60 degree azimuth coverage Initial Operating Sector (IOS) of the East Coast Radar System.

US COVERAGE

Official designation of the system is AN/FPS-118. Transmission frequency is 5-28MHz, with an output power of 1,200kW. A system with four sites was planned. One would be in Maine, the other three on the US West coast, Central USA and Alaska. Intended to provide early-warning of aircraft or missile threats approaching the continental USA, it has effectively been closed down with the ending of the Cold War.

The Raytheon AN/TPS-71 Relocatable OTH Radar (ROTHR) is much smaller than the FPS-118, and is designed to allow rapid deployment to prepared sites. Developed for the US Navy, it consists of two sites – a transmitter and a combined operations centre/receiver – spaced up to 110 miles (180km) apart. It transmits at frequencies of 5-28MHz, and has a power output of 200kW. Maximum range is 1,875 miles (3,000km).

The possibility that OTH radars could be used to track stealth aircraft emerged in the summer of 1986 when Dr. D.H. Sinnott, a senior principal research scientist of the Australian Department of Defence's Research Centre at Salisbury, stated during a defence conference in Canberra that the entire airframe of a stealth aircraft would reflect energy at HF frequencies.

An OTH radar system has a severe limitation in terms of minimum range. Since the radar signal must reach the ionosphere, reflect and then return to the earth's surface, an OTH radar cannot detect targets operating within a radius of about 500nm (900km). Aware of this fact, the crew of a stealth aircraft would be able to initiate a change in course or other evasive tactics once they were confident that their aircraft was no longer visible to the OTH radar.

Russia has an equivalent to the AN/FPS-118. Known as OTH-B, this has been in service since the 1970s. It transmits at a frequency of 4-30MHz, and has a power output of 30MW. An OTH radar system is also being

developed in China. Expected to have a range of 2,190 miles (3,500km), it operates between 5-28MHz, and emits 1000kW of power.

On the other side of the globe, Australia has the need for an OTH system and vast tracts of desert in which to locate antennas. Under the Jindalee programme, a single test site has been built at Alice Springs in the centre of the country. This will later form part of a three-site operation system due to enter service in the mid-1990s. The other sites will be in the north-east and the south-west.

It remains to be seen just how effectively OTH and VHF radars could "hand over" stealthy targets to microwave band radars. Much of the secret test flying of the F-117A and earlier XST stealth fighters in Nevada against threat systems will have been intended to investigate this problem.

"Can the F-117 or B-2 be tracked by radar? The answer to that question is yes," says USAF Director of Operational Requirements Maj. Gen. Bruce Carlson. "All vehicles can be tracked by radar. However, the key here is to know when you're being tracked by radar, what

radars are tracking you and what the fidelity of that track is. For instance, a very low frequency radar – whether it's tracking a conventional, first-generation or a third-generation stealth airplane – has very little capability to track it with precision. They know the general area that the airplane may be in, but they can't track it with precision needed to guide either another airplane to it or a SAM to it. So what you need then is the target-tracking

radars, the higher frequency radars that are much more accurate, and that's where the stealth airplanes that are designed from the bottom up have their significant advantages."

Another possible technique for detecting stealth aircraft involves inter-netting a series of fixed-site and mobile radars, using them intermittently as active search systems and for the rest of the time as passive direction-

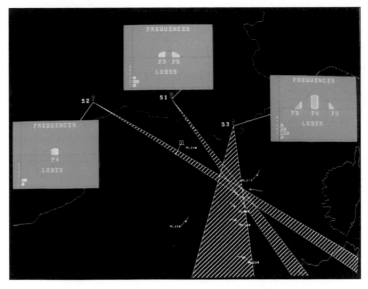

Left: Upgrades have allowed this US Army Patriot radar station to control improved versions of the Patriot missile, including the PAC-3 anti-missile variant.

Right: Triangulation locates the position of a hostile emitter. Stealth aircraft must remain radar- and radio-silent while in range of enemy ESM stations.

finders. This was first done as a way of avoiding ARM attacks. The enemy is faced with a series of blinking emitters which ESMs and ARMs "see" as only intermittent signals whose location and characteristics change rapidly. Even if one or more sites can be attacked and knocked out, the network will continue to function.

Detection of stealth targets would involve the use of a group of netted radars able to transmit on a wide range of frequencies. As a result of the inevitable compromises in the design process, stealth measures cannot be equally effective at all angles and frequencies. The greater the number of frequencies and directions of the signals arriving at a stealth aircraft, the greater the chances that one or more might create a usable echo.

One promising countermeasure to stealth is bi-static radar. In a normal (mono-static) radar, the transmitter and receiver are at the same location and often share a common antenna. In a bi-static radar, they are located some distance apart and several receivers may share a single transmitter. An

Below: The Ballistic Missile Early Warning System at Fylingdales in the UK has been upgraded to deal with new threats, which may include stealthy re-entry vehicles.

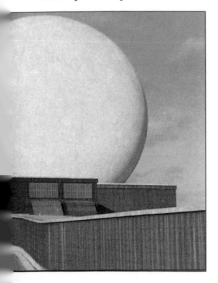

aircraft which relies on shaping or faceting to reduce its RCS is designed to ensure that an incoming radar signal is not reflected directly back to the radar. This works well against a conventional mono-static radar but could result in the incoming radar energy being "dumped" in the direction of a listening receiver forming part of a bi-static system.

In France, Thomson-CSF has developed the D-Fence bi-static warning radar to detect stealthy threats. Like the Parasol radar mentioned earlier, this operates in the HF band (3 to 30MHz), and was built under contract from the French MoD. D-Fence is reported to be able to detect stealth aircraft, UAVs and cruise missiles, and to have a range of tens of kilometres.

Being passive, receiver sites are immune to the attentions of threats such a directional jammers, anti-radiation missiles and "Wild Weasel" aircraft. In a bi-static radar, there are several potential ways of protecting the transmitter. The concept known as "sanctuary radar" involves installing the transmitter in a safe location from which it may serve a number of front-line receiving sites. Suitable locations for the transmitter could be far back from the battle area, either at a ground location heavily protected by air defences or in a high-flying aircraft. Another possibility would involve mounting the transmitter unit in a geo-stationary satellite.

Bi-static radar systems need not incorporate a transmitter, but could exploit the RF energy from other emitters. Lockheed Martin's Silent Sentry system uses a passive receiver to detect and track airborne targets via the reflected energy from television and FM radio stations.

Since these signal sources broadcast at VHF and UHF frequencies, their transmissions may be strongly reflected by stealth aircraft.

During tests of this concept, Lockheed Martin is reported to have used signals from FM radio stations in Gaithersburg, Maryland, to track commercial aircraft flying in and out of Baltimore-Washington International Airport. However, like VHF and UHF radars, Silent Sentry is not accurate enough to be used for targeting. It can be used only to detect a target, and to alert a separate tracking radar.

ADVANCED RADARS

Perhaps the best prospect for an anti-stealth radar is a technique only just emerging from the laboratory. This is known as a "carrierless radar". Tiny low-powered radars of this type are already used for some commercial applications such as creating images of the interior of concrete structures. However, larger and vastly more powerful systems could be developed for air surveillance and target tracking.

At first sight, the concept of a carrierless radar seems like a contradiction in terms. Engineers use the word "carrier" to describe the basic radio-frequency signal to which modulation is applied. Such modulation can be speech or data (in the case of a communications link), pulses (in the case of pulsed radar) or variations in frequency (in the case of a continuous-wave radar). Remove the carrier and it might seem that nothing is left to carry the modulation.

All the radar engineer needs is a pulse (probably of rectangular shape) with which to illuminate his target. Using a mathematical technique

known as Fourier Expansion, any waveform can be broken down into a series of sinusoidal components – a main component, known as the fundamental, and multiples of this fundamental, known as harmonics. Vary the shape and frequency of the waveform being analysed and the resulting "mix" of fundamental and harmonics will also change. For every shape of waveform, a "cocktail" of these components can be obtained.

The exact operating principles of carrierless radar are classified but the broad idea seems to be to reverse the process. Instead of transmitting the desired waveform, transmit the correct mix of frequencies which will recreate it. These could mostly be of low power and could stretch across most or even all of the frequency bands used for radar. The resulting synthesised pulse would not be affected by radar-absorbent materials.

OPTICAL SYSTEMS

Stealth technology may also be partially nullified by the use of sensors operating at frequencies far above those of traditional microwave radars. For decades, the highest frequencies used for military radars were in J-band (10-20GHz), but growing use is now being made of K band (20-40GHz) and M band (40-100GHz). Strictly speaking, the term "millimetre-wave" should be reserved for M band and higher, but in practice it is often applied to a growing number of systems operating at or near 35GHz.

An early application for millimetre-wave radar was in short-range air-defence. Hollandse Signaalapparaten offers several 35GHz radars such as the ASADS gun-mounted radar for AA weapons such as 40mm guns, Spear 35GHz radar/TV fire-control system for low-level air-defence units, and LIROD (Lightweight Radar/Optronic Detector) naval fire-control system.

Ericsson chose K-band for its Eagle fire-control radar so that the resulting narrow beam, high-gain antenna, and minimal sidelobes would help give the equipment a low radar signature. Their success lead to an improved version being selected as part of the RBS 23 BAMSE SAM system. Radars that combined millimetric and conventional microwave frequencies in a single tracker could use the lower frequency to detect targets, and the higher frequency for subsequent tracking. A common combination teams I-band and K-band.

Above: SAM systems which don't use radar will pose a threat to stealth aircraft. Shorts' Javelin is command guided and has an IR surveillance system.

Hollandse Signaalapparaten is probably the best-known manufacturer of this type of dual-frequency radar, offering its Flycatcher radar, Sting radar/EO naval fire-control system, and STIR naval tracking radar. However, the concept has also been used by other companies including Elta Electronic Industries in the EL/M-221 naval fire-control radar, and Bharat Dynamics in the PIW 519 weapon control radar. Russian designers used I and K-band in the radar controlling the Kinzhal (SA-N-9) naval SAM system, and are thought to have used the same dual frequencies in the MR-114, -145, and -185 radars for 100mm AK-100 naval gun mount.

The ability of a laser radar (lidar) to detect hydrocarbons in the atmosphere could provide a useful anti-stealth sensor. According to a paper on remote laser sensing published by Carlo

Right: One possible stealth detector is bi-static radar, a system whose transmitter and receiver are in different locations. The "sanctuary" concept shown here is probably the ultimate bi-static system. Ground-based receiving sites operate in conjunction with a transmitter in a high-flying aircraft (whose position is measured using ground-based DME stations), or even in a satellite.

Kopp in *Air Chronicles*, "a jet aircraft exhaust trail will contain concentrations of hydrocarbons of the order of parts per million, which can be 100 or more times the background atmospheric concentration. Should we see a proliferation of stealth technology in the next century, the ability to track such aircraft even under VFR conditions would significantly limit an opponent's opportunities to use his stealth aircraft productively. By constraining hostile stealth aircraft operations to IFR conditions where lidar is ineffective, an opponent will be at the mercy of the weather and thus more predictable in terms of operational activity." Since helicopters in NOE (Nap-Of-the-Earth) flight and hover are in a moderate to high engine power regime, and generating large amounts of exhaust gas, Kopp believes that a battlefield-surveillance lidar could also detect stealthy battlefield

helicopters in the class of the RAH-66 Comanche.

IR DETECTION

Techniques such as direct shielding, active cooling and passive surface treatments such as special paints and coatings have reduced the IR signature of stealthy aircraft and missiles, but not to the degree that RF signatures have been reduced. IR thus remains a viable method of detecting threats. The long-term goal of stealth engineers must be to reduce IR detectability in the 3-5 and 8-12 micron bands to levels which would make IR sensors as blunted in range as their RF counterparts, but until this has been achieved, IR and other EO sensors may prove valuable short-range anti-stealth sensors, particularly against missile threats. Their usefulness against manned aircraft may be limited, since high-value stealth aircraft

are likely to stay well above the combat ceiling of point-defence systems, attacking using guided munitions such as laser-guided bombs, or well away from the defences and attacking with stand-off missiles.

The ability of an EO system to track a stealth aircraft was shown at the 1996 Farnborough Air Show when a military crew demonstrating the BAe (now Matra BAe Dynamics) Jernas version of Rapier used the system's EO tracking system to acquire and track the Northrop Grumman B-2 Spirit stealth bomber at a range of 3.75 miles (6km). In practice, a B-2 tasked with attacking Farnborough would never have come within Rapier range of the airfield, so the entire exercise said nothing about the aircraft's potential vulnerability to ground-based sensors.

The B-2 may have some IR suppression tricks up its sleeve. Northrop Grumman's only

Bi-Static "Sanctuary" Concept

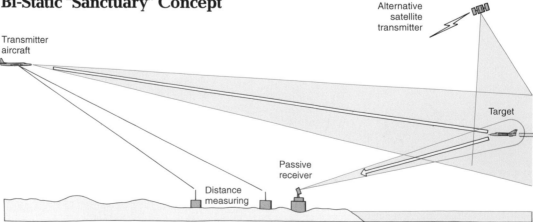

comment on the Farnborough incident was that, "It's easier to detect the B-2 at air shows than in combat," so it is possible that any IR-suppression system fitted to the aircraft would not be activated while the bomber could be observed by non-US sensors.

Some idea of the current level of Western capabilities can be gleaned from the AN/AAS-42. This has a 91lb (41kg) chin-mounted sensor head that contains the optics and detector assembly, plus a three-axis internally stabilised gimbal system. It operates in conjunction with a 37lb (16.3kg)

Left: **The Antey 9K33 Osa (SA-8 "Gecko") uses radar guidance but has a back-up optical tracking mode which could be used against stealth aircraft.**

Below: **Advanced IR-guided weapons such as the Stinger SAM (seen here in vehicle-mounted form) might be able to home in on the jetpipes of stealth fighters.**

controller/processor unit mounted within the aircraft. Unofficially reported to be a dual-band device operating at 3-5 microns and 8-12 microns, the system has six operating modes, which are similar to those of the aircraft's Hughes AN/APG-71 radar. Azimuth and elevation scan volumes are selectable, and separately controlled by the aircrew. Scanning can be done manually or under the control of the pilot.

The MiG bureau are enthusiastic proponents of EO sensors, and the stabilised EO system carried by the MiG-29 and Su-27 combines an infra-red search and track (IRST) sensor and a laser rangefinder which share a common stabilised Cassegrain optional system. The Sukhoi team takes a more conservative view of the virtues of EO sensors, but installed a similar system on the Su-27.

EO sensors are also carried by the Eurofighter 2000, Rafale, and the Mitsubishi F-2. The

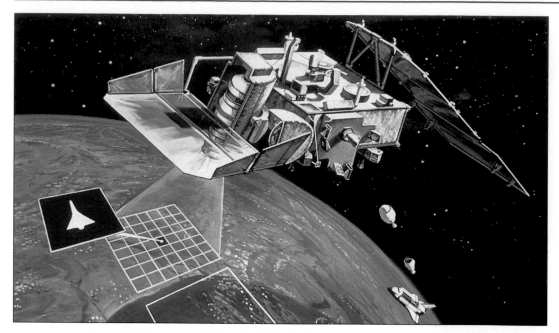

mid-course updating facility of the semi-active radar-guided R-27R1 and R-27ER1 models, so must be locked on before launch, yet have maximum ranges of 45 miles (72km) and 81 miles (130km), respectively.

In 1997 press reports suggested that Iraq was about to obtain the ability to track US stealth fighters by purchasing Tesla-Pardubice Tamara ESM systems from the Czech Republic. A year earlier Maj. Gen. Oldrizhikh Barak, president of the Tesla-Pardubice, told the Russian newspaper *Pravda* that a Tamara system consisting of three units spaced several miles apart can track stealth or similar low-signature aircraft from distances of about 12 miles (19km).

Tamara monitors the spectrum from 820MHz to 18GHz, and normally consists of three

proposed dual-band IRST originally planned for Eurofighter 2000 proved too expensive, so the specification was relaxed, allowing contractors to offer single-band or dual-band systems. In August 1992, a development contract was finally awarded to the Eurofist consortium for the Pirate (Passive Infra-Red Airborne Tracking Equipment) single-band system. FIAR acts as lead contractor, while Thorn EMI is the system design authority. Spanish team member was Eurotronica, which has since been replaced by Tecnobit.

The Defence Optronics division of Thomson-CSF is working with SAT to develop the forward-looking optronic system for Rafale. The system is mounted behind the radar, and has two sensor heads on the upper fuselage just ahead of the canopy. The IR search and imaging unit uses infra-red and high-definition CCD technology, and is mounted to port. The identification and rangefinding unit (based on an eye-safe laser rangefinder) is to starboard, while a common processing unit is located in the lower fuselage. The combined system will allow passive detection, visual identification, and damage assessment of targets in air-to-air combat.

Relatively little is known about the Japan Aviation Electronics laser/EO system on the Mitsubishi F-2. It is probably a dual-band (3-5 micron and 8-18 micron) sensor suitable for air-to-air and air-to-ground use.

The range at which aircraft can be detected by today's fighter-mounted EO systems is classified, but some clues can be obtained from the published performance of the IR-guided Vympel R-27T1 and R-27ET1 air-to-air missiles. These lack the

Above left: The Teal Ruby infra-red sensor was devised as a research tool into the problems of detecting air targets by observing their IR signature from orbit.

Left: The Almaz S-300PM (SA-10b "Grumble") uses a Track-Via-Missile (TVM) guidance system which may have been designed with low-RCS targets in mind.

Below: The likely operating altitude and location of Western surveillance aircraft would bring them within the firepower of long-range surface-to-air systems such as those operated by the Russians. This diagram was prepared before the deployment of the US Air Force's E-8 Joint Stars and retirement of the EF-111, but the potential problem remains. Plans to develop a stealthy aircraft in place of the E-8 were abandoned.

Ranges of Russian SAM Systems

Right: **The Improved Hawk is NATO's most common medium range SAM. Further upgrades are needed to counter future stealth aircraft developments.**

stations mounted on Tatra 815 8x8 trucks. By comparing the time of arrival of detected signals at the three stations, the system is able to derive the bearing of the emitter, then identify it by comparison with a built-in threat library. Tamara provides coverage over a 100 degree arc, while its maximum range is determined by the radar horizon. The Czech company has been promoting Tamara as an anti-stealth measure, but has not identified the nature of the RF signal emitted from stealth aircraft which would allow these to be tracked. The range of 12 miles mentioned above suggests a relatively low level signal.

It is unlikely that any one single technology will dramatically decrease the vulnerability of steath aircraft. By pooling the information from several sensors, no one of which is giving reliable data, the "signal-to-noise" ratio may be improved to the point were stealthy targets can be distinguished.

MULTI-SENSORS

Much of the effort currently being devoted to developing next-generation air defences is concentrating on the idea of netting different sensors, and particularly different types of sensor, then fusing the data from all sources to create a tactical picture. This technique is already being used on some modern air-defence tracking system such as Oerlikon Contraves Skyshield, which fuses data from the radar, TV and IR channels to help track difficult targets.

The Surveillance and Warning Systems Department of Bodenseewerke Gerätetechnik is testing a technology demonstrator for a multi-sensor system able to detect aircraft, helicopters, UAVs, and missiles. Developed under Germany's Aufklärung und Bekämpfung nicht-ballisticher Flugkörper (ABF) research and development programme, this will use a combination of IR and UV sensors that will scan an entire hemisphere. Fusing the target features seen in the two bands is expected to sort out potential targets from clutter and noise. A verification system consisting of a high-resolution IR sensor and a laser rangefinder will be used to examine these potential targets, obtaining additional information

Right: **The massive Antey S-300V (SA-12a "Gladiator") is part of a Russian SAM system designed to counter low-RCS missile targets.**

such as range, velocity and IR features. The equipment will then create three-dimensional tracks which will allow discrimination between real targets and clutter.

Conventional target association and tracking techniques such as probabilistic data association (PDA) and joint probabilistic data association (JPDA) work well given good data from a single tracking

sensor, but are less effective against the sort of poor-quality and intermittent data likely to be obtained when attempting to track a low-RCS target. Research work carried out at the National University of Defense Technology, in Hunan, China, has devised track initiation, data association, and tracking techniques suitable for use with a network of distributed tracking sensors. Such a network might be able to maintain a reliable track by combining individual detections or fragmentary tracks from every sensor in the system. Work has also been carried out at the Tsinghua University in China to develop new data-fusion techniques which would allow stealthy targets to be tracked by netted radars.

ANTI-STEALTH SAMS

The latest generation of

medium-range SAM systems offer anti-stealth capability. Following Desert Storm, the requirement for Patriot PAC-3 was extended to cover not only conventional aircraft, UAVs, and ballistic missiles, but also tactical air-to-surface missiles, anti-radiation missiles, tactical ballistic missiles, and what a Fiscal Year 97 report by the US Director, Operational Test and Evaluation (DOT&E), described as "additional performance requirements needed to counter advanced stealth technology". The minimum RCS Patriot PAC-3 can engage has never been released – Russian sources claim 1.08sq ft (0.1sq m), but this figure may not be reliable.

The previous chapter (Stealth in Action) described how Yugoslavian S-125 Pechora (SA-3 "Goa") surface-to-air missile systems had been upgraded to improve their anti-stealth capability. This did not mark the end of S-125 upgrades. Under a programme in which Russia's Rosvooruzheniye organisation is to upgrade 50 Egyptian Pechora systems to the Pechora-2 standard, the detection range against stealth aircraft is being increased from up to 10 miles (16km) to more than 19 miles (30km), say the system's designers.

Since the USA has been

Above: **Jamming strobes designed to mask large targets will be even more effective when used to protect stealth aircraft.**

Left: **In the absence of stealthy threats, the US is focusing future developments of the Standard naval SAM on the anti-ballistic missile role.**

openly developing small cruise missiles since the mid-1970s, it is only to be expected that the latest generation of Soviet SAMs has been designed to deal with such low-RCS targets. One of the first was the SA-10 Grumble, a weapon whose development may have been protracted by the need to cope with cruise missiles.

According to the US Department of Defense, at least 500 SA-10 sites would be needed in order to create an effective defence against cruise missiles. A system of this size would have at least some capability against stealth aircraft. The SA-10 systems are inter-netted (a technique described earlier when describing anti-stealth radar operations) and in 1987 the US DoD confirmed that the weapons have "a capability against low-altitude targets with small radar cross-sections such as cruise missiles".

The Antey S-300V (SA-12a Gladiator) will be a much more significant threat, particularly to B-2 operations. Like the SA-10b this is a mobile system, in this case with tracked rather than wheeled vehicles, and was first fielded in the mid-1980s.

The S-300 and S-300V systems were extensively modernised during the 1990s, to

Above: The display of a Patriot fire-control system shows several air targets. How well will the system cope with stealth aircraft?

Left: The original Patriot was designed to deal with aircraft targets. Improved versions will be used in the planned MEADS international SAM system.

create new and more combat-effective variants. The 96L6E phased-array target designation radar and 30N6E2 illumination and guidance radar of the Almaz/Fakel S-300PMU2 Favorit SAM system (an upgraded S-300) are able to detect cruise missiles flying at extremely low altitude, and the manufacturers claim an improved capability to engage stealthy targets.

The most recent Russian SAM systems to be announced are the Antey 2500 and the S-400. Both are based on existing systems and were designed to counter low-RCS targets, but neither is able to deal with true stealth aircraft. The Antey 2500 is based on the earlier S-300V (SA-12 "Giant/Gladiator"), but uses the improved 9M82M and 9M83M missiles in place of the earlier 9M82 and 9M83, while its ground equipment has been upgraded to incorporate improved radar signal processing techniques.

In a magazine article describing the Antey 2500 SAM system, Antey General Designer Veniamin Yefremov and Yuri Svirin, director general of the Mariysky Mashinostroitel Production Association, say that the system is intended to counter "battlefield and theatre missiles and other high-speed, 'stealth' highly manoeuvrable and hard-to-hit targets". In practice, however, its anti-stealth capability seems limited. While the Antey S300V could deal with targets whose RCS was as low as 1.08 to 0.54 sq ft (0.1 - 0.05sq m), the minimum size of target which can be engaged by the Antey 2500 is 0.22sq ft (0.02sq m).

By 1999 Russia had begun trials of the S-400. Little is known about this system, which the Russians say can fire at least two types of missiles – one for use against aircraft, the other against ballistic missile targets. Like the Antey 2500, it may be based in part on improved versions of existing hardware.

THE SOLUTION

At present, the only realistic solution to the problem of engaging low-observable targets at other than short range is the use of multi-mode guidance coupled to data links for mid-course updating. Once a target has been located and a missile (whether surface-to-air or air-to-air) is launched against it, the weapon must be able to fly towards the target under autopilot/inertial control, relying on mid-course updates to get it close enough to its quarry to allow the seeker to lock on. This technique is used by all the SAM systems mentioned so far, and by the European Family of Anti-air Missile Systems (FAMS) based on the two-stage Aster 15 and Aster 30 missiles. This is due to be deployed in land-based and ship-board forms. Both systems will use Aerospatiale vertically launched missiles, a Thomson-CSF Arabel I/J band multifunction phased-array radar, plus common computers and displays. The radar is expected to be able to handle approximately 50 tracks, and to engage up to 10 targets at the same time.with rounds being fired at rates of up to one per second.

Two types of round are planned, both vertical launched and ramjet powered. Aster 15 missile will have a range of between 6 and 10.5 miles (10-17km), while the Aster 30 – also known as Aster ER (Extended Range) – will have a tandem booster and greater range. During the initial stages of flight, the missiles will be inertially guided, receiving target updates via the Arabel radar. Once close to the target, the J-band Electronique Serge Dassault AD4A active pulse-Doppler seeker will be activated.

The US has no all-new long-range SAM on the drawing board, but the latest PAC-3 version of Patriot has an improved capability against ballistic missiles, stealth aircraft and stand-off jammers. It has a better radar, larger rocket motor giving greater range, a new 35GHz (K-band) seeker with three operating modes (including fully-active), and an improved warhead and fuze.

IMPROVED MISSILES

Stealth threats also demand the introduction of improved or even all-new air-to-air missiles. By the mid- to late-1990s, the ability to fly close to a target before engaging a terminal guidance mode was becoming an essential feature in the AIMs of all nations facing the threat of stealth aircraft or missiles. This capability first became available to USAF and other NATO air arms with the fielding of the Hughes (now Raytheon) AIM-120 AMRAAM, a missile which combines an active radar seeker with updateable inertial mid-course guidance. Developed to replace the AIM-7 Sparrow, AMRAAM is smaller and lighter, yet has a range of between 30 and 40nm (55-75km).

Matra BAe Dynamics says that its MICA (Missile

Above: The AIM-120 AMRAAM missile (seen here on test below the wing of an F-16) is now in service with the US and its main allies.

Right: The Rafale A prototype demonstrates an air-to-air armament of four Matra BAe Dynamics MICA "fire-and-forget" missiles and two wingtip-mounted Magics.

Below: Early test firings of the Matra BAe Dynamics MICA were from ground launchers. It is apparently in the same performance class as the US AMRAAM.

Intermediat de Combat Aerien) will match the performance of the US missile. Two alternative models of seeker are offered – a passive IR unit for air-combat missions, and an active-radar seeker for interception sorties.

In short-range combat, MICA is locked on to its target before launch. Medium-range engagements would be flown under strap-down inertial guidance, with the seeker being activated later in the flight. During long-range shots, the inertial system would be given an in-flight update. MICA is 10.17ft (3.1m) long and weighs around 240lb (110kg). Its solid-propellant rocket motor gives a maximum range of between 31 to 37 miles (50-60km), and its aerodynamic control surfaces are supplemented by a thrust-vectoring system to ensure high agility.

The Russian equivalent of the AMRAAM is the R-77. In its basic form, this is powered by a solid-propellant rocket motor, but a ramjet-powered RV-AAE version is known to be under development. It is unlikely that Russia will be able to afford to field the RV-AAE in the near future, but China is reported to be funding the project.

Even for these high-performance missiles, downing a stealthy aircraft or cruise missile will not be easy. New patterns of multispectral seeker may be needed. For example, one US project is developing a seeker intended to detect the small amount of energy emitted by the radar altimeter and engine of cruise missiles.

In the late 1980s Gen. Larry D. Welch, then the US Air Force chief of staff, predicted that, "It would take an incredible density of radars" to create a workable defence against the B-1B and B-2. In a war, the US bombers would fly through gaps in radar coverage, potential weaknesses that are plotted and regularly monitored by US intelligence-gathering.

STEALTHY CRUISE

In the absence of any Russian stealth aircraft, the US DoD sees stealthy cruise missiles as a more likely future threat. Such missiles could appear in the inventories of Russia, China, and several Middle Eastern nations, either as the result of exports of the weapons themselves, or as a

result of stealth technology being sold to nations engaged in developing ballistic or cruise missiles.

During 1997 hearings of the US Senate Armed Services Committee, General Howell M. Estes III, Commander in Chief of the North American Aerospace Defense Command (NORAD), and the Commander in Chief of the United States Space Command (USSPACECOM), said, "We are working on issues to give us better defensive capabilities against the cruise missile threat. Fighter upgrades and next generation fighters, such as the F-22, will improve our ability to defend against such weapons. We do not have the capability today that we would like to have to defend North America against cruise missiles ... we will need to ensure we have the necessary defensive systems in place before the threat becomes painfully real in the future."

Under the Radar System Improvement Program (RSIP), USAF E-3 Sentry AWACS aircraft are being given an upgraded and more reliable radar. A new pulse-compressed waveform will improve its ability to detect low-RCS targets, while other classified improvements will help the aircraft detect and track cruise missiles. When all the planned

modifications are completed, the upgraded E-3 should be able to detect a stealthy cruise missile at a range of more than 100 miles (160km), passing this data to an E-8 Joint Stars aircraft. Originally developed to detect and track ground targets (a capability used to great effect during the 1991 Gulf War), the E-8 will be given the ability to track low-flying aircraft, helicopters and missiles attempting to hide in ground clutter. It should be able to detect and track stealthy cruise missiles, and direct the fire of air- or ground-launched missiles. Fighters or SAM sites would not have to acquire the target, but would launch missiles into a "basket" in the sky so that the E-8 could take control of the weapon and direct the interception.

Similar upgrades are being planned by the US Navy to improve its E-2C early-warning aircraft. The Radar Modernization Program (RMP) will fit the aircraft with a new 18-radar-channel ADS-18 antenna, solid-state transmitters, and digital receivers. The upgraded radar will offer improved target

Right: This MiG-29 Fulcrum fighter is armed with a pair of medium-range AA-10 Alamo missiles, plus four short-range AA-8 Aphid dogfight weapons.

Above: **Another electronic platform that made an impressive debut in the Gulf War was the E-8 Joint-** Surveilance Target Attack Radar System (J-STARS), subsequently used over the former Yugoslavia.

tracking in high-clutter environments and over land. In the longer term, the USN hopes to replace the ADS-18 antenna with a new UHF electronically scanned array (UESA). Both changes will allow the radar to concentrate its RF energy against specific high-priority targets, so should improve performance against low-RCS threats.

Many of the techniques needed to detect and track stealth aircraft and missiles have been tested at the Pacific Missile Range Facility in Kauai, Hawaii. A project designated Mountain Top has investigated methods of extracting the tiny radar returns from stealthy targets from background clutter. This effort was expected to lead to a follow-on Mountain Top 2 series of experiments intended to prove the techniques needed to deal with stealth aircraft and stealthy cruise missiles.

Russia is carrying out its own investigation of potential anti-stealth techniques. Scientists have successfully tracked low-observable targets against a forest background, and a new version of at least one air-to-air missile has been developed for the anti-stealth role.

Similar work is under way in other countries, but on a smaller scale. Late in 2000, the UK announced that Thomson Racal Defence, the Defence Evaluation and Research Agency (DERA) and University

College London would be undertaking a three year programme into "innovative radar research related to counterstealth". This work would include 10 individual projects, and covers detection, tracking and classification of "difficult" and stealthy targets in land, sea and air environments.

For the foreseeable future, stealthy targets and small missiles will pose problems for air-defence systems. Most defence systems cost more than the weapon they are intended to counter, and coping with stealth technology is no exception to this rule. A late-

1990s article in the magazine *Lockheed Horizons* warned, "It will, in all probability, take a generation for the world to re-arm with yet undeveloped anti-stealth weapons. And, in that time, stealth technology will likewise continue to improve."

As the defences improve, the designers of stealth aircraft are beginning to react. "There has been continuous improvement in both analytical and experimental methods, particularly with respect to integration of shaping and materials," F-117A project manager Alan Brown noted in a technical paper. "At the same

Above: **The Vympel R-33 (AA-9 "Amos") missile was designed for use on the MiG-31 "Foxhound" but may be used to arm the Su-27 "Flanker". Unlike AMRAAM, it does not use active-radar guidance.**

time, the counter stealth faction is developing an increasing understanding of its requirements, forcing the stealth community into another round of improvements. The message is, that with all the dramatic improvements of the last two decades, there is little evidence of leveling off in capability."

INDEX

A-12 Avenger II, 86 et seq
Advance Technology Fighter (ATF), 13
Advanced Combat eXperimental programme (ACX), 114
Advanced Cruise Missile (ACM), 77 et seq
Advanced Manned Strategic Aircraft, 63
Advanced Tactical Aircraft (ATA), 86 et seq
Advanced Tactical Fighter (ATF), 56, 78 et seq
Advanced Technology Bomber (ATB), 67 et seq, 73 et seq
"Advanced Transport Technology Mission Analysis", 93
AGM-129A, 77 et seq
AGM-28 Hound Dog missile, 61, 62
Aircraft factories, 22, 23
Airfields, 22, 23
Airframe heat, 50
Airship Industries/Westinghouse YEZ-2A airship, 170
Alcatel Defense Systems missile-defence radar, 172
ALCMs (Air-Launched Cruise Missiles), 76 et seq
Anti-stealth air-to-air missiles, 182
Anti-stealth SAMs, 180
Aurora, 90 et seq
Avro (Hawker Siddeley) Vulcan, 56
AX (AFX) programme, 86

B
BAe Experimental Aircraft Programme II, 100, 112
BAe UAV, 101
Balkans, 159 et seq
Bell
  AH-1G, 35
  AH-1J, 35
  AH-1S Cobra, 35, 36
  Model 67 (X-16), 59
  OH-58D Stealth Kiowa Warrior, 95, 96
Bi-static radar, 175
"Black Manta", 93
"Black" programmes, 68 et seq
Boeing
  AGM-86B ALSM, 35

B-52, 35, 56, 57
E-3 Sentry, 131, 169
X-32 JSF, 89 et seq, 122
X-45A UCAV, 104
Boeing Sikorsky RAH-66 Comanche, 96, 128
"B-X bomber", 94

C
Camouflage and markings, 14 et seq
Canberra bomber, 18
Cancellation systems, 48 et seq
"Carrierless" radar, 175
Cavities, 36
Chaff and flares, 139
Chain Home early-warning radars, 27, 29
Chinese stealth technology, 100
CIA (Central Intelligence Agency), 58, 60, 106, 108
Circuit Analogue Absorbers, 47
Cobra Dane radar system, 173
Cockpits, 38
"Combat Dawn" programme, 102
"Compass Arrow" programme, 102
Composites, 42
Contrails, 22
Convair F-102 Delta Dagger, 40
Counter-stealth technology, 168 et seq
Cruise missiles, 75 et seq
Cuban Missile Crisis, 63

D
Dallenbach Layer, 43
DASA (EADS) Mako (Shark), 101
Dassault Aviation Aéronef de Validation Expérimentale (AVE) UAV, 105
Dassault Mirage 2000, 35
Dassault-Breguet Rafale, 48, 52, 100, 114
Dazzle camouflage, 17
de Havilland Mosquito, 42
Decoy RPVs, 144
Decoys, 138
Desert Fox, Operation, Persian Gulf, 159
Desert Shield, Operation, Persian Gulf, 148 et seq
Desert Storm, Operation, Persian Gulf, 152 et seq
DEW line radar network, 170
Diffraction, 30
Dihedrals, 31

Dornier LA-2000, 100

E
El Dorado Canyon, Operation, Libya, 146
Electromagnetic waves, 24
Electronic aids to stealth, 130 et seq
Electro-optical detection of stealth aircraft, 176
Electro-optical systems, 133
Engine inlets, 37 et seq
Engine noise, 51
Engine nozzles, 49, 50
Eurocopter Deutschland helicopter blade control, 95
Eurofighter Typhoon, 100, 112, 178
European stealth technology, 100
European UAVs, 105

F
"F-19", 11, 69, 116
Faceting, 11, 36, 69
Fairchild A-10, 20, 21, 50
Fan Song radar, 61
Ferris, Chris, 20, 21
Ferrite paint, 46, 47, 60, 106
FI-X (Japanese next-generation fighter), 99
Folland Gnat, 56
FS-X (Japanese Fighter, Support eXperimental) project, 99
Fuhs, Professor Allen E., 12, 56
Future Airborne Weapon System (FAWS, Germany), 105

G
General Atomics Predator UAV, 163
General Dynamics F-16, 20
General Dynamics/McDonnell Douglas A-12 ATA, 86 et seq
German stealth technology, 100
Gotha Go.229, 59
"Granger" electronic warfare unit, 60
"Grassblade" stealth helicopter, 97
Groom Lake test facility, 90
Grumman
  A-6 Intruder, 33
  A-6F Intruder, 86
  EA-6B Prowler, 38
  EF-111A, 57
  F-14 Tomcat, 18, 21, 40
  FB-111H, 67
Gulf War, 21, 143, 148 et seq
"Gusto" (CIA project), 60

H

Handley Page
 0/400, 15
 Hampden, 15
 Victor, 36
Harrier GR3, 19, 22
Harrier, 37
"Have Rust" programme, 75
Hawker Hunter, 56
Hertz, Heinrich, 25
HMS *Revenge*, 16
Horten Ho IX, 59
"Hot spots", 52 et seq
Hunting 126 research aircraft, 50
Hyper-X UAV, 90 et seq
HyTech project, 91

I

Indian stealth technology, 100
Infrared
 detection of stealth aircraft, 176
 emissions, 48 et seq
 jammers, 140
Iraq, 13, 21, 148 et seq
Iraqi air defences in Gulf War, 151
 et seq
Israel Aircraft Industries HA-10
 UAV, 105
Italian stealth technology, 100
Izmaylov, Col. Vladimir, 97

J

Jamming aircraft, 141 et seq
Jamming of SAMs, 57
Japanese stealth technology, 99
Jaumann absorber, 45
Johnson, Clarence "Kelly", 59
Joint Air-to-Surface Stand-Off
 Missile (JASSM), 78
Joint STARS, 88
Joint Strike Fighter, 88 et seq, 122
Just Cause, Operation, Panama,
 146 et seq

K

Kamov Ka-60 Kasatka, 97
Keldysh Research Centre, 48, 124
Kongsberg Nytt Sjomalsmissile, 78
Kosovo, 141, 159 et seq

L

Lampyridae (Firefly) programme, 101
Laser radar, 133
Laser radar anti-stealth sensors, 176
Lebanon, 146

LFI (Russian lightweight front-line
 fighter), 98
LFS (Russian lightweight frontal
 aircraft), 98
Light Helicopter Experimental
 (LHX) programme, 96
LMFI (Russian lightweight
 multifunctional front-line fighter), 98
Lockheed
 A-series aircraft, 60
 A-11, 61, 108
 A-12, 58, 61, 68, 108
 ATF, 35
 CL-282 (variant of F-104
  Starfighter), 59
 CL-400 "Suntan", 60
 D-21 reconnaissance RPV, 62
 Echo 1 RCS prediction
  programme, 53
 F-117 Nighthawk, 11 et seq, 34, 36,
  37, 39, 49, 53, 56, 64, 68 et seq, 79,
  90, 116, 132, 146
 Have Blue, 13, 21, 40, 49, 53, 63, 68, 78
 Mach 5 stealth concept, 52
 Q-Star, 53
 Senior Prom, 64 et seq
 "Skunk Works", 59 et seq
 SR-71 Blackbird, 35, 46, 51, 60, 90, 108
 Tier II and Tier III UAV, 103
 TR-1, 47, 59, 106, 108
 U-2 series, 18, 45, 60 et seq, 68, 106
 U-2R, 59, 106
 U-2S, 59, 106
 YF-12A, 61
 YMQM-105 Acquila RPV, 102, 103
 YO-3A, 53
Lockheed Martin A/F-117X, 69
 F-22A Raptor, 42, 47, 80, 120, 132
 X-35 JSF, 89 et seq, 122
Lockheed Martin/Boeing
 DarkStar UAV, 103
Long Range Cruise Missile
 (LRCM), 78

M

Martin 294 (RB-57D), 59
Martin Marietta X-24, 64
Matra Apache, 77
Matra BAe Dynamics Storm
 Shadow, 78
MCA (Indian Medium Combat
 Aircraft), 100
McDonnell Douglas (Boeing)
 F-4 Phantom, 21, 22-15 Eagle, 19
 F-15 Eagle STOL demonstrator, 50

 F/A-18E/F Super Hornet, 87
McDonnell Douglas Harpoon
 missile, 38
McDonnell Douglas No Tail Rotar
 (NOTAR), 95
McDonnell Douglas/Bell LHX, 95
MC-X transport, 93
Messerschmitt Bf 109, 15
Mikoyan 1.42 and 1.44 MFI, 98, 124
Mikoyan I-2000, 98
Mikoyan-Gurevich
 MiG-3, 16
 MiG-25, 53, 169
 MiG-29 Fulcrum, 33
Mission Adaptive Wing, 40
Mitsubishi F-2, 47, 99, 178
Mountain Top stealth detection
 programme, 185
Multi-sensor stealth-tracking
 systems, 179

N

NASA/Boeing X-36 UAV, 104
Navaids, 134
Night colours, 15
Night vision goggles (NVG), 134
Nitel stealth-detecting radar, 171
Noriega, General Manuel
 Antonio, 146, 147
North American
 F-107A, 52, 53
 F-108, 61
 XB-70, 60 et seq
 YF-93A, 38, 39
Northrop
 B-2 Spirit, 12, 13, 36, 39, 48, 49, 54,
  64, 67, 70 et seq, 92, 94, 118, 132,
  161 et seq, 168
 N-1M, 66
 Tacit Blue, 13, 88. 90
 Tacit Rainbow drone, 143, 144
 YB-49/XB-49, 66
 YF-23, 49, 80 et seq
Northrop Grumman
 Global Hawk, 103 et seq
 Pegasus UAV, 102

O

Over the horizon (OTH) radar
 systems, 171 et seq
Overholser, Denys, 63

P

P-50 Barlock radar, 63
Panama, 13, 146

Panavia Tornado IDS, 39
Parasol alerting radar, 171
Patriot radar system, 175
Pave Paws radar system, 173
Plasma cloud, 48, 124
Powers, Francis Gary, 18, 60, 62, 106
"Prime Chance" operation, 96
Pulse detonation engines, 91

R
Radar
  and radar cross-section, 24 et seq
  beam shapes, 131
  counters to stealth, 168 et seq
  cross-section (RCS) and aircraft
    size, 57
  cross-section (RCS) reduction, 56
  cross-section (RCS) test ranges
    (indoor/outdoor), 54, 55
  ranges, 56 et seq
  waveforms, 130
  wavelengths, 30
  waves, 24
Radar-Absorbent Structural (RAS)
  materials, 47
Radar-absorbing (and radar-
  absorbent) materials (RAM), 11, 24
Rainbow (CIA project), 60
RAM, 36, 42 et seq
Rayleigh scattering, 29
Raytheon AIM-120A AMRAAM, 42
"Red Wagon" project, 62
Rich, Ben R., 63 et seq, 70 et seq, 116
Rickenbacker, Eddie, 14
Rockwell International
  ATF proposal, 78
  B-1, 35, 38, 39, 63, 67
  B-1A, 49, 56, 58, 59, 108
  B-1B, 44, 49, 56, 57, 66, 72, 110, 137,
    158, 164 et seq
  B-1C, 72
RPVs (remotely piloted vehicles),
  101 et seq
Russian stealth technology, 97 et seq
Ryan
  "Lucy Lee" project, 62
  Model 136, 62
  Model 147A Fire Fly RPV, 62
  Model 147B Fire Fly RPV, 62, 101
  Q-2 Firebee target drone, 62

S
Saab
  J35 Draken, 36
  JAS-39 Gripen, 39

"Saber Penetrator" programme, 65
Salisbury Screen, 43 et seq, 60
SAMs against stealth aircraft, 57
Schwarzkopf, General Norman
  H., 148
Secrecy, 68 eq seq
"Senior Citzen" transport, 93
"Senior CJ", 71
"Senior Ice", 65, 71
"Senior Peg", 65
"Senior Trend", 68, 116
"Shamu", 88
"Skyquake", 90
"Smart skins", 145
Smoke and light, 22
Sopwith Snipe, 15
Spad fighter, 14
Spad XIII C.1, 15
Special Access Programs (SAPs),
  68 et seq
Stealth aircraft "sightings", 93, 94
Stealth helicopters, 95, 96
Stealthy cruise missiles, 183
Sukhoi
  S-37 Berkut (Golden Eagle), 98, 126
  T-60S (S-60), 98
Supermarine Spitfire, 16
Surveillance radars, 170
Swedish Highly Advanced
  Research Configuration (SHARC)
  UAV, 105
Sweetman, Bill, 12, 91, 109
SX-3 (Japanese stealth aircraft
  project), 99

T
Tamara ESM system, 178
"Teal Dawn" programme, 65, 76
"Teal Ruby" space-based infrared
  sensor, 51, 178
Teledyne
  Model 147T RPV, 102
  Model 154 (AQM-91A Compass
    Arrow) RPV, 35, 102
  Model 324 RPV, 35
  Model 350 RPV, 35
  RPVs, 61
Teledyne Ryan Tier II Plus UAV, 103
Terrain reference navigation
  (TRN), 133 et seq
Testor/Italeri "F-19" kit, 11, 12
Thermal signatures, 48 et seq
Thomson-CSF
  RCS-prediction software, 53
  TRS-22XX radar, 25

Thorn EMI RCS prediction polar
  diagram, 54
Tier 3A, 93
"TR-3A", 93

Travelling Waves, 30, 39 et seq
Tupolev
  Tu-95 and -142 Bear, 132
  Tu-160 Blackjack bomber, 96 et seq

U
UAVs (unmanned air vehicles), 101
  et seq
UCAVs (Unmanned combat air
  vehicles), 104
Ufmitsev, Pyotr, 33, 63
Urgent Fury, Operation, Grenada, 146

V
Vietnam War, 18, 19, 22, 28, 42, 61,
  63, 95, 101

W
Watson-Watt, Sir Robert, 27
Wavelengths, 25
Weapons carriage, 41
"Wild Weasel" anti-radar aircraft, 143
Windecker
  AC-7 Eagle 1, 63
  YE-5A, 63
Wing sweep angle, 36
World War II stealth aircraft, 59

X
X-30 National Aerospace Plane
  (NASP), 91
XST (Experimental Stealth
  Tactical aircraft), 59, 64, 66

Y
"Yehudi" lights, 22
YF-113G. 93
Yugoslav air defences, 56, 161
Yugoslavia, 161 et seq

Z
Zuiho (Japanese carrier), 18

DATE DUE

FEB 1 4 2012		

GAYLORD | PRINTED IN U.S.A.